This book is dedicated to my mother

Henrietta Ellen Birkel

for without her love and guidance, this endeavor would have never been a "reality." This woman has given of herself with an unselfish mind, she has always put her family before her, and has never received the fame or recognition that she deserves.

"Thank you, Mom"

L
O
V
E

Bobby

Library of Congress Cataloging in Publication Data
Vanderstigchel, Armand/Birkel, Robert Jr.

THE ADIRONDACK COOKBOOK by Armand C. Vanderstigchel *and*
   Robert E. Birkel, Jr.
P. CM.
Includes Index
ISBN 0964162601

CONCEPT: Armand C. Vanderstigchel *and* Robert Birkel, Jr.
EDITORS: Kay Mogusar *and* Vanders & Birkel
COVER PHOTOGRAPHS: Robert Birkel, Jr.
INSIDE PHOTOGRAPHS: Robert Birkel, Jr., Armand C. Vanderstigchel, *and*
                    contributing photographers and establishments
ILLUSTRATIONS: June Clow, Ardis Hughes, Brett Cohen, Alexander
                    Katsaros, John Sessions Hudson Armstrong, *and*
                    contributing artists and establishments
POEMS: June Clow *and* Robert Birkel, Jr.

THE ADIRONDACK COOKBOOK is available at special discounts when purchased in bulk for premiums and sales promotions as well as for fundraising or educational use. Special personalized editions can also be produced in large quantities. For details, contact:

Visit us at: www.adirondackcookbook.com

Vanders & Birkel Publishing
38 McAlester Avenue
Hicksville, NY 11801

E-mail us: info@ligourmettv.com

Distribution by North Country Books, Utica, NY, (315) 735-4877

For additional copies, or write to the address above. Ask us about our special Adirondack Cookbook merchandise products. These are great gifts for anyone who loves cooking and the Adirondacks.

MANUFACTURED IN THE UNITED STATES OF AMERICA.

No meals or free lodging were accepted by authors in gathering information for this book.

Introduction

Welcome to the ADIRONDACKS and to our publication focused on the cooking and cuisine of this nature wonderland.

Before we focus our attention on the cooking part, we would like to inform you on the Adirondacks as a State Park and, of course, its history and inhabitants. Using this as a reference, you will be able to understand the development of its cuisine and food-sources, which can be traced back as far as the seventeenth century.

You will be surprised to hear that the ADIRONDACK PARK has one of the most diversified sceneries in this great country. With approximately 3,000 lakes and ponds in an array of forest clad mountains—of which 42 peaks exceeding 4,000 feet in elevation; 2.5 million acres of protected and preserved land; an abundance of rare fauna and flora; and an endless, interwoven network of sparkling brooks and streams—the above mentioned statement speaks for itself.

What stirs more uniqueness is the fact that 130,000 year-round residents live within this park in a manner our ancestors did when they discovered this virgin land. In other words . . . they respect nature and live by its rule. The inner concern is present among these people to preserve and fight to keep the Adirondacks as we know it . . . beautiful. Once again we would like to express our gratitude to the organizations we mentioned in the acknowledgement section who are fighting to keep the Adirondacks out of harm's way.

Each year a reported 9 million visitors visit the park and explore the 105 scenic towns and villages connected with well kept roads which acclaims the Adirondacks as a motorist's paradise. And those thousands of visitors share together a common wealth and knowledge that will be carried on to the overlookers and those ignorant to think that you must travel far for a splendid vacation or weekend getaway.

Lakes and mountains rival in beauty abounding you with vivid imagery; equal to those in Switzerland; towering more than a mile above the sea level; and hosting a home for abundant wildlife like deer, bears, the bald eagle, lynx, moose, coyote, and many more. Every game fish to be found on the Eastern sea border—like brook trout, northern pike, small mouthed black bass, pickerel, and land-locked salmon (steelhead)—is found plentiful, a propelling call to the fisherman in us.

The hospitality industry people in this area have labored for years to make this region an Eden for visitors in every season, providing your favorite pastimes referring to hunting, fishing, swimming, skiing, boating, golf, tennis, horseback riding, hiking, mountain climbing, country dancing, concerts, or whatever floats your boat . . . oh yes, let's not forget cooking and eating.

What is ADIRONDACK COOKING?

This question has been repeatedly hurled in our direction by newpaper editors, TV reporters, friends and collegues, and probably you, dear reader.

Subsequently during our recipe search and footwork period, we revealed a red line running through the foundation and style of most of the recipes submitted by homecooks, chefs, and proprietors. The red line we detected dates back to the days the Algonquin and Mohawk Indians roamed the endless forests, soon to be adjoined by the first European settlers, whose daily provisions consisted of game, fish, fruits, maple syrup, wild mushrooms, nuts, and wild berries.

Throughout the following centuries, as mankind developed his agricultural skills and people from all over the world brought their culinary knowledge, the combination of natural resources, farming techniques, and cooking skills/equipment evolved the inception of Adirondack Cooking.

As you browse through the recipes in the book, you will acknowledge our view. Besides the enormous amount of baking recipes, you will see the combination of fruits with, for instance, poultry; where instead of traditional gravies, fruit sauces are incorporated into the recipe, which fits well with the current lowfat food craze sweeping the nation.

The majority of Restaurants and Bed & Breakfast establishments we visited or contacted were notorious for their high standards in food, atmosphere, and service. With fond memories we recall the evening we arrived at the "Bent Finial Manor" in Warrensburg after a photo shoot in Saratoga. Early snow had fallen on this chilly October night. We arrived late, with our host Pat Scully already calling it a day, leaving a welcome note on the unlocked door, a crackling fireplace, some snacks, and a carafe of wine . . . you call it daring (if you're from New York City) . . . we call it . . . ADIRONDACK HOSPITALITY!!!!!!

Dining at the Restaurants, you will notice that the overall dishes are made from scratch, down to the homebaked breads, pies, ice cream, and even the freshly squeezed lemonade. Because of the remote location of many places, especially in the winter, cooking skills must rely on local products and ingenuity.

As you travel throughout the area in the summertime, you will observe the many farmstands along the way . . . S T O P! You must check out the wonderful produce, crafts, and, oh yes, delicious baking goods. Wonderful, chunky fruit pies, zucchini breads, apple cider donuts, fresh squeezed apple cider, and just as I was writing this, Robert pressed me to mention the many Antique shops along the way . . . nothing to do with food, but worth checking out.

On the homecook front, we have had our share of adventure. During our research period in the Adirondacks, we often enjoyed homecooked meals from Gram Harris (check out her recipes) at the "Rustic Barn Campsite." We had her "Poorman's Stew," which spreads a savory aroma throughout the campsite. You know after that, we were not eating alone; a crowd of hungry campers and trailer enthusiasts gathered around Gram's infamous site and dug into the simmering pot of stew. Even camp custodian Bruce, who swears by his lake trout, stopped by for a bite. Adirondack hospitality at its finest hour.

Of course, we can provide you with some sour notes. The Adirondacks people are very down to earth, which made it understandably hard for us to approach their establishment, requesting a recipe or information for our book. How can we forget our visit at a restaurant in Lake Placid, where we enjoyed one of the best homestyle cooked meals in the Adirondacks, where the women proprietor thought we came from Mars when approaching her about the book. Some thought we were salesmen, trying to sell an advertising publication, hanging up the phone after two words.

Like in every walk of life, there will be obstacles and resistance when a new idea is being developed. It's the support from people like you and everyone who committed themselves to this book that made "ADIRONDACK COOKING" happen.

We hope with this book, to establish ADIRONDACK CUISINE as a new cooking trend, and most of all, bring the ADIRONDACKS closer to you.

ARMAND C. VANDERSTIGCHEL

FROM THE ADIRONDACK CHAIR WE GREET YOU

ARMAND *and* ROBERT

AUTHORS

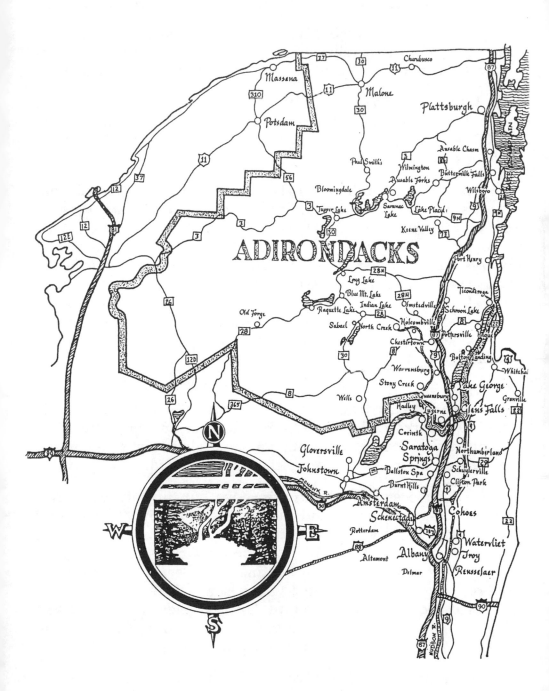

ADIRONDACKS

Author Note

"This is God's Country!" . . . the Lake Luzerne Real Estate agent meant it from the bottom of his heart; this slogan would always surface whenever we made our way through the Adirondacks.

What seemed a sales pitch turned into true reality . . . a summer up in the Adirondacks was enough to get hooked for life, and best of all, write this book about a wonderful region and its friendly inhabitants.

For many, the Adirondacks is an unsettled name, especially out of state, just like it was for Robert and me a few years back. Robert's father, Mr. Birkel, Sr., is an employee of the New York Racing Association, the organization involved in the Saratoga Racetrack. Every year, all of its New York City employees spend four to six weeks working at the racetrack in July and August. We were invited to make a visit at the Saratoga Racetrack in August of 1992. Leaving Long Island and heading up north on the beautiful Taconic Parkway, it became clear to us that New York State is a beautiful, diversified one . . . more than we tend to realize.

Once we arrived in Saratoga, a distinctness of lifestyle became apparent . . . relaxed, calm, friendly, and helpful. Hello there . . . is this New York?????? Strolling through Saratoga Main Street, the historic town—known for its mineral spas, horse racing, and the old casino—a prolonged visit can certainly be justified.

In the bookstores and souvenir shops, our curiosity was drawn by publications, posters, and calendars showcasing the beautiful Adirondack scenery. We decided to explore this region which we discovered is a sight to behold . . . for instance, Lake Placid, the former Winter Olympics town. Visiting Lake Placid further up north is like being beamed up into a village somewhere in the Swiss or Austrian Alps of Europe. Beautiful lakes, splendor mountains, and cozy alpine style villages await you, with an array of recreational facilities to excite any jaded traveller amongst us.

A person can only wonder . . . "Can it get any better?"

It sure can!! See and explore for yourself. Head up north on 87, get off on any exit, examine your map, and enter an exciting new world you never thought to exist in New York State . . . ladies and gentlemen,

WELCOME TO THE ADIRONDACKS!!!!!!

CO-AUTHOR: ARMAND C. VANDERSTIGCHEL

Acknowledgements

Front Cover Adirondack Cookbook Illustration:
  Brett Cohen

Front/Back Cover Photography:
  Robert E. Birkel, Jr.

Front Cover Location:
  Indian Lake, New York

Back Cover Location:
  Ausable Chasm - Keesville, New York

Front/Back Cover Design by:
  Armand C. Vanderstigchel • Robert E. Birkel, Jr.

Animal and Scenery Illustrations:
  June M. Clow - Wilmington, New York

Adirondack Map, Scenery, and Food Illustrations by:
 John Hudson Sessions Armstrong - Saratoga Springs, New York

Historic Saratoga Victorian Illustrations by:
  Ardis Hughes - Saratoga Springs, New York

Poems by:
  June M. Clow • Robert E. Birkel, Jr.

Adirondack Humor Illustrations:
  Alexander Katsaros - Sayville, New York

&a. &a. &a.

Special Thanks:
Victoria Verner and Staff - Adirondack Museum, Blue Mountain
Lake, New York • North Country Books (Sheila and Bob) - Utica,
New York • WRGB Channel "6" (Liz Bishop, Richard Bamberger,
Steve LaPointe) - Schnectady, New York • TV "10" (Richard
Lillpop) - Albany, New York • Adirondack Life Magazine (Steve
Parisi, Elizabeth Folwell, Howard Fish, Tom Hughes, Ann Eastman,
Lisa Richmond, Nathan Farb, Janine Rock, and the Staff at
Adirondack Life) • The Adirondack Center Museum • Paul Smith
Institute • Adirondack Discovery Organization • Adirondack

Nature Conservancy • National Audubon Society (Adirondack Campaign) • National Wildlife Organization • Bennett Lerner Associates • Weber & Foster • Able Photography • Cameta Camera • Design Color Labs • Elite Photography

᷌ ᷌ ᷌

Special Thanks to Our Production Coordinator:
Karen Graff

᷌ ᷌ ᷌

The Media Who Interviewed and Published the Editorials:
The Adirondack Journal (Diane) • Adirondack Daily Enterprise (John Penney) • The Record (Heidi Legenbauer) • Daily Gazette (Steve Williams) • Post Star (Pam Brooks, Tamara Dietrich, Sharlene Comstock) • The Saratogian (Jennifer Pruden and Lois Carson) • Leader Herald (Nancy Powers and Colleen) • The Lake Placid News (Kristen Young) • Times Union (Michael Vertanen) • North Creek News (Jerry Gardner) • The Chronicle (Brian Perry) • North Country Living (William Studley) • Plattsburgh News • Tupper Lake Free Press (Dan McLaren) • Ballston Spa Journal (Charles Hogan) • The Recorder (Kathy Smith) • Evening Telegram (Donna Thompson) • Evening Times (Erik Janicky) • The Observer (Barbara Charzun) • Hamilton County News (Chris Meisner) • Boonville Herald (Livingston Landsing) • Ogdensburg Courier Observer (Charles Kelly) • Malone Telegram • The Fulton Valley News (Vincent Caravan) • The Chateugay Record (John Sheehan) • The Adirondack Record Post (William Denton) • The Press Post (Barbara Willkinson) • Essex.County Republican (Fred and Christine) • Ken Gimball and All of Channel "12" News • L.I.

᷌ ᷌ ᷌

Long Island Crew:
Bob Sr., Brian, Jeanne, and Jackie Birkel; Shashana, Bill, Kaitlin, and Christopher Graff; and Paul Cummo (Desk Top Publishing); Sal, Pa, and Michael Morrison • Marie and Paul Gallowitsch (Skippers Pub) - Northport, New York • Dana Riggs, John Byers (Able Conklins Steak and Chop House) - Huntington, New York • Raymond Romaine (Computer Support Group) • Robert S. Kelly (Commercial Freight) • Michael Pistritto (Photography Consultant) • Harry and Debbie

Paige, Sharon Hill, Cindy and Tom Heller (Publishing Consultants) • James Sibree and John Keenan (N.Y.R.A.)

૭ ૭ ૭

Upstate Crew:
Barbara Beck, Cyndee Doherty, and Staff (The Inn at Saratoga) • Eleanor and Fred Harris (Grams) • Bill, Debbie, Tommy, Jerry, Ruth, Ann, Frank, Bob, Roberta, Mr. and Mrs. Mancini, Bruce, June, Jerry, John, June (The Rustic Barn Campsites) - the beautiful Adirondack Park • Patricia and William Stanley, Max and Joan McDonough - Saratoga Springs, New York • Dan Murphy (The Uncommon Grounds Coffee Shop) - Main Street Saratoga Springs, New York • Enterprise Rent-a-Car

૭ ૭ ૭

We would like to thank all of our cooks and chefs
from the Adirondacks
who submitted all these creative recipes—
some handed down from generation to generation.
These recipes that were developed from
the inner sanctum of the beholder's mind
will tempt you from page to page.

૭ ૭ ૭

A Very Special Thanks to:
Kay Mogusar, Joyce Hursman, and the Staff and Crew of Cookbook Publishers, Inc.

૭ ૭ ૭

"We would like to take this time to salute you all!!"
Armand and Robert

Table of Contents

❦

BED & BREAKFAST 1

VEGETABLES 101

SOUPS AND CHOWDERS 111

ENTREES
    Beef 115
    Poultry 123
    Pork 135
    Wild Game 141
    Miscellaneous 149

BREADS AND PASTRIES 153

CAKES, COOKIES, DESSERTS
    Cakes and Icings 165
    Cookies 179
    Desserts 183

PIES AND PUDDINGS
    Pies 189
    Puddings 195

MISCELLANEOUS 199

HINTS 205

❧ FAVORITE RECIPES ❧

FROM MY COOKBOOK

❧ Recipe Name	❧ Page Number

Adirondack

Bed & Breakfast
Resorts
Restaurants
and Purveyors

Bed & Breakfasts
Restaurants & Purveyors

The Cornerstone Victorian...1

Alynn's Butterfly Inn 6

The Bark Eater 7

1852 Inn 13

Country Road Lodge 17

Pine Tree Inn...21

High Peaks Inn 25

The Lamplight Inn...27

The Inn at Saratoga 33

Fo'Castle Farms..38

The Friends Lake Inn.. 39

The Book & Blanket.. 47

The Point 51

Oscar's Adirondack Mountain Smokehouse 59

The Lodge on Lake Clear 61

Sweeney's 67

The Chester Inn 69

The Stagecoach Inn 75

Goose Pond Inn.. 79

Moose River House.. 83

Mirror Lake Inn...87

The Cornerstone Victorian

Victorian Accommodations
3921 Main Street
Warrensburg, NY 12885
518-623-3308

The Cornerstone Victorian is definitely one of the most elegant Bed & Breakfast establishments in the Lake George region. Formerly known as the Bent Finial Manor, the impressive 1904 Queen Anne mansion opened up in 1989 and has since then been beautifully restored to its original 1904 look. Innkeepers Doug and Louise Goettsche are two hospitality industry professionals, known for their acclaimed reputation in the Catskills.

Located in the center of the Adirondack Antique Capital Warrensburg across from Oscar's Smokehouse, the Inn is perfectly located near all attractions, especially the ski center at Gore Mountain. In the winter they offer special ski/lodging packages. Don't skip the award-winning complimentary 5 course candlelight breakfast. Lunch and dinner become obsolete after this feast!

The Cornerstone Victorian

Candelight Breakfast at the Cornerstone Victorian

SAVORY EGGS IN BAKED CROUSTADES

Per serving:

1 hard roll (slice the bottom off, scoop out center, leaving top on – butter cut section and broil till lightly toasted)
¼ c. country sausage, browned and drained

2 Tbsp. diced fresh tomato
1 tsp. thinly sliced green onion
Pinch dried basil

EGG MIXTURE:

3 eggs
2 Tbsp. heavy cream
Salt

Pepper
½ oz. cream cheese
1 slice American cheese

Beat well.

In frying pan, cook sausage, diced tomatoes and sliced green onions. Sprinkle with basil to taste. Add egg mixture and cook till done. Scoop egg mixture into center of rolls. Top with a green onion palm tree.

The Cornerstone Victorian
Warrensburg, NY

3

CORNERSTONE'S SWEET SOUFFLÉS

FILLING:

8 oz. softened cream cheese
2 c. cottage cheese
1 tsp. vanilla

2 egg yolks
¼ c. sugar

Place all ingredients in a food processor. Combine. Set aside.

BATTER:

1 stick butter, softened
½ c. sugar
1½ c. sour cream
6 eggs

½ c. orange juice
1 c. flour
2 tsp. baking powder
1 tsp. vanilla

Blend batter ingredients together till smooth.

Grease 2 muffin tins. Fill ½ full with batter. Use a small ice-cream scoop and drop filling in batter. This can be made to this point the night before and refrigerated till morning. Bring dish to room temperature. Bake at 350° for 30 minutes or until done. Carefully remove Soufflés from muffin tins. Use 3 or 4 per serving. Top with Raspberry Sauce, then fresh fruit such as: Strawberries, Raspberries and Blueberries, and whipped cream! Makes 24 soufflés.

RASPBERRY SAUCE:

Equal parts: Raspberry Jam and Butter. Heat till melted and warm.

The Cornerstone Victorian
Warrensburg, NY

4

The Cornerstone Victorian Welcomes You

Alynn's Butterfly Inn

Bed & Breakfast
P.O. Box 248, Route 28
Warrensburg, NY 12885
518-623-9390

*Warm up to the Inn's
cozy wood stove!*

For that cozy, typical country bed and breakfast, head out to innkeepers Al and Lynn's charming establishment near many attractions with a daily, hearty breakfast.

ALYNN'S BUTTERFLY INN
CARAMEL FRENCH TOAST

1 c. brown sugar
½ c. butter
6 eggs
1½ c. milk
1 tsp. vanilla

2 Tbsp. corn syrup
½ c. sugar & 1 tsp. cinnamon,
   mixed
10 to 12 slices wheat bread

    Melt butter, corn syrup and brown sugar on stove in saucepan. Spread on greased 9x11 inch pan. Dip bread in eggs, milk and vanilla mixture. Layer bread on bottom of pan over brown sugar mixture. Sprinkle cinnamon & sugar mixture between layers. Add next layer bread dipped in egg mixture. Pour remaining egg mixture over top of all. Cover and refrigerate overnight. Bake at 350° for 30 to 35 minutes, uncovered. Serves 8 to 10.

Alynn's Butterfly Inn
Warrensburg, NY

The Bark Eater

A TRUE COUNTRY INN
"Bark Eater" is the English translation
of the Indian word "Adirondack."

Alstead Mill Road
Keene, New York 12942
518-576-2221
Fax 518-576-2071
Joe-Pete Wilson, Innkeeper

Originally a stagecoach stopover, the Bark Eater has been in operation since the early 1800s. The atmosphere still reflects these early times. The farmhouse, with its wide board floors, stone fireplaces, and rooms filled with antiques compliments its natural setting. Located on a spacious farm in the heart of the Adirondack High Peaks, the Bark Eater is a place to relax and enjoy your vacation.

Featured in *Country Inns and Back Roads* and *Cross Country Ski Inns of the Northeast*.

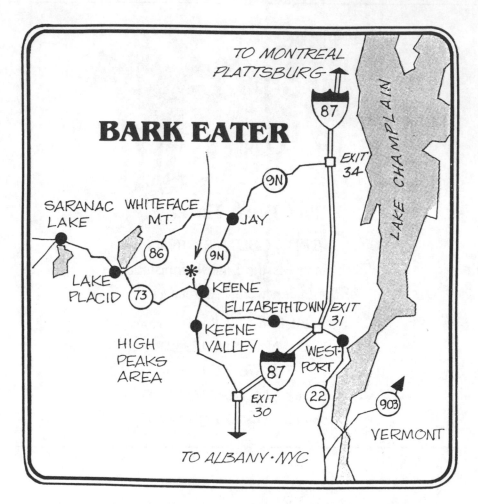

BARK EATER

TO MONTREAL
PLATTSBURG

87

EXIT 34

LAKE CHAMPLAIN

9N

SARANAC LAKE   WHITEFACE MT.   JAY

86   9N

LAKE PLACID   73   KEENE

ELIZABETHTOWN   EXIT 31

HIGH PEAKS AREA   KEENE VALLEY   87   WEST-PORT

EXIT 30   22   903

VERMONT

TO ALBANY · NYC

Hiking the Adirondacks

A favorite pastime among visitors and residents.

CHILLED TOMATO BISQUE

¼ c. olive oil
2 Tbs. crushed garlic
1 Tbs. paprika

1 (46 oz.) can tomato juice
⅓ c. cooking sherry
½ c. half & half

Place olive oil in a pan and heat until quite hot. Add garlic and saute for about 30 seconds. Stir in paprika and stir in tomato juice. Bring to a boil, and add cooking sherry. Heat for a couple of minutes. Remove from heat and cool. Chill in refrigerator. Stir in half & half and serve in chilled bowls. Garnish with fresh dill or basil.

Chef Peter Varns
The Bark Eater Inn
Alstead Mill Road
Keene, New York 12942

BARK EATER GRANOLA

DRY INGREDIENTS:

8 c. old-fashioned oats
1½ Tbs. cinnamon
1 c. coconut
½ c. wheat germ
½ c. sunflower seeds

¼ c. poppy seeds
¼ c. sesame seeds
¾ c. cashews
¾ c. almonds

WET INGREDIENTS:

¼ c. butter
1 c. oil
½ c. honey
¼ c. molasses

½ c. brown sugar
½ c. peanut butter
1 Tbs. vanilla

Combine all dry ingredients in a large bowl. Stir. Combine all wet ingredients in a microwaveable bowl. Heat on high for three minutes; stir well. Pour the mixture over the dry ingredients; stir well. Spread granola onto large baking sheet. Bake for 40 to 45 minutes at 375° stirring every 15 minutes. Let granola cool and add currants or raisins, if desired. Freezes well or keeps for up to 1 month in a sealed container.

Jodi Donns
The Bark Eater Inn
Alstead Mill Road
Keene, New York 12942

The Tradition of Adirondack hospitality is well served here . . . a tradition that began in the 19th century when the inn catered to stagecoach passengers traveling between Lake Champlain and Lake Placid.

JUNCO

1852 Inn

❧ *Very Reasonable Rates* ❧
Lake Shore Road
Willsboro, New York 12996-3421
518-963-4075
Lil & Isaac Iten

When this rambling farmhouse was built, Lake Champlain was the only connection with the outside world. The crops were sent, and supplies received, by graceful sloops that sailed south to New York and north to Montreal. Nearby Essex, an active lakeport in those days, still stands much as it did then. The hamlet boasts many Greek Revival and Federal homes of the same vintage, and is on the National Register of Historic Places.

The roads are still sparsely travelled—a cyclist's dream. The lakeshore is the eastern boundary of the 6 million acre Adirondack Park, the destination of nature-lovers from all over the globe. Bird watchers flock to this area, and fishermen and hikers love it.

The rooms are furnished in the simplicity of a 17th century farm. Fresh flowers from our perennial gardens welcome you, and our vegetable garden garnishes your full country breakfast.

At the farm, there's volleyball, ping pong, horseshoes, a picnic area, bicycles, a beaver pond to hike to, and cable TV.

The 1852 Inn is on Route 22, the Lake Shore Road, 1.7 miles north of the Essex-Charlotte (VT) ferry. Shuttle from and to the ferry or marinas provided.

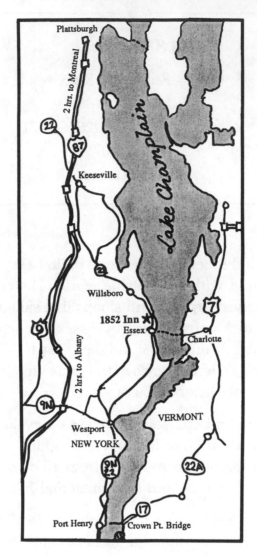

Area things to see and do:

Adirondack Center Museum
Art Galleries
AuSable Chasm
Biking
Bird Watching
Climbing the High Peaks
Essex and Willsboro Beach
Hiking
Historic Essex Hamlet
Lake Champlain Boat Tours

Meadowmount School of Music
Santa's North Pole
Shelburne Museum
Shelburne Farms
Vermont Wildflower Farm
Westport Depot Theatre
Whiteface Mountain Aerial Chairlift &
    Memorial Highway
Willsboro Golf Course
Willsboro Fish Ladder

1852 INN

SEPTEMBER FRIED GREEN TOMATOES
AND PUFFBALL MUSHROOMS

Surplus of unripened tomatoes
Plenty of wild giant puffball
   mushrooms
Seasoned bread crumbs

Parmesan cheese
Lots of garlic powder
A few eggs, beaten

     Slice green tomatoes about ¼ inch thick. Slice puffballs about ½ inch thick and peel. Mix equal parts of seasoned bread crumbs and Parmesan cheese and lots of garlic powder on a large plate. Beat a few eggs in a bowl. Press the tomato slice into the crumb mixture, then the egg, then back into the crumb mixture and saute in olive oil over low heat until golden brown. Repeat with the mushrooms. (The extra mushrooms can be frozen after cooling and being wrapped in plastic wrap.) Garnish with pickled fiddleheads, fresh herbs, and nasturtium flowers, pansies, or Johnny jump-ups, all edible.

Lil & Isaac Iten
1852 Inn
Willsboro, New York

15

CHICKADEE

Bed & Breakfast

Country Road Lodge

A secluded idyl at the end of a country road.
Since 1974

Hickory Hill Road (HCR 1 #227)
Warrensburgh, New York 12885
518-623-2207
Steve and Sandi Parisi, Innkeepers

Country Road Lodge

Awaken . . .

. . . to the aromas of freshly-brewed coffee and muffins baking in the oven. A full country breakfast of your choice, including home baked bread, is offered between 7:30 and 9 a.m. Bird watching from the breakfast table occasionally interrupts conversations with hosts and other guests. Panoramic views of the Hudson River and prominent Sugarloaf Mountain provide further distraction.

Originally a modest farmhouse and then a summer "camp" for a Warrensburgh family, **Country Road Lodge** came into being as a bed-and-breakfast and ski lodge in 1974.

A Word about Warrensburgh . . .

This town of 3,800 people, situated on the Schroon River, was once a river-powered mill town. The mills are gone but many of the graceful old homes built during the town's heyday remain, and enhance the quiet, tree-lined streets. The town is known for its antique shops and contains several very fine restaurants. Garage sales abound (including "The World's Largest Garage Sale," held in the fall, with more than 500 sellers!)

Warrensburgh is just five miles from famous Lake George with its beaches, scenic boat cruises, amusements, and fine restaurants. Saratoga Springs and its thoroughbred racetrack, harness racing, and Performing Arts Center are less than an hour away. You won't want to miss a visit to the Adirondack Museum at Blue Mountain Lake, in the heart of the Adirondacks, or a drive to Lake Placid and the High Peaks region.

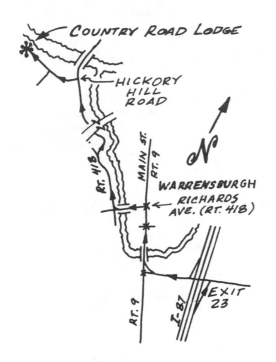

Directions

Take the Adirondack Northway, I-87 (NYS Thruway Exit 24 at Albany) to Warrensburgh Exit 23 (approximately 65 miles north of Albany) and follow signs into Warrensburgh. Turn left off Route 9 (Main St.) onto Route 418 (at traffic light in front of stone church). Follow Rt. 418 for 3 miles along river to Hickory Hill Road, on left. (If you find yourself crossing a bridge, you just missed the turn.) Country Road Lodge is ½ mile down Hickory Hill Road.

COUNTRY ROAD LODGE OATMEAL

3 c. water*
1½ c. oatmeal
¼ c. bran
¼ c. Wheatena

¼ tsp. pumpkin pie spice
1 Tbs. unsweetened coconut
    (optional)
3 Tbs. raisins

* Water may need to be adjusted, depending on type of oatmeal used.

Put all in small crockpot. Mix; turn on before going to bed. Wake up to delicious cooked oatmeal.

Serve with yogurt. Makes 3 to 4 servings.

Inkeepers: Steve & Sandi Parisi
Country Road Lodge
Warrensburgh, New York

🍎 🍎 🍎

HERBERT HOEGER'S APPLE RAISIN CAKE

1½ c. oil
2 c. sugar
3 eggs
1 tsp. vanilla
3 c. unbleached flour
1 tsp. baking soda
1 tsp. cinnamon

1 tsp. salt
3 medium apples, cored but
    unpeeled, thickly sliced
1 c. raisins
1 c. walnuts, chopped
Whipped cream

Preheat oven to 350°. In a mixing bowl combine the oil, sugar, eggs, and vanilla. Mix well. In a separate bowl combine the flour, baking soda, cinnamon, and salt to form a very stiff batter. Mix the dry ingredients into the wet. Stir the apples, raisins, and walnuts into the batter and spoon into a well-greased and floured Bundt pan. Bake 1 to 1¼ hours. Cool before removing from the pan. Serve plain or top with whipped cream.

Innkeepers: Steve & Sandi Parisi
Country Road Lodge
Warrensburgh, New York

PINE TREE INN
Bed and Breakfast

Route 9
North Hudson, New York 12855
518-532-9255
Peter & Patricia Schoch

ADIRONDACK STURDY

The main house was constructed circa 1865. It was known as the Schroon River Inn until the three story wing was added in 1928.

Original oak floors, together with a tin ceiling and hanging globe fixtures in the dining room are hallmarks of the period.

The inn today remains a classic Adirondack structure designated by the Town Board as a historic building.

COME HAVE BREAKFAST

Real maple syrup, homemade breads, eggs, French toast, or pancakes served with slab bacon or country sausage. Juices, freshly brewed coffee, and a variety of teas round out a filling meal.

LOCATION

½ mile north on Rt. 9 from I-87, exit 29 and Frontier Town.

INNKEEPERS

Pete and Pat will welcome you year round.
518-532-9255

OATMEAL APPLE RAISIN MUFFINS

1 egg
¾ c. raisins
½ c. oil
1 c. rolled oats
2 tsp. cinnamon
1 tsp. baking soda

¾ c. milk
1 large apple, chopped
1 c. whole wheat flour
¼ c. sugar
1 tsp. nutmeg

Beat egg. Stir in remaining ingredients, mixing just to moisten. Pour into 12 greased muffin pan or muffin cups until ¾ full. Bake in preheated 400° oven for 15 to 20 minutes. Allow to cool slightly in pan for 10 minutes. Serve warm. Makes 12 servings

Pine Tree Inn
North Hudson, New York
Bed & Breakfast

🍏 🍏 🍏

OVERNIGHT SWEET ROLLS

1 pkg. frozen dinner rolls (12 in a pkg.)
½ c. brown sugar

½ c. margarine
2 tsp. cinnamon

Place frozen pieces of dough in a lightly greased Bundt pan around the bottom of the pan. Melt margarine with brown sugar and cinnamon. Pour evenly over rolls in pan. Cover with foil and let rise overnight. Bake in a 350° preheated oven in the morning for 30 minutes. Let stand 10 minutes after removing from the oven. Invert onto serving plate and serve warm. Makes 12 servings.

Patricia B. Schoch
Pine Tree Inn
North Hudson, New York
Bed & Breakfast

THE OWL is taken from the Latin root word meaning "to howl."

Being nocturnal, the owl's keen sense of sight and acute sense of hearing, along with soft plumage that allows for noiseless flight, come in handy when hunting for meals. The great horned owl does not have a sense of smell which comes in handy when dining on skunk.

Common to the Northeast are the Eastern Screech Owl, Great Horned Owl, Long-Eared Owl, and the Barn Owl. Less common are the Barred Owl and Northern Saw-Whet Owl, seldom seen unless found roosting.

HIGH PEAKS INN

Route 73
P.O. Box 701
Keene Valley, New York 12943
518-576-2003
Linda & Jerry Limpert

Our Bed & Breakfast, built circa 1910, has been a guest home throughout most of its existence. My husband and I, former probation officers, have been owners since September, 1993. We try to provide a hearty breakfast as many of our guests are hikers, climbers, and skiers.

Linda Limpert

HIGH PEAKS INN CLOVE MUFFINS

¼ c. shortening
½ c. sugar
2 eggs
¼ c. orange juice
¾ c. milk

2 c. flour
½ tsp. salt
4 tsp. baking powder
1½ tsp. ground cloves

Cream together shortening and sugar. Add eggs and beat well. Mix dry ingredients together. Combine milk and orange juice. Add dry ingredients and liquid ingredients alternately to mixing bowl and beat until blended. Fill greased muffin tins ⅔ full. Bake at 450° for 10 to 12 minutes. Makes 1 dozen.

Linda Limpert
High Peaks Inn
Keene Valley, New York

The LAMPLIGHT INN

Bed and Breakfast

1992 "INN of the YEAR"

**The Complete Guide to Bed & Breakfasts,
Inns & Guest Houses in the U.S. & Canada**
2129 Lake Ave., P.O. Box 70
Lake Luzerne, New York 12846
(518) 696-5294 or 1-800-262-4668
INNKEEPERS: GENE & LINDA MERLINO

The Lamplight Inn is located in the picturesque village of Lake Luzerne, 18 miles north of Saratoga Springs and 10 miles south of Lake George. Built in 1890, this spacious Victorian was built as the summer residence of wealthy lumberman, Howard Conkling. Conkling spared no expense building his summer bachelor retreat.

Purchased as a whim in 1984, the innkeepers are the third owners of the home since 1890 and the first to live in the home through an Adirondack winter. It took a year to complete the first renovations and to officially open in September 1985. Today, the inn offers ten romantic bedrooms. Five have gas burning fireplaces, all private baths and central air conditioning. All the bedrooms are individually decorated, furnished with antiques and wicker, fluffy comforters and lace curtains. The memorable breakfast is served on a spacious sunporch with mountain view.

The Lamplight Inn has been voted the "1992 Inn of the Year" by the readers of the *Complete Guide to Bed & Breakfasts, Inns and Guesthouses in the United States and Canada*, by Pamela Lanier listing over 6000 inns. Most recently, the Lamplight Inn is proud to have a seven page article and photos in the December 1993 Christmas issue of *Country Inns Magazine*.

Directions

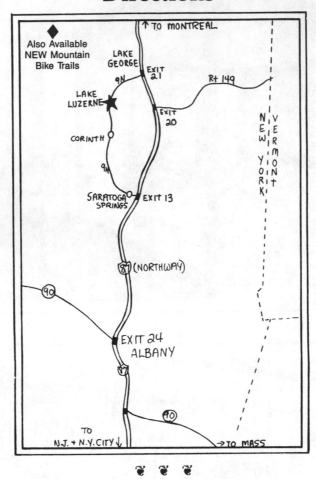

❦ ❦ ❦

LINDA'S STRAWBERRY BREAD

3 c. flour
1 tsp. baking soda
1 tsp. salt
3 tsp. cinnamon
2 c. sugar

2 c. frozen strawberries, thawed
  (not drained)
4 eggs, beaten
1¼ c. corn oil
1¼ c. walnuts, chopped

Mix dry ingredients. In large bowl mix wet ingredients. Stir in dry ingredients until well blended. Pour into greased loaf pans. Bake at 350°—check loaves after 40 minutes. Cool on rack. Makes 4 small loaves.

The Lamplight Inn
Lake Luzerne, New York
Bed & Breakfast

CINNAMON BUTTERMILK COFFEECAKE

2¼ c. flour	¼ tsp. ginger
1 c. light brown sugar	¾ c. corn oil
¾ c. granulated sugar	1 c. sliced almonds
2 tsp. cinnamon	1 tsp. baking powder
½ tsp. salt	1 tsp. baking soda
	1 egg
	1 c. buttermilk**

** Powdered buttermilk can be substituted for a quart of buttermilk. Works just as well.

Mix flour, sugars, 1 teaspoon cinnamon, salt, and ginger. Blend in oil until smooth. Remove ¾ cup of mixture and combine with almonds and remaining cinnamon. Mix and set aside. To remaining flour mixture add baking powder and baking soda, egg, and buttermilk; blend until smooth. Pour into a buttered 9x13 inch pan. Sprinkle almond mixture evenly over batter. Bake at 350° for 35 to 45 minutes. Cut into squares.

The Lamplight Inn
Lake Luzerne, New York
Bed & Breakfast

❧ ❧ ❧

LAMPLIGHT PEAR AND CRANBERRY CRISP

TOPPING:

1 c. flour	¼ tsp. salt
⅔ c. light brown sugar	½ c. butter, cut into pieces
½ c. old-fashioned oats	

FILLING:

8 to 10 firm, ripe pears	2 Tbs. flour
1 c. fresh cranberries	½ tsp. cinnamon
½ c. sugar	¼ tsp. nutmeg

Topping: Combine first 4 ingredients. Add butter and blend with fingertips until mixture is in crumbs.

Filling: Toss all ingredients in bowl to combine well. Transfer to a 9x11 Pyrex dish. Sprinkle topping over filling. Bake at 350° until top is golden and juices bubble (about 1 hour).

The Lamplight Inn
Lake Luzerne, New York
Bed & Breakfast

LAMPLIGHT APPLE OATMEAL CRISP

Granny Smith apples—	Sugar
1 per person	Melted butter
peeled, cored and	Rhubarb—if
sliced	available
Cinnamon	

TOPPING:

⅓ c. flour	½ tsp. salt
1 c. old-fashioned oatmeal	1 c. walnuts, chopped
½ c. light brown sugar	½ c. melted butter
1 tsp. cinnamon	

Toss apples with a little cinnamon, sugar, and melted butter. If rhubarb is available, chop and add to apples. Mix topping in separate bowl and spread topping over apples. Bake at 375° for 35 minutes.

Innkeepers: Linda & Gene Merlino
The Lamplight Inn
Lake Luzerne, New York
Bed & Breakfast

❦ ❦ ❦

MOM'S CHEESECAKE

All ingredients must be at room temperature.

4 (8 oz.) pkg. cream cheese	2 c. sugar
2 (16 oz.) containers sour cream	6 eggs
1 c. milk	2 Tbs. whiskey
1 Tbs. flour	Graham cracker crumbs

Sprinkle bottom of spring pan or tube pan with graham cracker crumbs to cover bottom of pan. Beat all ingredients and pour into prepared pan. Bake at 475° for 15 minutes. Lower heat to 225° and bake 1 hour longer. Turn off oven and let cake remain in oven for ½ hour. Remove to cool.

The Lamplight Inn
Lake Luzerne, New York
Bed & Breakfast

The Inn at Saratoga

231 Broadway
Exit 13N Off The Northway (I-87)
Saratoga Springs, NY 12866
518-583-1890
Fax 518-583-2543
Barbara Beck, General Manager

The Inn at Saratoga invites you to enjoy our delightful atmosphere and cozy surroundings which are sure to please you.

A testimony to Saratoga's vibrant presence, we offer you both the energetic atmosphere of professional boardroom suites plus all the comforts of a fully restored historic inn... with our own supreme cuisine and exceptional facilities.

Enjoy the charming old world ambiance of our intimate Cocktail Lounge while sipping your favorite beverage.

Good talk and relaxation abound, too in our Victorian appointed Restaurant where, along with our regular dining menu, we invite you to sample special selections offered nightly or enjoy the famous Sunday Jazz Brunch.

We feature harmonious and peaceful decor inside and a lovely lawn and garden for you to fully enjoy outside. Our accommodations include thirty-eight graciously furnished rooms and suites. A conference center and banquet area with a capacity for up to 150 people is also available. The reception area overlooks our delightful English garden which provides a lovely setting for weddings, parties, and other gatherings. Two boardroom suites are also available for meetings with seats for up to fourteen persons each.

Shop to your heart's content at the quaint and creative Saratoga shops and boutiques as well as the five nearby shopping centers and outlet malls.

The Inn at Saratoga is open year round. We're just south of some of the best skiing in the Northeast. We're centrally located to the world-famous Saratoga Thoroughbred Racetrack; the Saratoga Harness Track; the Saratoga National Historic Park, the National Museum of Dance; the National Museum of Racing; the Mineral Baths; and the Saratoga Performing Arts Center, summer home of the New York City Ballet and the Philadelphia Philharmonic Orchestra and a featured weekend with the Newport Jazz Festival. Saratoga is also the home of Skidmore College since 1903.

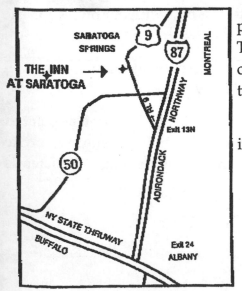

With a genuine and refined presence first established in 1880, The Inn At Saratoga bids you to celebrate the opulence of Saratoga today.

Join us please. Our pleasure is in serving you.

The Inn at Saratoga was built in 1880. Throughout the many years of existence, this Inn has been a famous landmark in Saratoga, where many weary racetrack visitors have found a comfortable stay.

General Manager Barbara Beck and Cindee Doherty have been a great help with our publication by assisting us with the Book/ Press release reception. Thank you!

APPETIZERS

Sauteed Artichoke Hearts over Spinach with Raspberry Vinaigrette

Shrimp Cocktail with Ancho Chili Cocktail Sauce

Salmon Cake with Red Pepper Tomato Coulis

SOUPS

Bisque of Lobster and Herbs

Chef's Soup Created Just for Today

SALADS

Grilled Italian Vegetables with Mixed Greens and Balsamic Vinaigrette

Baby Garden Greens, Herbs and Croutons with Buttermilk Dressing

PASTA

Tri-Colored Tortellini with Alfredo and Grilled Chicken

Linguini with Fresh Tomato Basil Sauce and Jumbo Shrimp

ENTREE

Chicken Piccata with Lemon, Capers and Mushrooms

Breast of Chicken, Sauteed in Virgin Olive Oil with Roasted Red Peppers,
    Artichoke Hearts and Pine Nuts

Marinated Pork Tenderloin, Grilled and served with a Black Currant Sauce

Broiled Scallops with Tri-Citrus Butter and White Wine

Gulf Shrimp Sauteed Scampi Style with Roasted Garlic

Grilled Filet of Salmon served with Lemon and Dill Beurre Blanc

Grilled New York Strip Steak with Parsley Fried Onions

Steak "Au Poivre" with Cognac Sauce

Filet Mignon served with Tomato, Mushrooms and Rosemary Ragout

Veal Medallions with Shitaki Mushrooms and finished with a
        Whole Grain Mustard Cream

Chefs at The Inn at Saratoga

GRILLED BREAST OF DUCK
WITH STRAWBERRY RHUBARB CHUTNEY

¼ c. sugar	2 c. strawberries, sliced
¼ c. cider vinegar	4 c. rhubarb stalk, diced
¾ c. red onion, chopped	Pinch of ground cloves
1 tsp. minced garlic	½ tsp. cinnamon
1 Tbs. minced ginger	½ tsp. ground cumin

Chutney: In saucepan, combine all ingredients except for onion, strawberries, and chutney. Bring to a simmer over medium heat until sugar dissolves. Add remaining ingredients and cook over low heat until rhubarb softens and mixture thickens, about 5 to 8 minutes. Cool until ready for use.

Duck: Trim fat and score the skin on four breasts of duck. Place skin side down in saute pan and render duck fat over low heat until skin is crispy, about 10 to 15 minutes. Finish by grilling duck meat side down on grill until desired temperature. Slice and serve with heated chutney. Any remaining chutney should be refrigerated. Also excellent with chicken or pork.

Dining Room Chef: Francois D' Aluiso
Banquet Chef: Dan Oyer
The Inn at Saratoga
Saratoga Springs, New York

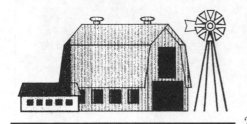

Fo'Castle Farms

166 Kingsley Road
Burnt Hills, New York 12027
518-399-8322

The favorite time of year is harvest, but anytime is a favorite time. Especially if you come from Burnt Hills and you're at Fo'Castle Farms. Where they have it all, a farm stand, a gift shop, a country-style coffee shop, and an apple orchard.

The business was established in 1908 and has grown. The on-premise bake shop is notorious for turning out homemade breads, pies, wonderful breakfast muffins, and my favorite, scrumptious doughnuts. Also stop in for breakfast or lunch as they have a fine array of choices to choose from. This place is a real find but don't keep it to yourself, bring a friend!!

HARVEST MAPLE PUMPKIN SOUP

4 lb. pumpkin, not peeled
5 Tbsp. oil
2 medium onions, sliced (2 cups)
2 tsp. salt
Freshly ground black pepper
⅛ tsp. cinnamon
5 c. chicken broth

Vegetable broth or commercial
    broth or bouillon cubes
1 c. light cream
¼ c. real maple syrup
1 stick unsalted butter, cut into
    cubes
Salt and pepper to taste

Preheat the oven to 425°. Cut the pumpkin into 2 inch slices. Do not peel, but scoop out the seeds and cut off the stringy mush. Brush 2 tablespoons olive oil over the slices and place on a cookie sheet lined with aluminum foil, peel against the paper. Roast for 30 minutes.

When pumpkin is cool enough to handle, slice off the peel with a large chef's knife. If any of the flesh has burned, cut that off, too. Cut the roasted pumpkin into 2-inch cubes (about 6 cups). Heat the remaining 3 tablespoons olive oil in a 6-quart heavy-bottomed soup pot and add the onions. Cover, reduce the heat, and braise the onions for 5 minutes without coloring. Stir in the pumpkin and sprinkle with salt, pepper, and nutmeg. Cover and braise for another 5 minutes. Pour in the broth, bring to a boil, cover, reduce the heat, and simmer for 20 minutes or until the pumpkin is very tender.

Puree the soup in a blender or food processor, ladle by ladle, or use an immersion blender. Reheat the soup; while it's reheating, add the cream, maple syrup and butter. Whisk until smooth. Season with salt and pepper as needed. Add more cream if soup is too thick. Serves 6 to 8.

Chef Debbie Smith, Fo'Castle Farms
Burnt Hills, NY

The Friends Lake Inn

Chestertown, New York
518-494-4751
Sharon & Greg Taylor, Innkeepers

Formerly known as Murphy's Friends Lake Inn, this landmark was built in 1860 as a boarding house to provide a "home-away-from-home" for men working in the local tannery, a main industry of early Chestertown. The Inn became a summer home for many as the Adirondacks developed into a popular retreat from the crowded city during the Prohibition Era. Horse-drawn buggies transported guests from the New York-North Creek rail stop at the "Glen" (Rt. #28) to the Inn for a summer stay, enjoying quiet days at the lake and nights at the "Grill" across the street.

As car travel became a way of life and motels popped up with the development of Lake George, the day of grand hotels ended in the Adirondacks. The Inn had been vacant for many years when we found it. We've tried our best to recreate the atmosphere, charm, and hospitality that the Murphy's began over 100 years ago. The physical restorations are as accurate as we could make them, while providing all the comforts of the modern era. We welcome old friends to come share what we've done and invite new friends to join us in enjoying the comforts of our home.

Our dining room captures the ambiance of the 19th century while specializing in sophisticated 20th century cuisine and service. Guests enjoy exquisite cuisine, homemade pates and breads, and irresistible international desserts. An Award Winning wine cellar reflects our passion in pairing fine food with wines. Eight original rooms and seven junior suites individually decorated offer our guests several comfortable options . . . including in-room jacuzzi tubs. Activity abounds year-round for our guests: hiking, biking, swimming, canoeing, & Nordic Skiing are all offered on site. Rafting, golfing, tennis, shopping, & downhill skiing can be found near-by. Come to Friends Lake Inn & enjoy all the Adirondacks has to offer in comfort and style.

Sharon & Greg Taylor, Innkeepers

Seasonal Menu Sample

Salad of Fresh Spring Greens, House Dressing

Entree Selections

Duck Breast, Pan Seared with Black Peppercorns
served with a Sherry Maple Demi-Glace

Salmon Filet Poached in Citrus Fruit Juices,
served with a Kiwi Butter Sauce

Pork Loin, Roasted and Topped with Stir Fry of Spring Vegetables

Saffron Angelhair Pasta with Shrimp, Scallops
and Fresh Vegetables

Dessert

A Spring Strawberry Shortcake

Coffee & Tea

Cappucino　　　　　　　Espresso

Friends Lake Inn uses fresh local mushrooms.

SNAPPING TURTLE SOUP

2 lb. veal bones
½ c. veal fat
2 onions, chopped with skin
1 stalk celery, chopped
2 carrots, chopped
½ tsp. marjoram
2 cloves
1 bay leaf
½ c. flour

2 qt. beef broth
1 c. tomatoes, chopped
1 lb. snapping turtle meat, cut
　　small
1 c. sherry
1 tsp. Tabasco sauce
2 tsp. kosher salt
1 hard-boiled egg

Heat oven to 400°. Place veal bones and fat in roasting pan with onions, celery, carrots, and spices. Place in oven and brown. Remove and dust with flour and stir in and return to oven for 25 to 30 minutes. Pour bones into large pot, add the broth and tomatoes. Simmer 4 to 6 hours and then strain. Add turtle meat with sherry, Tabasco, and salt. Allow to simmer 10 to 15 minutes. Serve and garnish with chopped egg.

Friends Lake Inn
Chestertown, New York

*The Inn has a beautiful flower garden
around the property*

VEGETARIAN CHILI

1 Tbs. canola oil
1 Tbs. garlic, minced
Crushed chippolte pepper
½ c. onion, diced
¼ c. bell pepper, diced
½ c. carrot, diced
1 c. cooked black beans, rinse if
    canned

1 c. cooked kidney beans, rinse if
    canned
1 c. white and yellow hominy
2 c. tomatoes, diced
3 c. tomato juice
1 tsp. dried oregano
2 tsp. ground cumin

Heat oil in a saucepan; add garlic, chippolte, onion, bell pepper, and carrot. Saute until you smell the garlic. Add remaining ingredients; simmer for 10 to 15 minutes. Serve hot with good bread and an earthy red wine.

*Friends Lake Inn
Chestertown, New York*

Pan Seared Duck Breast with Sherry Maple Sauce

PAN SEARED DUCK BREAST
WITH SHERRY MAPLE SAUCE

4 Mallard duck breasts, skin
   removed
1 Tbs. cracked black peppercorns
1 tsp. oil
1 Tbs. shallots, minced

¼ c. sherry vinegar
3 Tbs. maple syrup
½ c. Demi Glace
¼ tsp. salt
⅛ tsp. white pepper

Sprinkle black pepper over ducks and press into meat. In large saute pan warmed over medium-high heat, add oil and then duck breast. Allow to sear 2 minutes then turn over and cook for 3 minutes. Time will vary depending on thickness of breast. Duck breast is best when done medium rare. Remove breast from pan; keep warm. Add shallots and saute for 30 seconds; add vinegar and allow to reduce by ⅔. Add maple syrup and Demi Glace. Season with salt and pepper; allow to simmer 1 minute. Slice duck and spoon sauce over. Garnish with chopped parsley and pink peppercorns.

Friends Lake Inn
Chestertown, New York

Shop or ski at the nearby North Creek Village.

WILD BOAR CHOPS WITH APPLE CIDER SAUCE

12 center cut wild boar chops, 1
   inch thick
3 bay leaves
1 Tbs. coriander seed
1 Tbs. fennel seed
1 cinnamon stick
3 star anise
2-3 sprigs thyme

1 tsp. crushed red pepper
½ tsp. black peppercorns
⅛ tsp. nutmeg
5-6 sprigs parsley
1 Tbs. sugar
1 tsp. salt
⅛ tsp. white pepper
6 c. water

In saucepan add all ingredients, except chops, to the water. Bring to a simmer for 2 to 3 minutes; remove from heat and allow to cool. Place chops in spice liquid and allow to marinate for 24 hours. Grill and serve with apple cider sauce.

Friends Lake Inn
Chestertown, New York

APPLE CIDER SAUCE

½ c. cider vinegar
2 Tbs. shallots, minced
2 tsp. cracked black peppercorns
2 c. apple cider

¼ c. chicken broth
2 Tbs. arrowroot or cornstarch
½ tsp. kosher salt
¼ tsp. white pepper

In small saucepan, add vinegar, shallots, and peppercorns over high heat. Reduce volume by half. Add apple cider and allow to boil 2 to 3 minutes. Blend chicken broth with remainder of ingredients and add to boiling mixture. Allow to boil 2 more minutes. Remove from heat. Sauce may be cooled and refrigerated for several days.

Friends Lake Inn
Chestertown, New York

The Book & Blanket

Bed & Breakfast
P.O. Box 164, Rte. 9N
Jay, New York 12941
Kathy, Fred and Samuel, Hosts

Nestled in the charming hamlet of Jay, The Book & Blanket Bed & Breakfast is your jumping off point for a multitude of all-season activities and adventures in the Adirondack North Country. Less than 10 miles from Whiteface Mountain, our home offers skiers a roaring fire and plenty of books to relax with after an exhilarating day on the slopes. Mornings bring hearty breakfasts, including home-baked breads, muffins and fresh-ground coffee.

The Book & Blanket is just 17 miles from the bustle of Lake Placid and its Olympic venues. It is ideally situated in the Adirondacks on the east branch of the Ausable River, where fishing, swimming and hiking are literally a stone's throw away. Ausable Chasm, ferries to Vermont and Fort Ticonderoga are all easy day trips—even Montreal is less than 2 hours by car.

The Book & Blanket offers three spacious guest rooms (private bath available). Guests may choose from the Regency elegance of the Jane Austen room, the gentlemanly sophistication of the F. Scott Fitzgerald Room or the rustic comfort of the Jack London Room.

There's also a James Thurber nook (Thurber wrote one of his short stories on a stay in Jay), an extra-large porch (complete with swing), and an exuberant basset hound on the premises. But most of all there are books—in every room. Many of the books may be borrowed by guests "indefinitely." This means if you get interested in a novel, mystery, etc., you may take it with you to finish at your leisure. Perhaps on another visit you will leave a book of yours for another guest.

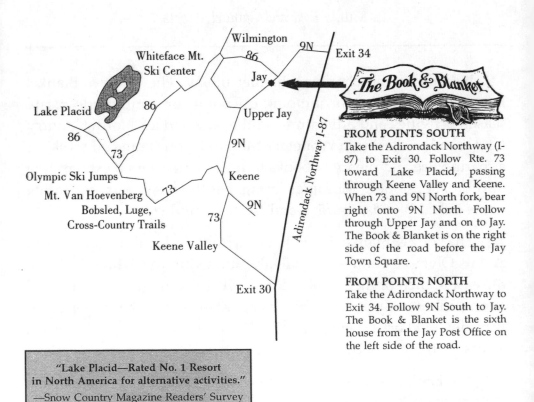

FROM POINTS SOUTH
Take the Adirondack Northway (I-87) to Exit 30. Follow Rte. 73 toward Lake Placid, passing through Keene Valley and Keene. When 73 and 9N North fork, bear right onto 9N North. Follow through Upper Jay and on to Jay. The Book & Blanket is on the right side of the road before the Jay Town Square.

FROM POINTS NORTH
Take the Adirondack Northway to Exit 34. Follow 9N South to Jay. The Book & Blanket is the sixth house from the Jay Post Office on the left side of the road.

"Lake Placid—Rated No. 1 Resort in North America for alternative activities."
—Snow Country Magazine Readers' Survey

NON-DAIRY (aka VEGAN) BANANA BREAD

1½ c. flour
½ tsp. salt
1 tsp. baking soda
½ c. olive oil

3 mashed ripe bananas (very ripe)
Egg Replacer (equivalent of 2
   eggs)
1 c. pure maple syrup

Preheat oven to 350°. Grease (with olive oil) and flour a loaf pan. In a large bowl mix the egg replacer, mash in the bananas, add the maple syrup and olive oil and continue mixing with a fork. In a separate bowl toss together the flour, salt and baking soda. (Optional: sprinkle in a little wheat germ too.)

Add the dry ingredients to the wet mixture and stir just until batter is blended. Pour into the prepared pan and bake for about 35 to 40 minutes, or until a skewer or toothpick comes out clean.

Remove from oven and let cool in pan for about 5 minutes; then turn onto a rack to cool completely.

My husband (who does not eat Vegan) likes this even better than the original recipe which calls for egg and sugar!

CARDINAL

THE POINT

Saranac Lake, New York 12983
518-891-5674 ❧ 800-255-3530 ❧ FAX 518-891-1152

THE POINT: AN ADIRONDACK GREAT CAMP

What is a Great Camp?

The Adirondack Great Camp represents a unique episode in American architectural history. From the end of the Civil War to the beginning of the Great Depression (1870-1930), a group of industrialists, financiers, and railroad magnates came to northern New York to build family vacation retreats. The Adirondack mountains provided them with an opportunity to assemble vast private holdings enclosing lakes, ponds, rivers, and forests. The newly wealthy rose to the challenge.

Attracted by the beauty, grandeur, and wilderness mystique of the region, they hired local craftsmen to build "camps" of native materials on a scale matching the "cottages" of Newport and "spa's" of Saratoga. As ownership of an Adirondack camp became fashionable, the Webbs, Vanderbilts, Whitneys, Lewisohns, and Rockefellers built their woodland retreats in isolated locales surrounded by hundreds of acres.

Collectively called Great Camps, these homes were constructed with a mixture of logs, native stone, and decorative rustic works of twigs and branches. They were built to co-exist with the surrounding environment, not to impose upon it, and as a result, a certain harmony exists between these "tree-houses" and the land on which they're built.

The Point . . . A Short History

The Point, originally named Camp Wonundra, was completed in 1933 for William Avery Rockefeller, a great-nephew of John D. Rockefeller. The last of the three camps designed by prominent Adirondack camp architect, William Distin, The Point stands on Whitney Point on the western shore of Upper Saranac Lake. Built in the Great Depression, this camp typified the post-World War I phase of Great Camp architecture with a reduction in the number of buildings, and closed the era of Great Camp construction.

The original estate consisted of an informal complex of nine buildings situated on the 10-acre peninsula that The Point currently encompasses. The nine buildings included the Main Lodge, the Boathouse, the Guest House, a garage/maintenance building (now a second guest house, renamed Eagle's Nest), a one-car garage (now a kitchen supply storage room), a garage/woodshed (where the office and management's quarters now stand), a small sap house (existing but non-functional), an Adirondack lean-to (still existing and functional), and a stone pump house which is still a working part of the Point's water system.

William A. Rockefeller built The Point as his private residence, and not only as a summer home but for year-round use. Consequently, The Point was winterized during its original construction. The foundation walls of the Main Lodge and the Guest House are massive, native cut stone. Both buildings are constructed with halved logs of Canadian pine set horizontally although corners have notched projecting logs, suggesting true log construction.

Progressions of logs project at the roof eaves and at the apex of the gables. The halved logs in the gables are peeled and set vertically. All the roofs are original slate, and most have a gable shape. The vestibule on the Main Lodge has the Queen Anne pyramid roof. Other exterior features are metal window sashes, bay windows, wrought-iron hardware, and massive chimneys made of local fieldstone boulders. Inside, most of the floors are pegged wood. The walls and ceilings are covered with wide-board pine wainscoting.

Camp Wonundra became "The Point" in 1980, with the need for additional local accommodations during the winter Olympics in Lake Placid, New York. Since that time, The Point has been offering its guests the warm hospitality of a private home, set amidst tradition and old romanticism. A retreat or hideaway for many, The Point offers the privacy and comforts of one's own home, and this is something The Point staff go to great lengths to ensure. Because many of our guests lead high-profile lives, in order to provide them with the atmosphere for which The Point is renowned, we always respect our guests' privacy and practice a strict code of utmost discretion regarding their identity.

Today The Point has 11 guest rooms, all with their own individual characters and appeal, and their own names. The Main Lodge has four guest rooms, the Eagle's Nest guest house has three (two upstairs above the Pub and one downstairs), the Guest House has three, and finally there is one very large accommodation above the Boathouse. The names of the guest rooms, by building, are as follows:

- Main Lodge: Mohawk, Algonquin, Iroquois, and Morningside
- Eagle's Nest: Sentinel, Lookout, and Trappers
- Guest House: Saranac, Weatherwatch, and Evensong
- Boathouse: the Boathouse.

A Relais & Chateaux Member

The Point has been a member of the prestigious Relais & Chateaux association since 1983. This Paris-based hotel group consists of 411 deluxe, highly individual hotels and gourmet restaurants in 36 countries throughout the world. The Relais & Chateaux properties offer the discerning traveler an intriguing alternative to large chain hotels; properties which reflect the personality and dedication of the hotelier, as well as the region in which each is located. The Point, as with all Relais & Chateaux members, has met very exacting entry requirements. But most importantly, it shares the steadfast commitment to the highest quality of warm, personal service and the five C's of Relais & Chateaux hospitality: Character, Courtesy, Calm, Comfort, and Cuisine.

About the Owners

David and Christie Garrett bought The Point from Ted Carter in October 1986. They first discovered this wonderful hideaway in 1981 when they visited on their anniversary. Needless to say, they fell in love with the property and its ambiance, and returned year after year. David, a stock broker, and his wife Christie, a landscape architect, reside in Burlington, Vermont. In 1986 when The Point went up for sale, the Garretts decided to try their hand at the business of being hoteliers, and have done very well, indeed.

About Your Host and Hostess

Bill and Claudia McNamee moved to the Adirondacks from Washington, D.C. in 1987 to manage The Point. Neither one of them had been involved in the management of hotels or inns previous to this; however, Bill is a chef and has worked in some of the finest restaurants in the world. It was Bill's culinary talents that initially brought them to The Point. Originally trained in Paris at Le Cordon Bleu, Bill has since worked as chef in a number of different restaurants including Le Pavillon in Washington, D.C., Le Chardon D'Or of The Morrison House in Alexandria, VA, and Michelin three-star restaurant, LeGavroche in London.

Claudia, on the other hand, had no previous experience in the hotel or restaurant business. She had spent her years in D.C. working as a hydrogeologist for a private environmental consulting firm, specializing in hazardous waste management. The move to The Point, for both Claudia and Bill, was a big change but came out of their mutual desire to take on something entirely different; something on which they could work together. As General Managers of The Point, their responsibilities cover many areas, including reservations, marketing, staffing, cuisine, wine selection, house and grounds maintenance, to name just a few.

About the Cuisine

When David and Christie Garrett bought The Point nearly eight years ago, one of their highest priorities was to upgrade the cuisine and the quality of food service. To this end, they sought the guidance of Michelin three-star chef, Albert Roux, who owns and operates one of the world's only 23 three-star restaurants, Le Gavroche in London. At the time that the Garretts were conferring with Mr. Roux, Bill McNamee had just returned to Washington, D.C. from his one-year sabbatical as one of the chefs at Le Gavroche. Mr. Roux subsequently asked Bill to represent him as a consultant to the Garrett's. It was at this time, in December 1987, that Bill initially became involved at The Point as a consultant to the kitchen. There is now a continuing affiliation between Albert Roux and The Point which ensures that The Point's kitchen staff is of the highest quality. Bill McNamee not only holds position of General Manager, but also acts as Executive Chef. To compliment Bill in the kitchen, young aspiring chefs are regularly brought over from Le Gavroche to work for 6 to 12-month periods. In this manner, The Point's cuisine is always fresh, with new ideas and new talent.

Things To Do

There are a multitude of activities that one can indulge in while staying at The Point. These activities differ, of course, with the changing seasons.

Winter is truly magical at The Point — deep pristine snow, frosted windows, and a remarkable quality of hushed stillness prevails. We provide ice skates and cross-country ski equipment for skating and skiing on the frozen lake. Snow-shoes are also available for treks through the woods. Enjoy a snow barbecue out on the point or on one of the nearby islands; set in front of a big bonfire, this is a favorite pastime of our winter guests. Ice-fishing if also available using The Point's custom-made ice-fishing shanty. Nearby there is downhill skiing, snowmobiling, dog sled rides, tobogganing, bobsledding, and horseback riding. A visit to Lake Placid is always fun, especially if you catch one of the exhibition sporting events such as the ski jumping at the Olympic ski jump facility. You can also go for a run on the Olympic luge or bobsled if you're up for it! And, of course, another favorite activity during the winter months is simply to curl up in front of a warm, crackling fire with a good book and a mug of hot chocolate or spiced apple cider.

Summer and autumn activities include boating, fishing, hiking, picnicking, swimming, water skiing, tennis, golf, bicycling, and horseback riding. Our boathouse harbors a small fleet of waterworthy vessels, including a 30-foot launch for cocktail cruises, a ski boat for water-skiing; smaller outboard motor boats and canoes for fishing and exploring; a sunfish and sailboard; and two classic, vintage mahogany runabouts for leisurely touring the lake. Fishing equipment is also available to our guests. Lake fish include trout, salmon, pike, and bass — all good fishing depending on the season. Also, enjoy nearby tennis and golf, and miles and miles of hiking in the area.

PEPPERED SEA BASS WITH RED WINE SAUCE

2 fresh sea bass (about 2½ lb.)

BRAISED SHALLOTS:

10 large shallots
3 c. Port
4 c. red wine

⅓ c. sugar
1 Tbs. cracked black pepper
Pinch of salt

RED WINE SAUCE:

8 shallots
½ box mushrooms
2 c. Port
6 c. red wine
1 sprig fresh thyme

1 bunch fresh basil
1 bay leaf
1 Tbs. black peppercorns
3 c. veal stock

GARNISH:

Sauteed spinach
Potato puree

Braised shallots

Sea Bass:

1. Descale, filet, and remove all bones from the fish. Trim belly part of the fish leaving a square filet about 4 inches long. With a sharp knife, make about 8 incisions across the back of the skin side.

2. Gently flour the filets. Crush ½ cup peppercorns and place filets skin side down into the crushed peppercorns, allowing the peppercorns to go into the incisions. The fish is now ready to be sauteed.

Braised Shallots:

1. Pour the wine and Port into a saucepan. Add the sugar, salt, and pepper. Add the shallots. Bring to a boil then cover with a lid or foil and slowly cook in the oven at 325° for 3 to 4 hours until soft.

Red Wine Sauce:

1. Peel and slice shallots and mushrooms into a saucepan. Add the rest of the ingredients (except for the veal stock) and bring to a boil. After it boils, reduce heat and simmer until a syrup-like consistency.

2. Add the veal stock and reduce by half. Strain thru a fine strainer. Check the seasoning.

Assembly:

1. Saute the bass skin side down in whole butter with a little oil until skin is golden brown, then turn fish over and cook the flesh side about 2-3 minutes.

2. In the center of the plate spoon some of the potato puree. Place cooked spinach all around the plate. Place braised shallots on top of the fish. Pour red wine sauce around the plate and serve. Serves 4.

Chef James Byars
The Point ◆ *Saranac Lake, New York*

58

Oscar's Adirondack Mountain Smokehouse

22 Raymond Lane
Warrensburg, New York 12885
1-800-627-3431

The Quintal family is famous for outstanding smoked meats. Since Oscar's recent appearance on the Food Network, food connoisseurs as far as Hawaii, are ordering incredible hams, bacon, sausages, and cheese. Try our liverwurst sandwich recipe which Bob and I prepare on the tailgate of the truck while stopping at Oscar's for lunch ingredients. It has become an instant classic and a funny tale to tell.

If you are a breakfast lover, you will certainly enjoy the following nitrate-free bacon available:

- Maple smoked
- Pepper smoked
- Double smoked
- Cajun smoked
- Applewood
- Hickory

ARMAND & BOB'S FAMOUS TAILGATE SMOKED LIVERWURST SANDWICH

Makes 4 sandwiches

2 lb. Oscar's smoked liverwurst, hand cut in ½ inch slices
8 slices potato bread or fresh rye
1 jar Oscar's sweet mustard

1 can French's fried onions, (if on the road), optional or 1 large onion, sliced and sauteed until brown (if home), optional

Pull the tailgate down of your pick-up truck, SUV or station wagon. Lay out 8 slices of bread. Spread generously with mustard. Divide the liverwurst slices amongst 4 of the slices. Sprinkle with fried or sauteed onions. Top the sandwiches with remaining 4 slices. Pack in your lunchbag and wash it down with chocolate milk from Stewart's or Cumberland Farms.

Consult your physician for possible addiction regarding this sandwich.

The Lodge on Lake Clear

P.O. Box 46
Lake Clear, New York 12945
Phone/Fax 518-891-1489

History

Built by the Otis Family, The Lodge at Lake Clear began over 100 years ago catering to pioneer travelers when the rail line was a major linkage connecting NY City and Montreal. The Hohmeyer Sr.'s began operating The Lodge in 1965, adding their German heritage and European traditions. Their son Ernest and his wife Cathy, great niece of the Otis family, now own and operate the property.

Old World Eatery

Cathy spent two years apprenticing in Mrs. Hohmeyer's kitchen learning her authentic Old World style of cooking. This, combined with the Adirondack recipes preserved from the Otis family and a bit of personal flair, offers the current Adirondack traveler a unique blend of "Old World Traditions" and seasonal Adirondack tastes.

(Recommended by SKI Magazine, Nov '93). Hearty roasts, healthy sautees and bountiful soups are prepared nightly on a 1946 Magic Chef stove. Currently we offer our traditional, hearty, five-course dinners to the public. For folks staying with us or our co-op members, a variation of our five-course dinners or light "pub" fare is available. Dinners by reservation only.

Rathskellar

Our German/Adirondack Rathskellar is available to dinner guests, Lodge guests, and Co-op guests. We serve speciality coffees, teas and freshly-made juices as well as alcoholic beverages, including German and other specialty beers in front of the fireplace. Relax or challenge a friend to a board game, pool, or ping pong. When possible please give us a call before you arrive especially if you are a small group.

Menu Sample

The Lodge
on Lake Clear

P.O. Box 46 "An Old World Inn" Phone/FAX
Lake Clear, NY 12945 (518) 891-1489

The Lodge features a unique full-course German/Adirondack meal in a warm, informal, and personal atmosphere. Each evening meal is created just for that evening's guest list, therefore reservations are a must.

The Unique Full-Course Dinners include:

Appetizer

Usually a minimum of 6 choices to include:
Smoked oysters, marinated herring, marinated hearts of artichoke, fruit cup, chicken liver pate, vegetable pate, shrimp cocktail, escargot and others.

Soup

One soup per night:
Mrs. Hohmeyer's famous chicken soup, her beef version, or a unique onion or oxtail soup.

Salad

Two choices:
German marinated cucumber salad or a fresh greens that varies with the seasons.

Entree

Always a minimum of four entree choices:
Weinerschnitzel, Roast Pork Loin, Roast Long Island Duckling, Cornish Game Hen with Wild Rice, Rabbit Sautee, Venison Sautee, Saurbraten with Potato Dumplings, Salmon & Haddock with a mustard caper sauce, Lamb Sautee, Roast Lamb, Lobster nestled in a caper and wine sauce, Pork Tenderloin Sautee, Fresh baked Trout with an herb sauce, German Beef Roulade and more.

Vegetables Served Family Style that vary with the Seasons

Dessert

Always homemade, vary with the seasons:
The Lodge cornucopia, German apple cake, German chocolate cake, apple strudel, homemade ice cream, blueberry pudding cake, Black forest cake, liqueur parfaits and many more
Served with our special blend of coffee at your request.

We celebrate an extensive red and white wine list. Also available are espresso and cappucino from our coffee bar.

The Lodge is ideal for intimate and fun small groups, also business oriented functions. Relax by the fireplace in our Rathskellar before or after your specially prepared meal. Since all items are not served nightly, you are welcome to request a special favorite if you wish—"first call, first choice."

We also feature Bed & Breakfast Rooms and Adirondack Chalets.

63

A typical Adirondack stove found in many lodges.

Although we serve some traditional German dishes, the Lodge never really uses recipes—but more a philosophy on blending fresh ingredients and tastes. On the next page is our Pork Tenderloin Saute. We vary meats and vegetables to season, freshness, and individual taste. For example, for our lamb saute we use fresh lamb (preferably with a bone), onions, potatoes, and green beans or a beef tenderloin with mushrooms and onions. The variations are as endless as your appetite and imagination.

PORK TENDERLOIN SAUTE

Saute a cup of onions, a clove or two of garlic, a couple pieces of bacon and 2 to 3 pork tenderloins (cut in 1 inch "cubes") in a deep saucepan. Simmer with a couple of handfuls each of sweet green peppers and mushrooms, a bay leaf, a couple of celery stalks, and a carrot. Add a little fresh hot pepper if you like a sharper taste. Simmer just until meat is done (approximately 20 minutes). Add a small amount of cornstarch mixed with water to thicken. Simmer 5 more minutes. Remove from heat and add ½ cup of good red wine. Serve over your choice of pasta for a light meal.

❦ ❦ ❦

GERMAN APPLE CAKE

Peel and core 6 to 8 large Granny Smith apples. Thinly slice into a bowl. Sprinkle on ½ cup sugar, 2 teaspoons cinnamon, and a dash of nutmeg. Set aside.

In a small bowl combine 1⅓ cups flour, ½ cup sugar, 1 egg, ¼ stick butter, 1 teaspoon salt, 1 teaspoon vanilla, and 2 teaspoons baking powder. Pat into a buttered springform pan bringing the dough 1 inch up the sides. Pour in apples.

Crumb ½ stick butter, ¼ cup sugar, and ⅔ cup flour and crumble on top.

Bake 30 minutes in 350° oven. Top should be slightly brown. Serve plain or with vanilla ice cream or whipped cream.

THE GREAT BLUE HERON is the largest of the North American herons.

He wades slowly through shallows or stands with his head hunched on shoulders when hunting. You will see him in the Ausable River dining on frogs and small fish during the Adirondack summers. He spends the winter months south of the Mason-Dixon line.

SWEENEY'S

Bruin Haven Inn
Restaurant & Cabins

Route 30
Sabael, New York 12864
518-648-5450
Alicia M. & Patrick M. Sweeney

OVEN OMELET

¼ c. butter or margarine	1 c. milk
1½ dozen eggs	2 tsp. salt
1 c. sour cream	¼ c. onions or scallions, chopped

Preheat oven to 325°. Melt butter or margarine in a 13½x9x2 inch baking dish by placing in oven. Take out of oven and tilt dish to coat bottom with the melted butter.

In a large bowl beat eggs, sour cream, milk, and salt until blended. Stir in the onions. Pour into dish and bake until the eggs are set, but still moist, about 35 minutes. Serves 12.

Alicia M. Sweeney
Sweeney's Restaurant & Cabins
Sabael, New York

ROBIN

June '94

A Graciously Restored
1837 Country Gentleman's Greek Revival

The
Chester Inn

BED & BREAKFAST

On the National Register of Historic Places
in the Historic District of
Chestertown, N.Y.

PHONE: (518) 494-4148

The Chester Inn
P.O. Box 163   Main Street
Chestertown, N.Y. 12817

Bruce and Suzanne Robbins & family welcome you to:

THE CHESTER INN

SITUATED: on 13 acres of meadowlands amidst 19th century barns, carriage stalls, and its own smoke house . . . in the heart of the beautiful Adirondacks.

HISTORY OF THE CHESTER INN: Built by Charles Fowler, a merchant from Albany, N.Y. One of the early pioneer salesmen, Mr. Fowler became a prosperous banker and businessman.

IN THE MID 1880s Harry Downs acquired the Fowler estate and the "Chester House," a large Adirondack hotel which was adjacent to the Fowler home.

THE HORSES AND CARRIAGES: were stabled in barns (which still stand) behind the house, for the use of guests staying at the Chester House.

Map of Area around Chester Inn

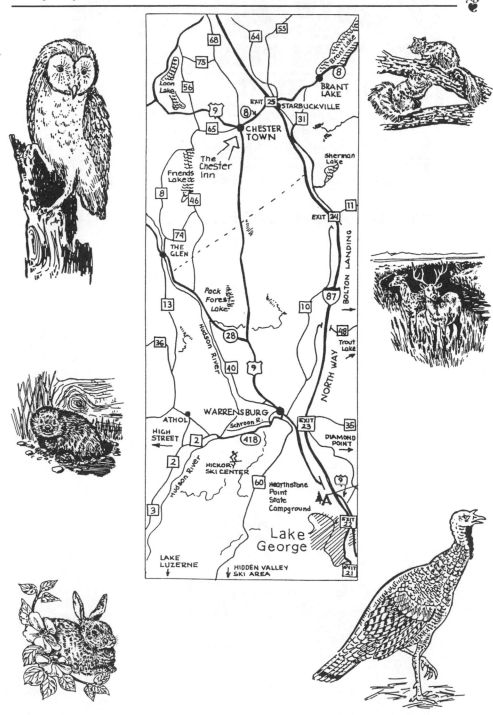

TOMATO MUSHROOM AND BASIL SOUP

1 lb. mushrooms	5 c. all-purpose tomatoes
1 red onion	1½ tsp. salt
5 Tbs. margarine	1½ tsp. sugar
5 Tbs. flour	Basil to taste
5 c. milk	

Mix together the mushrooms, onion, and margarine. Add the 5 tablespoons of flour sprinkled over the above and cook for one minute. Then gradually pour in 5 cups of milk, heated over low heat, then add 5 cups of all-purpose tomatoes with 1 teaspoon of baking soda. Then add 1½ teaspoon salt, 1½ teaspoon sugar, and basil to taste

Bruce Robbins, Sr.
Main St. Ice Cream
The Chester Inn

ADIRONDACK BAKED FRENCH BREAD

6 large eggs
1½ c. milk
1 c. light cream
1¼ tsp. vanilla
¼ tsp. cinnamon
¼ tsp. nutmeg

1 loaf French bread
¼ c. butter, softened
½ c. light brown sugar
½ c. walnuts, chopped
1 Tbs. maple syrup

Butter large baking dish. In medium bowl, beat eggs, milk, cream, vanilla, cinnamon, and nutmeg. Cut bread into 1 inch slices. Place sliced bread in baking dish, single layer with sides touching. Pour entire mixture over bread. In small bowl combine topping mixture (melt in microwave if necessary). Spread evenly over bread. Cover and refrigerate overnight. In morning, preheat oven to 350°, bake 40 minutes or until puffed and golden brown. Serves 6 to 8.

Innkeeper Bruce Robbins
The Chester Inn
Chestertown, NY

🍒 🍒 🍒

CHESTER INN STRAWBERRY CREAM DRESSING

½ c. mayonnaise
1 (8 oz.) pkg. cream cheese,
   softened
1 (3 oz.) pkg. cream cheese,
   softened

½ pt. sour cream
1 c. fresh strawberries
½ c. powdered sugar

Place all ingredients in food processor with steel blade, or use blender. Process until smooth and creamy. Spoon over individual plates of fresh fruit—kiwi, strawberry, banana, and melon—sprig of mint to the side.

Innkeeper Bruce Robbins
The Chester Inn
Chestertown, NY

HOUSE FINCH

THE STAGECOACH INN — SINCE 1833
370 OLD MILITARY ROAD, LAKE PLACID, N.Y. 12946   (518) 523-9474   TLX 858383

THE STAGECOACH INN
(SINCE 1833)

Directions —

From the South: I-87 (Adirondack Northway) to exit 30, to Rt. 73 to Lake Placid—left on Old Military Rd.

From the North: I-87 (Adirondack Northway) to exit 34 to Rt. 9N to Rt. 86 to Lake Placid—left on Rt. 73— Right on Averyville Rd.—left on Old Military Rd.

From the West: I-81 to Watertown, Rt. 3 to Saranac Lake, Rt. 86 to Lake Placid—right on Old Military Rd.

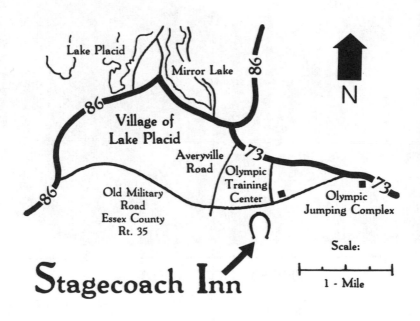

STAGECOACH INN PANCAKES

2 c. oatmeal
2 c. buttermilk
2 eggs
¼ c. butter/margarine, melted
Zest from one orange
½ c. flour

2 Tbs. sugar
½ tsp. baking powder
½ tsp. baking soda
½ tsp. ground cinnamon
¼ tsp. ground nutmeg

Soak the oatmeal and buttermilk overnight. Combine the orange zest with the sugar and let it sit overnight as well.

The next day, mix the eggs and cooled melted butter together and add to the oatmeal mixture.

Mix the remaining ingredients together and mix into the oatmeal/egg mixture.

Makes twelve to fifteen pancakes. Serve with maple syrup and orange butter.

❦ ❦ ❦

ORANGE BUTTER

½ lb. butter, softened
Zest from two oranges

2 Tbs. sugar
¼ c. orange juice

Mix the softened butter with the orange zest and sugar. Slowly add the orange juice to blend well. Can be stored in the refrigerator or frozen.

Andrea Terwillegar, Cook

BLUE JAY

Goose Pond Inn

A Country Bed & Breakfast

Main Street, P.O. Box 273
North Creek, New York 12853
(518) 251-3434
Beverly & Jim Englert

A turn of the century bed and breakfast offering travelers respite in comfortable surroundings. The Inn has four guest rooms with a private bath, each filled with antiques and collectibles. It is truly a Bed & Breakfast adhering to the charm of an earlier time.

The Inn's celebrated gourmet breakfast is served each morning in our country dining room overlooking our pond, featuring such delicacies as Jim's brandied French toast with sautéed apples being a special favorite. Special blended coffees, homemade Belgian waffles with flambéed bananas, pancakes with seasonal fruit and crêpes with rhubarb sauce are a few of our daily specials.

A friendly place to stay while you enjoy four seasons of the Adirondacks. The Inn has a charming setting at the edge of town with a one-mile ride to Gore Mountain Ski Center. Cross-country ski trails are practically right in our back yard.

Late March through mid-June and again in the fall, Hudson River rafting tours offer incredible whitewater excitement.

Our summer season is beautiful; relax in a tube in the Hudson River, hike in the Siamese Wilderness area, mountain bike on the ski trails or browse for antiques, collectibles and handcrafts nearby.

Nothing can surpass the beauty of the Adirondacks in the fall. Foliage is at its peak late September into October.

After a full day of Adirondack adventure relax by a warm fire in our cozy living room or enjoy a game of pool or darts in our separate game room. A great getaway at any time of the year. Come feed the geese!

DIRECTIONS: Route 87 to exit 23, follow signs for Gore Mountain, North Creek. Travel along route 9 to route 28 into North Creek. Make a right turn at Business District sign on to Main Street. We are located one mile down the road on the right.

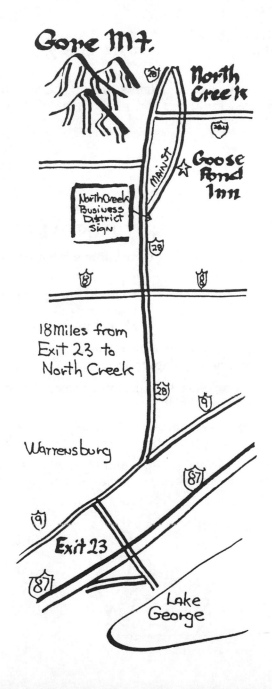

BRANDIED FRENCH TOAST
WITH SAUTEED APPLES

APPLES:

2 Granny Smith apples, peeled & thinly sliced

Dash of cinnamon & nutmeg
Clarified or melted butter

FRENCH TOAST:

6 slices hard crust Italian bread, sliced ½ inch thick
4 eggs

¼ c. milk
1 Tbs. brandy

Soak bread in combined ingredients, turning several times. Bake on lightly greased preheated griddle or flat pan 2 minutes on each side until browned. Add more butter if desired. Yield 2 servings.

Jim Englert
Goose Pond Inn
North Creek, New York

❧ ❧ ❧

CARROT-WALNUT PANCAKES

Use your favorite pancake mix or use this scratch pancake recipe.

3 eggs, separated
3 Tbs. butter, melted
1 Tbs. sugar
1½ c. sifted flour

1 tsp. soda
1 tsp. baking powder
½ tsp. salt
1⅔ c. buttermilk

Egg mixture: Beat 3 egg yolks with mixer at medium speed. Beat in 3 tablespoons melted butter and 1 tablespoon sugar.

Flour mixture: Sift together 1½ cup flour, 1 teaspoon soda, 1 teaspoon baking powder, and ½ teaspoon salt.

Beat flour mixture into egg mixture alternately with 1⅔ cups buttermilk at low speed. Fold in at same speed 3 stiffly beaten egg whites. Bake on griddle.

Add ½ cup grated carrots, ¼ cup walnuts, and ¼ teaspoon cinnamon. Fold these ingredients into your choice of pancake mix. Bake on griddle! Bon Appetit!

Jim Englert
Goose Pond Inn
North Creek, New York

MOOSE RIVER HOUSE
BED and BREAKFAST
12 Birch Street / P.O. Box 184
Thendara, N.Y. 13472
(at Old Forge)
315-369-3104

Built circa 1884 as a small hotel, Moose River House was accessible only by boat. The double-decked "Fawn," a tiny side-wheeler, steamed upstream from Minnehaha where the only wooden train rails ended.

Today, refurbished in Victorian style, we delight in sharing its guest rooms overlooking the river which offers miles of canoeing, fishing, or just enjoying the wild life in its natural habitat. Enjoy the comfort of your room or the fireplaced living room where you can read, watch television, play games, or just visit with the other guests.

It is our desire that you feel like "an honored, special guest in our home" at Moose River House.

Originating here is the canoe trip through the eight lakes of the Fulton Chain and Raquette, Forked, Long, and Saranac Lakes. A summer chairlift and picnicking are available on McCauley Mountain, which in winter offers 11 alpine trails and 20 kilometers of cross-country skiing.

Summer recreation includes golfing, horseback riding, hiking, and water sports. Nearby Old Forge has fine gift and antique shops to browse and many restaurants to enjoy. Spend a day at the Enchanted Forest or the Blue Mountain Museum.

Breakfast is included in the price of each room and is served between 8:30 and 9:00 in the dining room or outside deck, both of which overlook the river.

Members of:
Bed & Breakfast Association of New York State
Central Adirondack Association

Owners: Kate and Bill Labbate & Family

315-369-3104

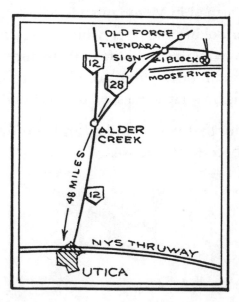

APPLE MUFFINS

1 egg
½ c. milk
¼ c. oil
1 c. apple, grated
1½ c. all-purpose flour

½ c. sugar
½ tsp. cinnamon
2 tsp. baking powder
½ tsp. salt

TOPPING:

¼ c. brown sugar, packed
¼ c. broken nuts

½ tsp. cinnamon

Beat egg in small bowl and add milk, oil, and apple, mixing well. In large bowl combine flour, sugar, cinnamon, baking powder, and salt. Add apple mixture to dry ingredients; batter will be lumpy. Fill greased muffin pan ⅔ full. Mix together topping mix. Sprinkle over batter. Bake in 400° oven for 25 to 30 minutes. Serve warm.

Makes 12 muffins

Kathleen Labbate
Moose River House Bed & Breakfast

PHOEBE

June '94

Mirror Lake Inn

ADIRONDACK MOUNTAINS - LAKE PLACID, NEW YORK 12946
518-523-2544

This modern resort hotel is located on a hillside overlooking Mirror Lake. The many conveniences available (spa, gym, hair salon, tennis court, pools, private beach, winter skating rink), make this a popular spot in Lake Placid for those who want it all!!

Favorites are "The Placid Suites," with king size beds, whirlpool baths, private lakeview balconies and champagne and flowers upon arrival.

The Mirror Lake has a marvelous restaurant with a relaxful bar for the weary traveler. There is a dress code for dinner so don't show up in hiking gear . . .

The Inn is popular for its conference facility for large or small groups. In December the Inn is beautifully decorated in Christmas holiday lights and garments . . . a sight to behold.

VENISON SIRLOIN WITH
CHERRY & MELON COMPOTE

4 (4 oz.) venison steaks
4 pieces bacon
2 Tbs. dried cherry
¼ honeydew melon
¼ cantalope

2 Tbs. bourbon
½ c. maple syrup
Salt and pepper to taste
1 tsp. butter, melted

Compote: Combine the dried cherries and bourbon with a small amount of water and simmer to almost dry. Use a melon baller to scoop melons. Add the melons and syrup to the finished cherries. Cook for 5 minutes.

Prepare the venison by wrapping a slice of bacon around and picking. Heat a sauté pan with butter. Season the steaks and sauté to the desired tenderness.

Serve ¼ cup of compote over each steak.

Executive Chef Scott Wolcott
Mirror Lake Inn

❧ *AuSable Chasm* ❧
Keesville, New York

❧ *AuSable Chasm* ❧

Keesville, New York

← *White Face Mountain*
Wilmington, New York

Entrance to White Face Mountain
Wilmington, New York
↓

🥬 *Great Sacandaga Lake* 🥬

🥬 *Hudson River* 🥬
Upstate New York

❧ Santa's North Pole ❧
Wilmington, New York

❧ Lake George ❧
New York

← **Whiteface Mountain**
Wilmington, New York

→
Pottersville
Natural Stone Caves

✦ *Balloon Festival* ✦
Glen Falls, New York

&@ *Photographer/Author Robert E. Birkel, Jr.* @&
Blue Mountain Lake, New York

&@ *Saratoga Racetrack* @&

ếa Saratoga Springs, New York ấa

CANFIELD CASINO

BATCHELLER HOUSE

🍃 *The Adelphi Hotel* 🍃
Saratoga Springs, New York
Painting by Ardis Hughes

❧ *Saratoga Horse Racing* ❧

Vegetables

FOOD QUANTITIES FOR 25, 50, AND 100 SERVINGS

FOOD	25 SERVINGS	50 SERVINGS	100 SERVINGS
Rolls	4 doz.	8 doz.	16 doz.
Bread	50 slices or 3 1-lb. loaves	100 slices or 6 1-lb. loaves	200 slices or 12 1-lb. loaves
Butter	½ lb.	¾ to 1 lb.	1½ lb.
Mayonnaise	1 c.	2 to 3 c.	4 to 6 c.
Mixed filling for sandwiches (meat, eggs, fish)	1½ qt.	2½ to 3 qt.	5 to 6 qt.
Mixed filling (sweet-fruit)	1 qt.	1¾ to 2 qt.	2½ to 4 qt.
Jams & preserves	1½ lb.	3 lb.	6 lb.
Crackers	1½ lb.	3 lb.	6 lb.
Cheese (2 oz. per serving)	3 lb.	6 lb.	12 lb.
Soup	1½ gal.	3 gal.	6 gal.
Salad dressings	1 pt.	2½ pt.	½ gal.
Meat, Poultry, or Fish:			
Wieners (beef)	6½ lb.	13 lb.	25 lb.
Hamburger	9 lb.	18 lb.	35 lb.
Turkey or chicken	13 lb.	25 to 35 lb.	50 to 75 lb.
Fish, large whole (round)	13 lb.	25 lb.	50 lb.
Fish, fillets or steaks	7½ lb.	15 lb.	30 lb.
Salads, Casseroles, Vegetables:			
Potato salad	4¼ qt.	2¼ gal.	4½ gal.
Scalloped potatoes	4½ qt. or 1 12x20" pan	8½ qt.	17 qt.
Mashed potatoes	9 lb.	18-20 lb.	25-35 lb.
Spaghetti	1¼ gal.	2½ gal.	5 gal.
Baked beans	¾ gal.	1¼ gal.	2½ gal.
Jello salad	¾ gal.	1¼ gal.	2½ gal.
Canned vegetables	1 #10 can	2½ #10 cans	4 #10 cans
Fresh Vegetables:			
Lettuce (for salads)	4 heads	8 heads	15 heads
Carrots (3 oz. or ½ c.)	6¼ lb.	12½ lb.	25 lb.
Tomatoes	3-5 lb.	7-10 lb.	14-20 lb.
Desserts:			
Watermelon	37½ lb.	75 lb.	150 lb.
Fruit cup (½ c. per serving)	3 qt.	6 qt.	12 qt.
Cake	1 10x12" sheet cake 1½ 10" layer cakes	1 12x20" sheet cake 3 10" layer cakes	2 12x20" sheet cakes 6 10" layer cakes
Whipping cream	¾ pt.	1½ to 2 pt.	3 pt.
Ice Cream:			
Brick	3¼ qt.	6½ qt.	12½ qt.
Bulk	2¼ qt.	4½ qt. or 1¼ gal.	9 qt. or 2½ gal.
Beverages:			
Coffee	½ lb. and 1½ gal. water	1 lb. and 3 gal. water	2 lb. and 6 gal. water
Tea	¹⁄₁₂ lb. and 1½ gal. water	⅙ lb. and 3 gal. water	⅓ lb. and 6 gal. water
Lemonade	10 to 15 lemons, 1½ gal. water	20 to 30 lemons, 3 gal. water	40 to 60 lemons, 6 gal. water

VEGETABLES 🍎

ASPARAGUS AU RASPBERRY

1 lb. thin, locally grown
    asparagus
1 small Bermuda onion
¼ c. raspberry vinegar

3 Tbs. lite olive oil
3 Tbs. lemon juice
1 Tbs. lemon pepper

Steam asparagus until just tender — about 3 to 4 minutes. Mix vinegar, oil, lemon juice, and lemon pepper. Shake. Cut onion into thin slices; add to asparagus and pour dressing over all. Chill. Serve on Romaine leaves or red lettuce leaves.

Lee James, Kings Park, New York

MATUMBLA BAKED BEANS

Great Northern beans
1 small onion, peeled
2 to 3 slices salt pork

1 Tbs. brown sugar
½ tsp. dry mustard

Soak 1 package of beans overnight in water. The next day rinse and drain beans; cover with fresh water and simmer on stove until slightly tender. Layer the bottom of a bean crock with beans about 1½ inches deep and place onion in the middle of this layer of beans. Surround the onion with the slices of salt pork and brown sugar and mustard. Continue the layers of beans and salt pork with the seasonings, ending with a layer of salt pork on the top. Ladle in enough of the bean cooking liquid to come within 2 inches of the top level of the beans. Cover crock and cook in preheated 300° oven for 3 hours. Uncover and cook an additional 1 to 1½ hours.

Linda and Fred Robare, Pierce Field, New York

AUSABLE BEANS

1½ c. navy beans, small whites, or
  great Northern beans (dry)
1 c. stewed tomatoes, drained
1 c. chicken broth

1 onion, chopped fine
2 cloves garlic, minced
4 Tbs. butter
Salt and pepper to taste

Wash the beans. Soak overnight, or use the short method. Preheat oven to 300°. Drain beans and place in a bean pot with remaining ingredients. Stir, cover, and bake until liquid is nearly absorbed, about 2 hours.

For variation, substitute 1½ cups of dried rice for the beans. Add chopped tomatoes and 1 cup of chicken stock. If you are a garlic person, increase the minced garlic. You can also increase butter to one whole stick.

June M. Clow, Wilmington, New York

HIKER'S BAKED BEANS

1 lb. pea beans
½ lb. salt pork
½ tsp. baking soda (to reduce gas
    formation)

Pepper
Catsup
1 Tbs. shortening

Wash and soak beans overnight. In the morning, pour the water off and replace with fresh water. Bring to a boil for a few minutes. Pour off water and replace with fresh water, just covering the beans. You can add the baking soda to reduce gas formation. Add salt pork; can slice thinly before or after cooking. Boil until beans begin to get tender. Let the water boil down some before putting beans in a shallow 9 x 11 pan. Stir occasionally while boiling. When beans are ready, transfer to shallow pan, shake a little pepper on them, and add a small amount of catsup. Stir in shortening. Arrange the salt pork on top of the beans. Bake in a hot oven for about 2 hours. When pork browns on one side, turn it over. May need to add broth to the beans as they cook. Check occasionally. Test doneness by tasting.

Linda Naone, Tupper Lake, New York

Jay, New York

NORTHERN RED CABBAGE

¾ c. water
1 small head (2 lb.) red cabbage,
    finely sliced
3 tart apples, cored, peeled, cut
    into small cubes

¼ c. brown sugar, packed
½ tsp. cinnamon
¼ tsp. allspice
¼ tsp. cloves
2 Tbs. butter, divided

In large saucepan, bring all ingredients except 1 tablespoon butter to a boil. Reduce heat; cover, stirring occasionally. Simmer 45 minutes, or until cabbage is crisp tender. Stir in remaining butter; serve hot.

Helen Witts, Schenectady, New York

CARROTS PIEDMONTESE

1 lb. carrots, pared
3 Tbs. margarine
1 small onion, sliced very thin
1 small clove garlic
½ tsp. salt
1 Tbs. vinegar
1 Tbs. chives, finely chopped

Slice carrots into thin rings about ⅛-inch thick (approximately 3 cups). Cook in boiling salted water in a covered saucepan for 3 minutes; drain. Return parboiled carrots to saucepan; add margarine, onion, and garlic clove. Cover and cook over low heat for 10 minutes or until carrots are crisply tender. Remove and discard garlic; stir in vinegar. Place carrots in serving dish; sprinkle with chives.

Lynn Paska, Schenectady, New York

FRESH CORN FRITTERS

1½ c. fresh corn, sliced from cobs
3 eggs, separated
¾ c. flour
¾ tsp. baking powder
1 tsp. salt
¼ tsp. freshly ground black
pepper

Combine corn and egg yolks. Sift flour, baking powder, salt, and pepper together. Add to first mixture. Mix well. Beat egg whites until they stand in soft peaks. Fold into the corn mixture. Drop from a tablespoon into hot vegetable oil. Fry until a golden brown. Makes 1 dozen.

Carol M. Miller, Northumberland, New York

Carol M. Miller of Colebrook Farm in Northumberland, who runs an antique shop, sent us a large number of fantastic Adirondack recipes. The ample incorporation of fruits into her dishes is not only clever, but the fruits are also low-calorie substitutes for gravy. (See Carol Miller's pork chop recipe.) The baking is delicious. "We'll be over for coffee real soon, Carol!"

CORN SOUFFLE

1 (12 oz.) can creamed corn
1 (12 oz.) can whole corn
1 stick margarine
¼ c. sour cream
2 eggs, beaten
1 (8 oz.) corn bread mix
4 oz. Velveeta cheese, cubed

Mix all together and pour in casserole dish. Bake 50 to 60 minutes uncovered at 350°.

Ruth Lebanon, Corinth, New York

Lake Sacandaga, New York

EGGPLANT CORLEONE

3 to 4 eggplants	Italian sauce
6 to 8 Italian frying peppers	Frying oil
1 whole large onion	2 to 3 cloves of garlic
1 package Mozzarella, shredded	4 to 5 eggs for egg wash (beaten)

Peel eggplants; slice ¼-inch slices and let stand a few hours for moisture to evaporate. Egg wash the eggplant and dip into seasoned Italian bread crumbs. Fry to golden brown and drain — very important — on paper toweling. Slice peppers and onions; saute until soft, in oil and garlic, then drain. Next take pan, put the sauce in the bottom. Then put first layer of eggplant on bottom, then a layer of peppers and onions, then another layer of eggplant. Put some sauce on top of eggplant and then some cheese; continue layering until you end with a layer of eggplant with sauce on top with cheese. Bake at 375° until hot.

Al Retzlaff, Saratoga Springs, New York

Al Retzlaff of Saratoga Springs was the first to send in a recipe. His Eggplant Corleone was featured on Channel 10 TV. His "Original Saratoga Brownie" disappears fast at any of his many parties he orchestrates. "Bring them to the Book Release Party, Al!"

DEVILED GREEN BEANS

8 oz. whole green beans
1 Tbs. butter
2 tsp. prepared mustard

½ tsp. Worcestershire sauce
Pepper
Bread crumbs

Mix first 5 ingredients together. Place in casserole. Sprinkle with bread crumbs. Place in 325° oven until hot. Mushrooms and pimientos can be added, if desired. Serves 2.

Shirley Fahey, Hadley, New York

HENRIETTA'S KARTOFFOGLAZE

½ c. plus 2 Tbs. butter
1 c. fine dry white bread crumbs
3 slices bread with edges off
½ c. flour
½ c. farina (NOT quick cook)
3½ tsp. salt

¼ tsp. nutmeg
¼ tsp. white pepper
2 eggs
3½ c. riced potatoes (5 baked
   potatoes forced through a
   screen or rice masher)

In a heavy 8-inch skillet, melt ½ cup butter over medium heat. When butter is melted, drop in bread crumbs and toast them. Drain and put on side. With a knife cut the bread into ½-inch squares. Melt the remaining butter in a skillet and add the bread. Cook over moderate heat. Add bread cubes; stir until brown all over. Put croutons on paper towels and let dry. Combine flour, farina, 1½ teaspoons salt, nutmeg, and white pepper in small bowl. Beat with large spoon a few tablespoons at a time into the riced pot. Beat 2 eggs and put in potato mixture. Beat until dough holds spoon lightly. If too thin, add more flour 1 teaspoon at a time. Flour your hands. Scoop 2 teaspoons and roll into a ball. Press a hole in the center and put in 2 croutons; roll into a ball again. Bring 4 quarts of water with remaining salt to a boil. Drop in all balls and stir. Gently simmer for 12 to 15 minutes. Wait for dumplings to rise to surface, then cook for 1 minute longer. Remove dumplings. Serve on a platter. Makes 20 dumplings.

Henrietta Ellen Birkel, Corinth, New York

MAPLEWOOD BAKED POTATOES

4 medium potatoes, peeled and
   thinly sliced
3 slices bacon, diced
1 medium onion, chopped
¼ c. vinegar

¼ c. molasses
¼ c. packed brown sugar
1 tsp. mustard
1 tsp. flour
1 tsp. salt

Mix or toss above ingredients. Add to greased 2-quart casserole. Cover and bake 45 to 50 minutes at 475° until potatoes are tender.

Beverly A. Gillespie, Gloversville, New York

TWICE-TASTY POTATOES

4 baking potatoes
2 eggs
4 Tbs. butter or margarine
4 Tbs. whipping cream
Salt and pepper

¾ c. Cheddar or Monterey Jack
    cheese, shredded
1 Tbs. snipped chives
1 Tbs. carrot, thinly sliced

Rinse and scrub potatoes. Pat dry. Prick a few times with a fork. Bake at 375° for about 1 hour or until soft. Cut a thin slice off the top of each potato. Carefully scoop out the pulp. Put pulp in a bowl. Separate eggs. Add egg yolks to potato pulp. Stir and blend until smooth. Fold in butter, cream, chives, and carrots. Season to taste with salt and pepper. Beat egg whites until stiff peaks form. Fold into potato mixture. Fill potato shells with mixture. Sprinkle with cheese. Bake in oven at 375° for 15 minutes or until heated through. Serves 4.

Jackie Birkel, Corinth, New York

DODSON POTATO CAKES

1 c. leftover mashed potatoes
1 egg
¼ tsp. baking powder
4 rounded tsp. flour

1 tsp. salt
¼ c. milk
1½ c. sharp cheese, grated
1 small onion, grated

Mix all ingredients together. Fry in melted shortening in skillet until brown and edges are well set. Turn and cook other side until brown. Serves 4.

Mary Dodson, Burnt Hill, New York

Mary Dodson, a lifelong resident of the Adirondack, is a fervent collector of cookbooks and recipes. She started collecting her own family recipes when she was a young child. Check out her old homestyle recipes from her Adirondack families.

GRANDMA HARRIS' HOME FRIES

White potatoes, cooked
½ stick butter or margarine
Diced onions

Diced green peppers
Salt and pepper
Poultry seasoning

Cut up white cooked potatoes home-fry style. In fry pan melt butter. Add potatoes, onions, and green peppers. Add salt and pepper; sprinkle with poultry seasoning. Brown to desired doneness.

Gram Harris, Ballston Spa, New York

SLICED BAKED POTATOES

4 medium potatoes
1 tsp. salt
2 to 3 Tbs. butter, melted
2 to 3 Tbs. fresh herbs, chopped
  or 2 to 3 tsp. dried herbs

4 Tbs. Cheddar cheese, grated
1½ Tbs. Parmesan cheese

Scrub and rinse potatoes. Cut potatoes into thin slices, but not all the way through. Put potatoes in a baking dish, fanning them slightly. Sprinkle with salt and drizzle with butter. Sprinkle with herbs. Bake potatoes at 425° for 50 minutes. Remove from oven and sprinkle with cheeses. Bake for another 10 to 15 minutes. Serves 4.

Karen Graff, Clifton Park, New York

POTATO PUFFS

4 to 6 potatoes, peeled and
  cooked, then mashed
2 egg yolks, well beaten
2 egg whites, beaten until peaks
  form

1 small onion, diced
1 clove garlic, diced
1 Tbs. butter or margarine

Fold 2 stiffly beaten egg whites into fluffy mashed potatoes. Put aside. Saute onion and garlic until tender, but not brown. Add to mashed potatoes with the egg yolks. Mix together. Put into a greased casserole and bake for 30 minutes at 350° or until puffed and brown. Serves 4 to 6.

Shirley Fahey, Hadley, New York

SQUASH DELIGHT

Hubbard squash, cooked
1 onion, grated
1 carrot, grated
½ pint sour cream
1 stick butter or margarine,
  melted

1 can cream of chicken soup
½ pkg. stuffing mix
Salt and pepper

Bake squash in oven until shell is very soft, approximately 1 hour. Remove and allow to cool to handle. Remove skin and seeds. Mash squash until smooth. Add remaining ingredients. Put in casserole and bake for 30 minutes at 350° or until hot. Other types of squash can be substituted. Serves 6 to 8.

Shirley Fahey, Hadley, New York

SWEET POTATOES AND APPLES

4 medium size sweet potatoes
½ tsp. cinnamon
4 medium size apples
1 tsp. lemon juice
¾ c. light brown sugar, firmly packed
½ tsp. salt
2 Tbs. butter or margarine
½ c. water

Parboil sweet potatoes until tender; cool and skin. Cut into thick slices. Peel, core, and slice apples into ½-inch rings. Mix the sugar, salt, and cinnamon. Arrange alternate layers of sweet potatoes and apples in greased baking dish. Sprinkle each layer with sugar mixture and lemon juice. Top with apple rings. Dot with butter. Add water. Bake covered in a 375° oven for about 35 minutes. Remove cover and cook until apples are tender and top is browned, about 15 minutes or less. Serves 6.

Carol M. Miller, Northumberland, New York

VEGETABLE QUICHE

10 oz. broccoli
½ c. onion, chopped
½ c. green pepper
1 c. Cheddar cheese, shredded
3 eggs
1½ c. milk
¼ tsp. pepper
¾ c. Bisquick
1 tsp. salt

Combine uncooked broccoli, onion, green pepper, and cheese in pie plate. Beat remaining ingredients until smooth. Pour into pie plate. Bake until golden brown for 35 to 40 minutes at 300°. Test center with wooden toothpick. Should be dry. Serves 6.

Laura Roberts, Clifton Park, New York

IMPOSSIBLE GARDEN PIE

2 c. zucchini, chopped
1 c. tomato, chopped
½ c. onion, chopped
⅓ c. Parmesan cheese, grated
1 c. milk
⅓ c. Bisquick baking mix
2 eggs
½ tsp. salt
¼ tsp. pepper

Heat oven to 400°. Lightly grease 9-inch pie plate. Sprinkle zucchini, tomato, onion, and cheese in pie plate. Beat remaining ingredients until smooth, 15 seconds in blender on high speed. Pour into pie plate. Bake until golden brown and knife inserted in center comes out clean, about 30 minutes. Let stand 5 minutes. Garnish with tomato and zucchini slices if desired. Refrigerate remaining pie. Serves 6.

Lynn Paska, Schenectady, New York

Soups
and Chowders

COOKING SUGGESTIONS

To toast coconut for cakes, put in pie pan and place in moderate oven. Stir often from edges, to brown evenly.

*   *   *   *   *

Flour should be sifted once before measuring. Fill the cup without packing.

*   *   *   *   *

Do not grease the sides of cake pans, grease only the bottom.

*   *   *   *   *

When beating egg whites do not tap beater on bowl of egg whites. The jarring of beater will cause the whites to lose a great deal of their fluffiness. The beater should be tapped on the hand to clear off the whites.

*   *   *   *   *

Rub the bottom of the soup cup with a sliced whole garlic to accent the flavor of Navy Bean Soup.

*   *   *   *   *

Eggs should be at least three days old before using in cakes.

*   *   *   *   *

```
SLOW OVEN................250 to 325 degrees
MODERATE OVEN.......350 to 375 degrees
HOT OVEN....................400 to 450 degrees
VERY HOT OVEN.........450 to 500 degrees
```

*   *   *   *   *

When making cake icing or candy consisting of milk or cream and sugar, add one teaspoon of ordinary table syrup for each cup of sugar used. Boil in the usual way. Your finished product will be much smoother and not so apt to become sugary.

SOUPS AND CHOWDERS 🦌

CAMP CHILI

1½ lb. venison steak, cubed
2 Tbs. olive oil
1 Tbs. olive oil
1 medium onion, chopped
1 medium green pepper, chopped
2 garlic cloves, minced
1 (12 oz.) can beef broth
1 (6 oz.) can tomato paste

1 tsp. seasoned pepper
1 tsp. dry oregano
1 tsp. dry basil
3 Tbs. chili powder
6 whole bay leaves
½ tsp. salt
3 small dried hot red chili peppers
1 can pinto beans, drained

Saute steaks in 2 tablespoons of olive oil until browned. In Dutch oven, in 1 tablespoon of olive oil, saute onion, green pepper, and garlic. Add beef broth and tomato paste and stir to combine. Return the meat to this mixture and add oregano, basil, chili powder, bay leaves, pepper, chili pepper, and salt. Stir well. Add pinto beans. Simmer for 1 hour, stirring occasionally. Remove bay leaves before serving. Serve with a dollop of sour cream, grated Cheddar cheese, and/or chopped raw onion. This is very spicy chili. For milder version, decrease the chili powder and eliminate the hot chili peppers. Can be made with regular ground beef.

Linda and Fred Robare, Piercefield, New York

Linda T. Robare, a Ohio girl, was introduced to the typical Adirondack lifestyle 30 years ago, when she met her husband, a Tupper Lake resident. His mountain hunting, fishing, and trapping knowledge shows through in the recipes sent to us. Over the years they cooked on an old wood stove which, according to her, makes any food taste better . . . whether real or imaginary, it just works magic.

ADIRONDACK HOT DOG SOUP

2 lb. hot dogs, diced
7 potatoes, diced
2 large carrots, diced
3 stalks celery, diced
½ qt. spaghetti sauce

1 tsp. oregano
1 Tbs. garlic powder
Water (as needed)
Parmesan cheese (as needed)

Use a 6 quart kettle. Add all ingredients together in the kettle and add water to cover everything. Bring to a boil and cook until all vegetables are tender and hot dogs are plump. Season to taste with Parmesan cheese.

Anna Bialahoski, Wells, New York

BAVARIAN LENTIL SOUP

1 (16 oz.) bag dried lentils
8 c. beef stock
2 large onions, chopped
3 medium carrots, chopped
3 green onions, chopped
2 Tbs. red wine vinegar
2 Tbs. sugar (Yes, sugar! No substitutes!)
3 bay leaves
Pepper
Ground thyme
Salt
1 potato, cooked and diced (optional)
8 oz. smoked ham, diced (optional)

Soak lentils overnight, or bring to a boil for 1 minute (in plain water). Take off the stove and let stand for 1 hour. Drain lentils. Cook potato separately. Dice and set aside. Put lentils, chopped onions, chopped carrots, chopped green onions, and bay leaves in 10 cups of beef stock and bring to a boil. Cook over low heat for about 45 minutes or until lentils are tender but not too mushy. Stir regularly to avoid scorching. When fully cooked, add red wine vinegar, sugar, and optional diced cooked potatoes and smoked ham. Remove bay leaves and add salt, pepper, and ground thyme to taste.

Shashana Roehl

NORTHWAY ONION SOUP

1½ lb. onions, thinly sliced
3 Tbs. butter
1 Tbs. oil
½ tsp. salt
3 Tbs. flour
2 qt. beef bouillon
½ c. white wine (optional)
1 lb. Swiss cheese
1 lb. Gouda cheese
French bread (dry)
Parmesan cheese

Cook onion in butter and oil for 15 minutes covered. Uncover, add salt and cook on medium high for 40 minutes until golden brown. Stir in flour for 3 minutes. Add bouillon and wine and bring to a boil. Reduce heat and simmer 30 to 40 minutes. Grate cheese. Put soup in ovenproof bowls. Place thick slice of bread on soup. Put mixture of grated cheeses on top. Sprinkle Parmesan cheese on top. Bake 25 minutes at 350°; then broil until brown and bubbly.

Marilyn Mauro, Clifton Park, New York

ORANGE CARROT SOUP

1 tsp. fresh ginger, minced
8 carrots
4 scallions
3 Tbs. butter
3 c. chicken stock

Salt and pepper
6 navel oranges
2 Tbs. fresh coriander, chopped
for garnish

Mince ginger and cut carrots and scallions into thin slices. Melt butter in saucepan; add ginger, carrots, and scallions and saute over low heat until scallions are soft, but not brown (10 minutes). Add 2 cups of chicken stock, season with salt and pepper. Simmer, covered, until carrots are tender (about 10 minutes). Puree mixture in blender. Return puree to saucepan and add the remaining cup of chicken stock. Peel one orange and cut four thin slices for garnish. Squeeze 1½ cups juice from remaining oranges and add to saucepan. Season to taste. Chop coriander and sprinkle on top. Garnish with orange slice. Serves 4.

Chef Armand Vanderstigchel, Corinth, New York

POLISH POTATOES AND SAUSAGE SOUP

2 Tbs. butter
1 lb. (or more) kielbasa
1 c. onion, chopped
2 c. celery and leaves, chopped
4 to 6 c. pared carrots, sliced

3 c. pared potatoes, cubed
1 bay leaf
½ Tbs. thyme
½ c. beef bouillon or beef broth

In large kettle, melt butter. Add kielbasa, onion, and celery. Cook until onion and celery are tender. Add rest of ingredients except potatoes. Cover and cook 1½ hours. Add potatoes; cover and cook 20 minutes longer. Makes 3 cups.

William J. Davis, Clifton Park, New York

LUZERNE CHEESE AND CHEDDAR CHOWDER

4 c. water
3 c. cabbage, shredded
1 c. ham or Canadian Bacon,
   chopped
2 large carrots, thinly sliced

1 (5.5 oz.) pkg. dry au grautin
   potatoes
1 c. milk
1 Tbs. corn starch
1 c. frozen green beans

In a large kettle combine the first five ingredients. Bring to a boil, reduce heat. Simmer, covered, for 15 minutes. Combine milk; add corn starch. Add to soup along with frozen beans. Simmer, covered, for 10 to 15 minutes. Serves 4 to 6.

Mrs. Clarissa Mahr, Lake Luzerne, New York

FISH CHOWDER

Fish fillets
Carrot, grated
Onion, finely chopped
Celery with leaves, chopped
Bottled clam juice
Pimiento, chopped
Whole thyme
Whole tarragon

Bay leaves
White pepper
Old Bay Seasoning
1 quart half & half
Potatoes, cooked and diced
1 pint sour cream
1 stick butter
Flour

In Dutch oven or heavy soup pot, saute carrot, onion, and celery in melted butter for about 10 minutes. Add the fish and continue simmering for another 10 minutes or until fish flakes apart. To this mixture, add flour by spoonful until you have slightly thickened paste. Add clam juice, pimiento, thyme, tarragon, bay leaves, white pepper, Old Bay Seasoning, half and half, and potatoes. Slowly simmer all ingredients to blend flavors and then adjust seasonings to your taste. Just before serving, add sour cream and heat.

Linda and Fred Robare, Piercefield, New York

FISHERMAN'S CHOWDER

½ lb. diced bacon
1 large onion
6 potatoes
4 lb. fish
4 stalks celery, diced
Juice of 2 lemons
¼ lb. butter
4 garlic cloves, crushed

4 cloves
1 Tbs. ground pepper
1 tsp. Creole seasoning
1 tsp. salt
2 oz. bourbon
2 containers evaporated milk
2 c. water

Place 4 pounds fish in frying pan with enough water to half cover. Poach over low flame. Strain stock and put aside. Brown bacon in skillet and add onions and potatoes. Add fish and rest of ingredients, including stock. Serves 6.

William J. Davis, Clifton Park, New York

Entrees

MEAT ROASTING GUIDE

Cut	Weight Pounds	Approx. Time (Hours) (325° oven)	Internal Temperature
BEEF			
Standing rib roast			
(10 inch) ribs	4	1¾	140° (rare)
(If using shorter cut (8-inch)		2	160° (medium)
ribs, allow 30 min. longer)		2½	170° (well done)
	8	2½	140° (rare)
		3	160° (medium)
		4½	170° (well done)
Rolled ribs	4	2	140° (rare)
		2½	160° (medium)
		3	170° (well done)
	6	3	140° (rare)
		3¼	160° (medium)
		4	170° (well done)
Rolled rump	5	2¼	140° (rare)
(Roast only if high quality.	3	160° (medium)	
Otherwise, braise.)		3¼	170° (well done)
Sirloin tip	3	1½	140° (rare)
(Roast only if high quality.		2	160° (medium)
Otherwise, braise.)		2¼	170° (well done)
LAMB			
Leg	6	3	175° (medium)
		3½	180° (well done)
	8	4	175° (medium)
		4½	180° (well done)
VEAL			
Leg (piece)	5	2½ to 3	170° (well done)
Shoulder	6	3½	170° (well done)
Rolled shoulder	3 to 5	3 to 3½	170° (well done)

POULTRY ROASTING GUIDE

Type of Poultry	Ready-To-Cook Weight	Oven Temperature	Approx. Total Roasting Time
TURKEY	6 to 8 lb.	325°	2½ to 3 hr.
	8 to 12 lb.	325°	3 to 3½ hr.
	12 to 16 lb.	325°	3½ to 4 hr.
	16 to 20 lb.	325°	4 to 4½ hr.
	20 to 24 lb.	300°	5 to 6 hr.
CHICKEN (Unstuffed)	2 to 2½ lb.	400°	1 to 1½ hr.
	2½ to 4 lb.	400°	1½ to 2½ hr.
	4 to 8 lb.	325°	3 to 5 hr.
DUCK (Unstuffed)	3 to 5 lb.	325°	2½ to 3 hr.

NOTE: Small chickens are roasted at 400° so that they brown well in the short cooking time. They may also be done at 325° but will take longer and will not be as brown. Increase cooking time 15 to 20 minutes for stuffed chicken and duck.

Keeseville, New York

ENTREES 🍎

❧ BEEF ❧

SAUTEED BEEF AND WILD MUSHROOMS WITH BALSALMIC VINEGAR

1 lb. tender beef tips, cut into
    small pieces
½ c. shallots, minced
¼ c. olive oil
1 Tbs. garlic, minced
½ c. fresh basil, chopped
½ tsp. kosher salt
Pinch white pepper

¼ c. balsamic vinegar
½ lb. wild mushrooms (regular
    mushrooms will do!)
1 tsp. white sugar
½ c. red peppers, diced
1 c. beef bouillon stock (1
    bouillon cube to 1 cup of
    water; heat and set aside)

Note: Have all ingredients ready before you start your method. This saves time and avoids mistakes.

Saute quickly over high heat the beef, shallots, garlic, and mushrooms all at once in olive oil, stirring rapidly. Then add sugar and balsamic vinegar. Saute until beef is tender and then add diced red peppers. Pour bouillon stock in pan; a steaming effect will take place, so stand away from pan when pouring in liquid!! Stir and add sugar and basil leaves. Turn down heat and finish with salt and pepper. Serve hot over rice or bow tie pasta.

Note: You can thicken your sauce by mixing ¼ cup of corn starch to ½ cup of cold water. Mix. At end of method, pour into pan; stir until thick.

Chef Michael Morrison

HAYDEN STEW

1 lb. stew meat
Stew vegetables—carrots,
   turnips, potatoes, celery,
   onions

Bay leaf
Salt and pepper to taste

Braise meat by frying until all sides are brown. In same pan, add water and bay leaf to meat; cover and cook for 3 hours. Check periodically and add water when dry. Cook at medium temperature.

Add stew vegetables to beef stew and cook for 25 minutes. Serves 2.

Adirondack Stew is a simple and easy recipe. According to Hayden Young, it can be cooked on any campfire in the Adirondacks!

Hayden Young, Saranac Lake, New York

WARRENSBURG BEEF PROVENCALE

1¼ lb. beef tenderloin, middle cut
2 Tbs. butter or margarine
1½ tsp. salt
Dash ground pepper
¼ c. water

10 potatoes
6 Tbs. butter or margarine, room
   temperature
1 to 2 cloves garlic, minced
3 Tbs. parsley, finely chopped

Trim excess fat off meat, Remove tendon. In a skillet, heat butter until lightly browned. Add meat. Brown well on all sides. Sprinkle with half the salt and pepper. Reduce heat. Cover. Let meat cook for about 10 minutes, turning once during cooking time. Remove meat. Cover with foil. Place on a carving board. Add water to pan; heat. Scrape up brownings, strain juices. Peel potatoes, slice thinly. Layer potatoes on a lightly greased oven proof dish. Sprinkle remaining salt in between layers. Pour pan juices over. Bake potatoes at 425° for 30 minutes; remove from oven. Cut beef into 8 even slices. Place on top of potatoes. Stir together softened butter, minced garlic and parsley. Spread butter over meat. Heat at 425° for 8 minutes.

Robert Birkel, Corinth, New York

NORTHERN MEATLOAF WITH CHEESE

¼ c. milk
2 tsp. dry mustard
1 lb. ground beef
⅓ c. quick oats, uncooked

¼ c. ketchup
¼ c. onion, finely chopped
½ lb. Velveeta, cubed

Preheat oven to 350°. Stir Velveeta, milk, and mustard in small saucepan over low heat until smooth. Reserve ¾ cup Velveeta cheese. Mix remaining ¼ cup Velveeta and remaining ingredients in large bowl until well blended. Shape into 8 x 3 loaf in a 10 x 6 baking dish. Bake for 40 minutes. Serve with reserved Velveeta. Serves 4.

Jean Birkel, Corinth, New York

HENRIETTA'S STUFFED PEPPERS

6 large bell peppers
1 onion
2 eggs
¼ oz. pepper

1 lb. chopped chuck
1 lb. ground round
1 lb. pork
Tomato soup

Mix 1 pound chopped chuck, 1 lb. ground round, and 1 pound ground pork, together with onion and bread pieces, one-half onion chopped up, with 2 eggs, and pepper. Cut off tops of bell peppers and stuff with contents. Put all stuffed peppers in a large pot. Fill pot with tomato soup, your own or you may use Campbell's tomato soup. (Make sure that the peppers are submerged in the soup and put on medium heat for about one hour.) The mixture will cook the meat along with the rest of the ingredients. Serve hot with potatoes and vegetables.

Henrietta Ellen Birkel, Corinth, New York

HENRIETTA'S SAUERBRATEN

1½ c. dry red wine
1½ c. red wine vinegar
6 c. cold water
1 medium onion, sliced
5 black peppercorns
4 whole juniper berries
2 small bay leaves
4 lb. boneless eye round of beef

2 Tbsp. flour
1 c. water
3 Tbsp. lard
½ c. onions, chopped
½ c. carrots, chopped
¼ c. celery, chopped
1 box gingersnaps (as needed)

In a saucepan, combine first seven ingredients. Bring to a boil; let cool. Place beef in a crock or plastic bowl. Pour in cooled mixture, making sure beef is covered in this marinade. Refrigerate beef for 3 days, occasionally turning the beef to fully marinate. Strain marinade, discard vegetable/spice mixture.

In a heavy 5 quart pot/Dutch Oven, put lard and over high heat brown the beef on all sides; remove beef from pot. Add the chopped onions, celery and carrots. Add the flour and stir all together absorbing the pan juices. Once the flour turns golden, add 3 cups of marinade. and one cup of water, stir and mix; bring to a boil. Place the meat back into the pot, cover and place in the oven at 375°F.; roast for 2 hours or until meat is fork tender.

Remove meat from the pot; set aside. Transfer all liquid to a large measuring cup and skim fat. Measure 2½ cups of pan juice liquid into a sauce pan. (If not enough liquid is available, add water to empty roasting pot and scrape particles from pot to produce flavor.) Bring the liquid to a simmering boil. Add gingersnaps, a few at a time, breaking them up with your hands (as needed). The snaps will thicken the sauce! Simmer for 5 minutes. Pour the sauce through a metal strainer, pressing and straining the vegetables in sauce firmly, to release all the juices. Return the sauce to the pan, season with salt and pepper as needed. *Serve with red cabbage and potato dumplings.* Serves 4 to 6.

Henrietta Ellen Birkel, Corinth, New York

FRENCH CANADIAN MEAT PIE

½ lb. pork
½ lb. lean beef, coarsely ground
¼ Tbs. celery salt
¼ Tbs. chili powder

½ Tbs. onion salt
1 Tbs. salt
1 Tbs. pepper
Pie crust

Cook meat in fry pan on medium heat, adding water to keep it moist. Do not brown. Simmer until cooked thoroughly, adding spices while cooking. Cover and let simmer. Do not add grease. Make pastry for double crust pie, except roll crusts a little thicker. Put meat into crust after it has cooled somewhat, adding some liquid left in fry pan. Slit top crust and crimp edges well. Bake until crust is done. May be kept in cool place or in freezer and used when wanted.

June Shone, Holcomb, New York

SCHENECTADY CON CARNE

1 Tbs. salad oil
2 medium onions, chopped
2 garlic cloves, minced
3 lb. beef, coarsely ground
2 Tbs. chili powder

1 tsp. salt
½ c. dark rum**
1 (6 oz.) can tomato paste
1 (1 lb. 12 oz.) can tomatoes
48 oz. red kidney beans, drained

Heat oil in large pot. Lightly saute onions and garlic. Add meat, breaking up and stirring with wooden spoon until color changes. Add remaining ingredients. Stir, cover, and simmer 2 hours. Check seasonings.

**The dark rum makes this a winner!

Lynn Paska, Schenectady, New York

POOR MAN'S STEW

8 medium potatoes
4 large carrots, thinly sliced
1 onion, thinly sliced

1 can corned beef
½ stick butter
Salt and pepper

Slice potatoes into ¼-inch-thick slices. Add thinly sliced carrots and onion. Cover with just enough water to top vegetables. Boil until tender. Add 1 can corned beef and butter; salt and pepper to taste. Bring to a boil until butter melts and corned beef heats through. Serves 6.

Gram Harris, Ballston Spa, New York

BILLY'S GOLF BALLS

1½ lb. ground beef
½ c. long grain rice, parboiled
½ c. onion, chopped
½ c. green pepper, chopped

½ tsp. salt
1 c. condensed tomato soup
1¼ c. water

Combine first 5 ingredients. Shape into 24 balls. Place in casserole dish very close together. Blend soup with water and pour over meatballs. Cover and bake at 350° for 1½ hours.

Karen Graff, Clifton Park, New York

SPICED POT ROAST

2 onions, chopped
¼ c. salad oil
1 (4 lb.) beef roast
¼ c. flour
1 tsp. salt
2½ c. cooked tomatoes

¼ tsp. pepper
1 bay leaf
¼ tsp. whole cloves
¼ c. vinegar
2 Tbs. brown sugar

Cook onions in fat in Dutch oven until tender. Dredge roast with flour; cook in Dutch oven with onions until brown on all sides. Place rack under roast. Combine salt, tomatoes, pepper, bay leaf, cloves, vinegar, and brown sugar. Pour over roast. Cover and simmer for about 3 hours or until roast is tender.

Mary Dodson, Burnt Hills, New York

OLD FASHIONED PUMPKIN MEATLOAF

1 medium size pumpkin
2 lb. ground beef
1 egg, beaten
2 Tbs. horseradish
¼ c. ketchup
¼ c. mustard
½ c. seasoned bread crumbs
1 tsp. garlic powder

1 small onion, finely chopped
½ c. green pepper, chopped
8 oz. tomato sauce
½ c. water
1 tsp. basil
1 tsp. oregano
1 tsp. seasoned pepper

Cut top of pumpkin off and clean out the pumpkin meat. Save the pumpkin meat for other uses, if desired. Wash the empty pumpkin shell; let set on towel while mixing meatloaf ingredients. Mix the meat, egg, horseradish, ketchup, mustard, bread crumbs, garlic powder, chopped onion, and chopped green pepper together. Form into a loaf and place in pumpkin shell. Use your finger to make several holes in the top of loaf. Combine topping ingredients, mixing well. Pour over the top of the meatloaf. Fill in the holes on top of meatloaf as well. Bake at 350° for 1½ hours in roasting pan covered with foil. Poke a few holes in foil to let steam escape.

Mary Dodson, Burnt Hills, New York

MEATLOAF BAKE

2 lb. ground beef
1 medium onion, chopped
1 small green pepper, chopped
2 stalks celery, chopped
¼ c. parsley, chopped
4 slices bread, crumbled
2 eggs
¼ tsp. pepper

4 unpeeled potatoes, scrubbed
and halved
2 green peppers, halved and
seeded
2 red peppers, halved and seeded
2 onions, quartered
Ketchup Topping

Combine beef, onion, green pepper, celery, parsley, bread, eggs, and pepper in a large bowl; mix well. Shape into a loaf. Place in a large shallow baking pan. Bake at 350° for 30 minutes.

Meanwhile, parboil the potatoes for 10 minutes. Place onions, peppers, and potatoes around the meatloaf. Spread Ketchup Topping over loaf. Return to oven and bake 1 hour longer, basting vegetables several times with pan liquids.

KETCHUP TOPPING:

½ c. ketchup
1 tsp. prepared mustard

¼ tsp. soy sauce

Combine ketchup, prepared mustard, and soy sauce in a cup. Mix well.

Lynn Paska, Schenectady, New York

Lynn Paska of Schenectady has a 3-minute recipe show on WHRL-FM 103 at 11:45 a.m. Monday through Friday. The program, which is in its tenth year, features "GREAT RECIPES" from area cooks. As an amateur gourmet cook, she enjoys her show and collecting recipes from friends, neighbors, magazines, newspapers, and of course . . . local chefs. Thanks for your extensive recipe input LYNN!!

ONIONY STEAK AND POTATOES

1 Tbs. salad oil
1 lb. beef round steak, cut ½-inch
    thick
1 pkg. onion soup mix
4 medium potatoes, sliced

1 tsp. pepper
Water
2 Tbs. flour
1 pkg. frozen green beans

In 12-inch skillet, over medium heat, heat oil. Saute steak in pan until well-browned on both sides. Stir in onion soup mix, potatoes, pepper, and 2½ cups water. Heat to boiling; reduce to low heat. Cover; simmer 20 minutes, stirring occasionally. Add green beans; cover, cooking 20 minutes longer or until meat and vegetables are tender. Remove meat and vegetables to platter; keep warm. Meanwhile, in a cup, blend flour and ½ cup water until smooth. Gradually stir mixture into hot liquid in skillet, cooking and stirring constantly until thickened. Serve gravy with meat and vegetables.

Lynn Paska, Schenectady, New York

UNCLE BUCK'S JUICY RIB STEAKS
(A Dedication)

4 rib steaks, 1 inch thick
4 tsp. cornstarch
1 small leek
1 Tbs. butter or margarine
Dash fresh pepper

⅓ c. beef broth
1 Tbs. vinegar
1 tsp. dried thyme or rosemary
2 Tbs. cold butter (optional)

Quickly rinse steaks. Pat dry. Rub a teaspoon of cornstarch on each steak. Rinse and slice leek. In a skillet, heat butter; add leek. Reduce heat. Saute, stirring until leek is soft; remove from pan. Set aside.

Add steaks to hot pan. Cook until steaks are done to your liking, 7 to 8 minutes for well-done. Remove steaks to heated platter. Add beef broth and vinegar to skillet. Stir to scrape up brownings. Add thyme or rosemary. Add butter if used, a small piece at a time, and cook until pan juices are smooth and shiny. Pour pan juices over steaks. Add leek to pan and heat quickly. Pour over steaks; serve immediately.

Vander & Birkel, Corinth, New York

CHRISTMAS EVE MEAT PIE

1 lb. chuck beef
1 lb. lean fresh pork
1 small onion
Salt and pepper

Ground sage
Ground cloves
Pie crust

Boil the meat until done and let cool. Salt and pepper while cooking. Let the broth cook down a little. Using the medium cutter of a food processor, grind meat and onion. Return ingredients to broth and continue to simmer. Add sage and cloves a little at a time. Continue to taste until it is just as spicy as you like it. It should make one pie. Put in pie shell and bake at 375° until crust is golden brown.

Linda Naone, Tupper Lake, New York

Linda Naone, whose mother came to Tupper Lake in 1914 and entered into a large French family when marrying Linda's father, inherited this recipe. Linda's mother's mother-in-law most likely taught her how to prepare this traditional meat pie recipe. Her mother sent Linda the recipe when she used to live in Hawaii, where she absolutely had to celebrate Christmas with this tradition.

LEAFY STUFFED CABBAGE

1 nice head of leafy green cabbage
1 lb. ground beef
1 egg
1 small onion, grated
2 Tbs. cooked rice

2 Tbs. brown sugar
Juice of ¼ lemon
Salt
16 ounces tomato sauce

Break off outside leaves of cabbage and wash in cold water. Take out core and place whole cabbage in large pot and cover. Bring to a boil. While that is parboiling, in large bowl add meat, egg, onion, rice, and salt; mix well. Cool off leaves. Take teaspoonful of meat mixture and put towards center of a cabbage leaf; roll well. Layer in large sauce pot. Pour tomato sauce over the rolls. Add brown sugar and lemon juice. Cook on medium heat. When it starts to cook, put lid on tightly and reduce to simmer. Cook 2½ to 3 hours; add more brown sugar and lemon juice to taste as cooking.

Marilyn Mauro, Clifton Park, New York

❧ POULTRY ❧

GRILLED ADIRONDACK
SWEET POTATO CHICKEN

1 sweet potato, boiled soft	1 qt. boiling water
⅛ c. honey	2 chicken breast halves, cleaned
1 Tbs. brown sugar	1 Tbs. thyme
1 Tbs. cooking oil	1 tsp. garlic, chopped fine
½ tsp. salt	1 Tbs. oil
¼ tsp. white pepper	1 tsp. red vinegar

Note: Have all ingredients ready before you start your recipe procedure; this saves time and mistakes!

Prepare sweet potato. Peel and leave whole; boil until soft. Cool and slice lengthwise. Mix honey, brown sugar, oil, salt, and pepper. Dip sliced sweet potato in mix and quickly saute until browned; do not burn. Remove from heat and set aside.

Mix together the thyme, garlic, oil, and red vinegar. Coat chicken breasts with this marinade. Grill chicken until tender. (On most household ovens, the bottom broiler can be used as a grill.) Shingle chicken breast and sweet potato slices on serving plate and serve. You should "fan" the pieces so they complement each other in color and taste. Garnish with chopped parsley.

Chef Michael J. Morrison

Mike Morrison, Armand C. Vanderstigchel,
Erin DeWeaver, Alexander Katsaris
(American Kidney Fund Foodshow)

ADIRONDACK WILDBERRY CHICKEN

4 boneless chicken breasts
1 c. raspberry vinegar
2 c. water
2 c. fresh blackberries
2 c. fresh blueberries
2 c. fresh strawberries
2 c. fresh raspberries
2 c. cranberry juice

½ c. brown sugar
½ c. honey
1 tsp. salt
1 c. cassis brandy (plain brandy
　　as substitute)
1 tsp. chopped fresh mint leaves
4 whole mint leaves for garnish

Combine vinegar and water in shallow bowl. Place chicken breasts in bowl. Marinate overnight or at least six hours.

Place marinated chicken on grill or bake in oven at 350 degrees until cooked. Set aside and keep warm.

Sauce: Combine 1 cup each of the berries with 2 cups cranberry juice in sauce pan. Bring to medium boil.

Add brown sugar, honey, salt and chopped mint leaves. Bring to slow boil.

Add brandy. Let alcohol cook out for two minutes. Sauce should have medium-thick consistency. Turn off heat.

Place chicken in center of plate. Spoon sauce over center of chicken leaving the outsides dry.

Sprinkle remaining berries over the chicken. Place the mint leaf in the 9 o'clock position of each plate.

Rice or salad accompanies this low-fat, delicious summer dish. Serves 4.

Chef Armand C. Vanderstigchel

CHICKEN A LA QUEENSBURY

4 chicken cutlets	1 lemon
1 c. olive oil	1 tsp. black pepper
1 c. white wine	1 tsp. cumin
1 c. white vinegar	1 tsp. salt
1 c. water	

Whip up ingredients for marinade in bowl until fully mixed. Place chicken cutlets in shallow bowl and pour marinade over cutlets. Marinate for 3 hours. Remove chicken from marinade. Grill or bake until thoroughly cooked. Keep warm and set aside, while preparing the sauce.

SAUCE:

1 c. sour cream	1 tsp. cumin
½ c. half and half	1 tsp. black pepper
½ c. pickle juice	1 tsp. salt
½ c. pickles, chopped	1 tsp. onion
1 c. corn kernels, cooked	1 tsp. garlic powder
1 c. cucumbers, diced	2 Tbs. sugar
1 Tbs. fresh dill, chopped	½ tsp. thyme

Mix sour cream, half and half, and pickle juice in bowl. Whip until smooth. Add spices and sugar; mix. Fold in corn, chopped pickles, cucumber, and dill.

Place grilled chicken on plate. Spoon over cold sauce. Garnish with lemon wedge and fresh dill sprig. Serve with rice, green salad, or pasta salad.

Chef Armand C. Vanderstigchel

CHICKEN CASSEROLE

1 large chicken, cooked and deboned	4½ qt. bread crumbs
	1 tsp. salt
1 c. butter	2 onions, minced
1 c. flour	1 tsp. poultry seasoning
2 c. milk	½ tsp. pepper
Salt and pepper	2 c. celery, chopped
6 eggs	

Cook and debone large chicken; cut meat into small chunks. Save all the liquid (5½ cups). Make a gravy by mixing the broth with the butter, milk, flour, salt, pepper, and eggs; heat. Make a chicken dressing with rest of ingredients. Layer dressing, meat, gravy in casserole dish. Repeat layers. Bake at 350° until done.

Laura Roberts, Clifton Park, New York

CHICKEN D'EBLEE

4 boneless chicken breasts, thinly
   sliced
Flour to coat
½ c. white cooking wine with
   lemon

1 Tbs. tarragon
1 Tbs. lemon juice
1 clove garlic, minced
2 red peppers, roasted (see
   instructions)

Mix wine, lemon juice, tarragon, and garlic. Marinate chicken for 1 hour uncovered in refrigerator. Turn after ½ hour.

Roasted Peppers: Core and seed. Place on baking sheet and place under broiler. Turn as peppers start to steam and burn. When black, remove and place in paper bag. Leave in bag for 15 to 20 minutes. Remove blackened skin; cut in half.

Coat chicken; brown in 3 tablespoons oil. When almost done, place one-half pepper and 2 slices of cheese on each breast. Remove when cheese is melted. Serve immediately with fresh salad, using locally-grown ingredients.

Debra Lorocco and Lee James, Kings Park, New York

GLAZED CHICKEN WITH GRAPE SAUCE

4 skinned boneless chicken
   breast halves
¾ c. seedless red grapes
¼ c. apple jelly

¼ c. grape jelly
2 Tbs. dry sherry
2 tsp. lemon juice
¼ tsp. salt

Wash chicken and pat dry. Spray large skillet with non-stick coating. Heat over medium-high heat. Add chicken. Cook 8 to 10 minutes, turning once. Transfer chicken to serving plates. Cover. Cut grapes in half. Melt jellies with sherry, lemon juice, and salt in saucepan. Add grapes. Spoon over chicken. Makes 4 servings.

Bob Birkel, Sr., Corinth, New York

Bob Birkel, Sr.

—author's father, a Nyra Saratoga Racetrack Veteran who introduced us to life in Saratoga, the Adirondacks, and beyond . . . we owe you. . . .

GLOVERVILLE CHICKEN BAKE

CRUST:

½ c. soft butter
8 oz. sour cream
1 egg
1 c. flour
1 tsp. salt
1 tsp. baking powder

1 tsp. rosemary, chopped
½ tsp. thyme
1 tsp. onion powder
1 c. Muenster cheese, shredded
Filling (recipe follows)

Combine butter, sour cream, and egg; beat at medium speed until of a smooth consistency. Mix in flour, salt, baking powder, rosemary, thyme, and onion powder. Blend at low speed. In a 9-inch pie pan, lightly greased, spread with a rubber spatula the mixture over bottom and sides up to 1 inch of the rim. Spoon Filling (recipe follows) into crust carefully. Sprinkle top evenly with Muenster cheese. Bake for 25 to 30 minutes at 350° until crust is golden brown. Let stand for approximately 15 minutes. Serve with salad or mashed potatoes.

FILLING:

½ c. red pepper, chopped
½ c. onions, chopped
½ c. celery, diced
½ c. green onions, chopped

2 Tbs. butter
2 c. cooked chicken, cubed
1 c. fresh mushrooms, sliced
1 can cream of chicken soup

In a large and deep frying pan, saute onions, celery, pepper, green onions, and mushrooms until al dente. Add cream soup and a dash of salt and pepper. Mix together and add as mentioned in first part of recipe.

Chef Armand Vanderstigchel

HENZLER CHICKEN BAKE

1 can cream of chicken soup
¾ c. milk
¼ tsp. salt
2 to 3 c. chicken, cut up
16 oz. broccoli, cauliflower,
    carrots, cut up

1 c. Cheddar cheese, shredded
1 (2.8 oz.) can Durkee French fried
    onions
1 c. biscuit mix
1 egg, slightly beaten

Combine soup, milk, chicken, veggies, ½ cup of cheese, ½ can of onions. Spread mixture into a greased 8"x12" baking dish. Bake uncovered at 425° for 10 minutes. Meanwhile, combine biscuit, egg, and milk to form a soft dough. Spoon over hot chicken mixture to form a lattice design. Bake uncovered at 425° for 20 minutes or until biscuits are golden brown. Top lattice with remaining cheese and onions until cheese melts. KEEP AN EYE ON IT!

Meribeth Henzler, Saratoga Springs, New York

OUTDOOR CHICKEN

2 chickens, cut up
¼ lb. butter, melted
3 Tbs. soy sauce

1 Tbs. lemon juice
½ tsp. pepper
Garlic powder

Make a sauce of all ingredients. Dip chicken pieces in sauce and put on broiler skin side down. Broil 20 minutes and then turn over and broil other side for 20 minutes.

Laura Roberts, Clifton Park, New York

PEPPERCORN CHICKEN BREASTS

4 large chicken breast halves,
    skinned and boned
1 Tbs. whole peppercorns,
    crushed

2 tsp. butter
½ c. dry sherry or orange juice
½ c. whipping cream
½ tsp. tarragon leaves

Place chicken between sheets of plastic wrap. Pound with flat edge of mallet to about ¼-inch thickness. Sprinkle with peppercorns. Heat heavy nonstick skillet. Add butter and chicken. Cook, turning once, until chicken is done, about 5 minutes. Remove chicken and keep warm. Increase heat to high. Add sherry or orange juice to pan and whisk in the cream and tarragon. Boil, stirring until sauce is glossy, thickened and reduced to about half the original volume. Spoon sauce over chicken. Serves 4.

Bob Birkel, Corinth, New York

ROB'S HOT CHICKEN AND RICE

2½ to 3 lb. chicken, cut into pieces
1 Tbs. butter or margarine
¼ lb. bacon, well chopped
1 c. onions, chopped
1 tsp. garlic, minced

1 tsp. red pepper
1 c. tomatoes, chopped
1½ c. uncooked rice
1 c. peas (optional)
3 c. boiling water

Dry chicken and sprinkle with salt and pepper. In big saucepan, melt butter over medium heat. Add chopped bacon and fry until brown. Drain bacon on paper towel, leaving fat in pan. Brown chicken on all sides. Remove chicken; drain almost all of the fat out of the pan and save. Add onions and garlic and cook until onions are soft but not brown. Add red pepper and tomatoes; boil, stirring constantly, until all liquid disappears. Mixture will be thick. Add chicken, fat, rice, peas, boiling water, and 1 teaspoon salt to saucepan. Stir lightly. Bring to a boil over high heat, then reduce to low heat. Cover and cook 30 minutes until chicken is tender and liquid is gone.

Robert Mauro, Clifton Park, New York

SARATOGA HONEY-CURRIED CHICKEN

1 (3 lb.) fryer, cut up
½ c. butter, melted
½ c. honey

¼ c. prepared mustard
1 tsp. salt
1 tsp. curry powder

Place chicken in shallow baking pan, skin up. Combine rest of ingredients; pour over chicken. Bake 1¼ hours at 350°. It can blacken easily, so watch it!!!

Joan Smith, Saratoga Springs, New York

Joan Smith, a Saratoga Springs resident, enjoys preparing her recipes, especially during the racing season when she has lots of company over. "When can we come over for dinner, Joan?!!" Sincerely . . . Robert and Armand.

SWISS CHICKEN CUTLETS

5 chicken cutlets
Salt
2 eggs, beaten
1 cup bread crumbs
¼ c. cooking oil

3 Tbs. butter or margarine
¼ c. flour
½ tsp. salt
2½ c. milk
1 c. Swiss cheese, shredded

Salt chicken cutlets lightly. Dip in beaten egg, then bread crumbs. Brown 2 minutes in 2 tablespoons oil on each side. Add remaining oil as needed. Set chicken aside. In pot, melt butter, blend in flour, salt, and pepper. Pour half of sauce into baking dish. Arrange cutlets on top of sauce. Top with remaining sauce. Bake covered at 350° until heated through, about 50 minutes. Sprinkle with cheese. Return to oven for 2 minutes or until cheese melts.

Karen Graff, Clifton Park, New York

TUPPER LAKE CHICKEN SQUASH SOUFFLE

3 chicken breasts
4 medium squash
2 slices white bread
½ c. corn meal
½ c. half and half
1 egg
1 c. green onion, diced

1 Tbs. fresh dill, chopped
½ Tbs. onion powder
1 tsp. paprika
Salt and pepper
Bread crumbs
Soft butter

Season chicken with salt and pepper; bake, grill, or saute until cooked. Let cook for 5 minutes. Cut into thin strips. Set aside until needed. Peel squash; cut into medium pieces. Boil in unsalted water until tender. Drain and mash. Soak bread in milk, blend into squash. Add whipped egg into mixture. Add green onions, salt, and pepper. Add in chicken. Spoon squash mixture into greased casserole and sprinkle with bread crumbs and corn meal; dot with butter. Bake at 350° for 30 minutes. Check every 10 minutes. Serve with salad or rice. Add dill, onion powder, and paprika if you want more zest.

Chef Armand C. Vanderstigchel

WATERVLIET CHICKEN CACCIATORE

2 tsp. olive oil
4 boneless chicken breasts
1 large green pepper, minced
1 large onion, diced
2 cloves garlic
Basil leaves
¼ c. sherry wine

16 oz. homemade tomato sauce
1 c. water
4 oz. whole mushrooms, cut up
Salt and pepper to taste
1 lb. linguini
¼ c. Parmesan cheese

Brown chicken in olive oil, remove chicken and in saucepan saute green peppers for 5 minutes. Add onion, garlic, and basil; saute until onions are soft. Add sherry, tomato sauce, and 1 cup of water. Bring to a boil; lower heat. Return chicken to saucepan; cook covered slowly for approximately ¾ hour. Prior to serving, add mushrooms. Cook linguini according to package. Remove chicken; add sauce to pasta. Cover with cheese. Serves 3 to 4.

Mary D. Quackenbush, Watervliet, New York

BIRCHTON TURKEY DIVAN

1 large head broccoli
1 c. brown rice
1 (10¾ oz.) can mushroom soup

2 c. turkey pieces
½ lb. Cheddar cheese, grated
8 oz. mushroom pieces

Cook rice and place in bottom of large casserole dish. Add all other ingredients, one by one, layer by layer, leaving part of cheese to place on top. Bake at 325° for 45 minutes to 1 hour.

Hope Geisler, Ballston Spa, New York

TURKEY A LA CHRISTOPHER

1 lb. turkey cutlets (can use
    chicken)
2 Tbs. butter
3 Tbs. flour
2 tsp. instant chicken bouillon

¼ tsp. garlic powder
1 c. water
½ c. Marsala wine
1 c. mushrooms

Melt 1 tablespoon butter in skillet over medium heat. When butter begins to brown, add half of the turkey. Cook 3 minutes; turn and cook 2 minutes more. Place turkey on serving platter. Repeat with remaining turkey and butter. Place turkey on platter. Combine flour, bouillon, and garlic powder in bowl. Gradually stir in water and wine. Add to skillet and cook over medium heat 5 minutes, stirring constantly until thickened. Add mushrooms and heat 1 more minute. Pour half over turkey; pass remaining sauce. Makes 4 servings.

Karen Graff, Clifton Park, New York

APPLE HERB STUFFING FOR CHICKEN OR PORK

3 medium onions (1½ c.), chopped
½ c. celery, sliced
6 Tbs. butter or margarine
3 c. baking apples, finely diced
3 c. whole wheat bread cubes
¼ c. fresh parsley, chopped

½ tsp. leaf sage, crumbled
¼ tsp. ground nutmeg
2 envelopes or 1 tsp. instant
    chicken broth
½ c. hot water

Saute onions and celery in butter in skillet until soft, about 5 minutes. Stir in apple; continue cooking and stirring 3 to 5 minutes. Remove from heat. Combine with bread, parsley, sage, thyme, nutmeg, chicken broth, and water in a large bowl. Toss until evenly moist. Makes 5 cups.

Carol M. Miller, Northumberland, New York

Adirondack Winter Scene

Blushing Mountain

Driving home from the printer's shop
On the road I had to stop
For there in front of me just ahead
Was Whiteface Mountain blushing red.

A sight like this I'd never seen
(a mountain in winter is white and green),
But when the sun sets bright and bold
It reflects a light of pink and gold.

The high peak's glow was fading fast—
This phenomena would not last.
Entranced, I sincerely hope and pray
That Whiteface will blush another day.

June Clow

June m Clow
1989

THE COTTONTAIL RABBIT typically weighs from 2 to 3 pounds and stretches out to about 18 inches. They have large eyes and ears which make it all the better to see and hear you with.

They require good cover and a ready supply of food. Simple vegetarians, they have a special love for young garden cabbages. In winter they can be found feeding on the spilled seed from your bird feeder at night.

The breeding season extends from March to September. Each doe may produce 3 to 4 litters of 5 or 6 young each year, the gestation period being less than 30 days.

Newborns are 4 inches long and weigh less than an ounce with dainty ½ inch long ears. Since they have many predators, only a third to a half of them will ever make it out of the nest. Of those who do, more than 80% will not survive their first year in the wild.

Blue Mountain Lake, Blue Mountain, New York

❧ PORK ❧

ADIRONDACK PORK

3 lb. loin of pork
1 qt. apple cider
2 c. white vinegar
2 c. water
1 c. brown sugar

1 c. honey
1 Tbs. pickling spice
4 bay leaves
2 apples, quartered
2 c. oil

Remove all outside fat from pork loin. Place in shallow glass or plastic bowl. Place remaining ingredients in saucepan. Bring to a boil. Turn fire off. Cool marinade. Once cooled, pour over pork loin. Marinate pork overnight in refrigerator. Turn occasionally.

Next Day: Remove pork from marinade. Place on drip rack. Save marinade. In large Dutch oven or roasting pan pour oil. On high flame bring to light smokey haze. Turn off fire. Place pork in pan. Turn fire back on high. Brown both sides of pork. Once browned, remove from pan. Remove also the grease. Place pork back in pan. Turn fire on. Add conserved marinade. Roast in oven at 350° while constantly basting and turning pork. The pork is done at internal temperature of 165° and above. Use meat thermometer. Remove pork, save juice. Let meat rest. Strain roasting juice through strainer and save.

Slice pork in layers on platter garnished with parsley, herbs, and orange wedges. Pour sauce over. Sprinkle walnuts and dried fruit over pork. (Use dried cherries, cranberries, or apricots.

Serve with mashed potatoes, corn bread, or biscuits. Serves 4 to 6.

Continued on following page.

Continued from previous page.

SAUCE:

1 c. applejack brandy	2 tsp. black pepper
2 c. apple cider	2 Tbs. brown sugar
1 c. orange juice	1 tsp. grated orange peel
2 c. roasting juice	1 tsp. cinnamon
2 c. apples, diced	1 tsp. rosemary
1 c. walnuts, chopped	2 Tbs. cornstarch**
½ Tbs. salt	

**This essential thickening agent performs best when mixed with cold water until smooth. Slowly pour the corn starch mixture into boiling liquid and stir with vigor until sauce is smooth and shiny. If sauce is still watery, mix another batch and stir in until demanded thickness.

Mix all sauce ingredients in saucepan including roasting juice. Bring to boil. Add in cornstarch slowly while stirring. Sauce should have slightly medium thickness.

Chef Armand S. Vanderstigchel

GLENS FALLS HARVEST STEW

1 lb. fresh sausage
2 lb. broccoli rabe (or fresh
   spinach)
8 large red potatoes
2 large onions
1 large cauliflower
2 carrots
4 corn cobs
1 red pepper
¾ c. corn/sunflower oil

1 qt. chicken stock
1 Tbs. black pepper
1 Tbs. salt
1 tsp. garlic powder
1 tsp. onion powder
1 tsp. thyme, rosemary
1 tsp. basil
1 c. anisette liquor
½ c. brown sugar

In pot of boiling water cook sausage until thoroughly done. Remove sausage from water. Place on platter; cool. Once cooled, slice up into 2-inch slices. Boil potatoes until almost cooked. You can test the potatoes by inserting a fork into them. If the potato slides slowly off the fork, it's done. Set aside. Cut florets off cauliflower. Blanch them in boiling water until halfway done. Scrape corn off the cob; peel carrots and cut into ½-inch-thick slices. Boil both vegetables until done. Drain; set aside. Peel and dice onions and garlic cloves. Cut red pepper in half. Clean out core and slice into small strips. Wash broccoli and cut off stems; set aside.

In large skillet heat oil until a light hazy smoke. Turn off fire. Place sausage, onions, and garlic into pan. Turn fire back on. Toss mixture around until golden brown over high heat. Carefully add anisette liquor. Cook alcohol out for approximately 5 minutes. Add carrots, corn, spices, and sugar. Add chicken stock and cauliflower. Bring to a simmer. Add broccoli and pepper strips. Bring to a simmer again. Add in potatoes. Cook for 5 to 10 minutes on medium heat while gently stirring without breaking the potatoes. Serve with pumpernickel bread. Serves 4 to 6.

Chef Armand Vanderstigchel

HAM NOODLE CASSEROLE

8 oz. noodles
1½ c. cooked ham, chopped
1 c. sharp cheese, grated
1 can cream of chicken soup

½ c. milk
½ tsp. curry powder
2 Tbs. butter or margarine

Preheat oven to 375°. Cook noodles; drain. Combine ham and ¾ cup cheese; alternate layers of noodles and ham in greased 1 quart dish. Mix soup, milk, and curry. Pour over noodles. Sprinkle top with remaining cheese. Dot with butter. Bake 20 to 25 minutes.

Karen Graff, Clifton Park, New York

NORTH CHURCH FRIED DUMPLINGS

1 lb. ground pork
½ c. Chinese cabbage, minced
3 scallions, minced
½ tsp. fresh ginger, minced
1 garlic clove, minced

3 Tbs. soy sauce
1 tsp. honey or pinch of sugar
½ tsp. sesame oil
Wonton wrappers

After mixing all ingredients (except wonton wrappers) very well, put 1 tablespoon of filling into the middle of wonton wrappers. Fold in half and seal by pinching along the edge.

To cook, heat 3 tablespoons of peanut or vegetable oil in a nonstick frying pan. Place dumplings in very hot pan (be careful they don't touch). Fry until bottoms are golden brown, then pour in a solution of 2 tablespoons soy sauce mixed in ¼ cup hot water. Cover immediately and cook for 3 minutes. Serve with sweet and sour sauce and/or dish of soy sauce with minced scallion and ginger. When sealing wontons, spread a little egg white or warm water along the edges before pressing together. Dumplings can be steamed, boiled, or fried.

Minced shrimp can be substituted for pork. Wonton wrappers are square; after folding in half and sealing, trim outer edge with scissors without cutting away seal.

Scott Johnson, Queensbury, New York

LAKE PLACID BOILED DINNER

1 small Daisy ham (modern hams
    contain much less fat, but
    the flavor is milder)
Potatoes

Whole onions
Carrots
Young green cabbage, quartered
Celery stalks

Boil ham in a large pot for ½ to 1 hour. Add vegetables (plus other available vegetables, if desired). Cook until tender. Serve with mustard.

Araxie Dunn, Lake Placid, New York

BAKED PORK CHOPS WITH FRESH FRUIT

6 loin pork chops, cut 1½ inch
   thick
1½ tsp. salt
½ tsp. freshly ground black
   pepper
⅛ tsp. thyme
2 eggs, beaten
1 c. dry bread crumbs

3 Tbs. butter
2 tsp. onions, chopped
1 c. peeled, cored, sliced apples
1 c. whole cranberries, washed
½ c. hot water
1 Tbs. Worcestershire sauce
2 Tbs. sugar

Trim the fat from the chops; rub with mixture of salt, pepper, and thyme. Dip the chops in the eggs, then in the crumbs, coating them well. Melt the butter in a heavy skillet; saute the onions 2 minutes. Add the chops and brown on both sides. Mix together the apples, cranberries, water, Worcestershire sauce, and sugar. Pour over the chops. Cover and bake in a 350° oven for 50 minutes or until chops are tender. Remove the cover for the last 15 minutes. Serves 6.

Carol M. Miller, Northumberland, New York

SPARERIBS AND KRAUT

4 lb. pork spareribs
½ lb. bacon, cut into ½-inch
   pieces
2 red onions, cut in wedges
¼ c. unsifted flour
3 c. apple juice

6 c. sauerkraut
2 tsp. caraway seeds
2 lb. small red potatoes
Lemon juice
3 red apples, cored and wedged

Cut ribs into 2 rib portions; trim excess fat. Brown bacon and remove. Cook onions in bacon drippings until tender, then remove. Brown ribs, a few at a time in remaining fat, and remove. Drain all but 2 tablespoons fat. Stir in flour and apple juice. Bring to a boil. Simmer 1 minute.

In colander, rinse sauerkraut with cold water and drain. Add ribs with bacon, onion, and caraway. Over medium heat, bring to a boil. Reduce heat and simmer covered for 1 hour, stirring occasionally until ribs are tender. With vegetable parer, cut a narrow spiral channel around each potato. Place in cold water mixed with a little lemon juice.

Rinse potatoes and place in 3-quart saucepan. Cover with cold water and 1 teaspoon salt. Cover and bring to a boil. Reduce heat and simmer until potatoes are tender (20 minutes). Drain and keep covered. Place apple wedges and chopped parsley on top of sauerkraut. Cover and simmer until apples are tender (5 minutes). Drain sauerkraut mixture. Arrange on serving platter with apples, ribs, and potatoes. Serves 4 to 6.

Chef Armand Vanderstigchel

THE SKUNK is endemic to the United States and southern Canada.

Perhaps because of his pungent defense mechanism he is a self-confident, easy-going, and gentle, although shy, little cat-sized creature.

He does not need keen senses for survival. He cannot climb or run very fast. But then, why should he? He has little to fear from potential predators who know better than to fool around with him.

Not true hibernators, they will den up, often communally, and sleep through the coldest months of winter.

Lake Saratoga, Saratoga Springs, Ballston Spa Area

❧ WILD GAME ❧

BERTH GOOSE WITH
VENISON-WILD RICE STUFFING

1 (12 to 14 lb.) goose
4 c. wild rice, cooked
1 lb. ground venison with pork
1 c. celery, diced
1 c. onions, minced
1 c. fresh mushrooms

½ c. butter
2 Tbs. parsley, snipped
3 drops Tabasco sauce
Cracked pepper to taste
1 egg
½ tsp. poultry seasoning

In a cast iron skillet over medium heat, melt butter. Add venison, celery, onions, mushrooms, parsley, Tabasco sauce, pepper, and poultry seasoning. Cook about 10 minutes or until venison is cooked. Add to rice, mix by hand. Add egg, mix by hand.

Stuff goose: Wipe goose inside and out and sprinkle with salt and cracked black pepper. Stuff the cavity with the stuffing. Place trussed bird on rack in a shallow pan. Roast in moderate (350°) oven for 4 to 4½ hours for a 12 to 14 pound bird. Drain fat as it accumulates.

William J. Davis, Clifton Park, New York

RACQUETTE RIVER RABBIT

1½ to 2 lb. wild or domestic
    rabbit, cut into pieces
Salt and pepper
Paprika
Olive oil
2 cans mushroom stems (save
    liquid)
2 large tomatoes, diced
½ c. celery with leaves, chopped

1 large onion, sliced
1 large garlic clove, minced
1 Tbs. lemon juice
1 tsp. whole thyme
1 tsp. rosemary
1 c. white wine
1 c. milk
1 Tbs. corn starch

Sprinkle meat with salt, pepper, and paprika. In iron skillet heat oil and brown meat pieces; drain. Add mushrooms with liquid, tomatoes, celery, onion, garlic clove, lemon juice, thyme, rosemary, and wine. Cover and simmer approximately 1 hour or until meat is tender. Remove meat to platter and keep warm. Shake the milk and corn starch in a jar until well mixed. On medium high heat, add mixture to pan juices while stirring constantly. When thickened to gravy consistency, simmer about 5 minutes and adjust seasonings to taste.

Linda and Fred Robare, Piercefield, New York

Adirondack Flair

With mornings so bright and crisp, and the green grass, all covered with dew, the air so warm and tender, and the flowers in a colorful splendor, make you feel all shiny and new. The aura of the land, the calmness of the waters, make you feel that your life is rewarded, with the mountains of heaven, and you suddenly realize that you are in "God's" country!!

Robert E. Birkel, Jr.

SECOND OF SEPTEMBER VENISON

1 (5 lb.) venison filet
1 Tbs. bacon, chopped
1 small red onion, finely chopped
1 stalk celery
3 Tbs. olive oil
¼ c. beef bouillon or beef stock

1 bay leaf
1 Tbs. flour
1 Tbs. parsley, finely chopped
10 peppercorns, crushed
1 pint half and half

Pierce holes in the venison with a toothpick or other small diameter instrument. Place venison in marinade of dry red wine for at least 4 hours. Place a thin onion slice on top of the meat and occasionally turn venison over during the marinade process. After marinating, lightly flour the venison then saute it until golden brown. Set aside.

Sauce: Finely chop bacon, onion, and celery. In a saucepan add oil and wait until sizzling. Add bacon, onion, and celery. Cover, and over medium heat fry for 8 to 10 minutes. Remove cover then fry until vegetables are almost translucent. Add flour and stir until mixture gains consistency. When mixture is golden brown or of even consistency, add in stock and continue to stir until boiling. Add remaining ingredients except half and half. With pot uncovered let simmer for 1 hour under medium to low heat. After 1 hour, add half and half stirring until creamy texture is achieved. Pour ingredients into a saucepan filling it half way. Set to medium high heat whisking frequently. When sauce begins to bubble, reduce to medium heat. Add venison at regular intervals. Test venison with fork. When desired doneness is achieved, place venison on serving plate; pour mixture over until covered and plate is filled. Serves 4.

William T. Neary, Olmstedville, New York

VENISON CHILI

4 large onions, thinly sliced
2 cloves garlic, finely chopped
½ c. vegetable oil
8 oz. mushrooms
2 lb. venison, diced or cubed
2 Tbs. chili powder
1 tsp. ground coriander
½ tsp. ground cumin
Dash of Tabasco

2 Tbs. parsley
1 tsp. Creole seasoning
½ tsp. cayenne pepper
½ tsp. oregano
1 c. beer
½ c. tomato paste
1½ tsp. salt
2 to 3 (No. 303) cans kidney beans

Saute the onions and garlic in oil until they are limp and colored. Add the venison and mushrooms and brown. Add the rest of the ingredients and blend, except the beans. Reduce the heat and simmer for 1 to 1½ hours. Add more beer if the mixture gets too dry. Cook until it is well thickened and rich in flavor. Just before serving, blend in drained kidney beans until they are well heated. Pinto beans may be substituted for kidney beans. Serves 4 to 6.

William J. Davis, Clifton Park, New York

VENISON MAGGIE

Venison steaks or chops   **Butter (generous pieces)**

Tenderize steaks or chops by pounding well with the back of the butcher knife to break up sinews. (Will resemble cubed steak.) Heat heavy cast iron skillet to "piping" hot. Add a generous piece of butter, and then meat as soon as butter melts. (If more than one panful is to be cooked, keep cooked pieces warm.) Turn pieces once. They should be done "well". Pour pan juices on top; add a piece of butter if desired. Serve immediately.

Mary E. Kays, Olmstedville, New York

The "Venison Maggie" recipe, was Ms. Kays' grandmother's (Margaret "Mag" Brannon Kay). The Kays' place was in North Minerva. From 1880, she served venison, trout, veal, lamb, goose, and duckling from their farm at the Stagecoach relay. Travelers were well pleased with the fare "Mag" provided them during the stop.

VENISON STEW

5 lb. venison, cut up into cubes   **24 oz. tomato puree**
3 green peppers   **16 oz. stewed tomatoes**
2 red hot peppers, packed in oil   **8 oz. mushrooms with juice**
6 onions, sliced   **½ c. burgundy wine**
½ cube garlic   **Potatoes and carrots**

Brown venison in butter or oil. Add tomato puree, stewed tomatoes, red hot peppers, garlic, wine, and salt and pepper to taste. Cook until almost tender. Add carrots, potatoes, onions, pepper, and mushrooms. Cook until tender and serve hot.

Helen Witts, Schenectady, New York

Helen Witts, a Schenectady resident who spends leisure time in the village of Northville, sent us a great "Venison Stew" recipe. Thanks!!

WHITETAIL STEW

2 lb. venison steak, cut into stew-
    size pieces
Olive oil
½ c. flour
4 medium onions, quartered
2 garlic cloves, minced

1 (10½ oz.) can condensed beef
    broth
1 bottle beer
1 c. fresh parsley, chopped
4 bay leaves
1 tsp. whole thyme

Heat oil in Dutch oven. Put flour in a plastic bag; add meat pieces a few at a time, shaking them in closed bag in order to coat with flour. Shake excess flour off meat; place meat in hot oil and brown on all sides. Continue until all meat is nicely browned. Drain pan and return all meat to Dutch oven. Add onions, garlic, beef broth, beer, parsley, bay leaves, and thyme. Cover pan and simmer 1 to 1½ hours or until meat is tender. Stir occasionally and add water if necessary to keep mixture from sticking. Sprinkle additional fresh parsley and fresh ground pepper on top of serving dish. Serve over boiled or mashed potatoes.

Linda and Fred Robare, Piercefield, New York

"Adirondack Humor"

WORKMAN'S NOODLES

2 slices bacon
½ c. onion, chopped
1 lb. ground beef
1 can tomatoes, cut up

½ c. green peppers, chopped
¼ c. chili sauce
1 tsp. salt
3 c. medium-sized noodles

In large skillet, cook bacon crisp. Remove from pan and drain. Crumble and set aside. Add onion to bacon drippings in skillet. Cook until tender, but not brown. Add meat. Cook until browned. Stir in tomatoes, peppers, chili sauce, salt, and pepper. Add uncooked noodles. Cook covered over low heat for 30 minutes until noodles are tender, stirring frequently. Add bacon. Serves 4.

Marilyn Mauro, Clifton Park, New York

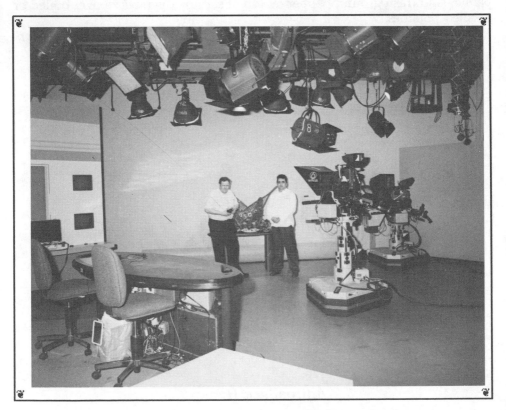

WRGB Channel 6, Schnectady, New York
Authors promoting the Adirondack Cookbook

THE BLACK BEAR was the model for the original Teddy bear, though hardly cuddly.

Normally shy, they can be aggressive when provoked and downright dangerous when they loose their fear of man as they do around dumps or parks where food is available.

In the autumn they den up to sleep although they do not truly hibernate. This is the time when the mother bear will have her cubs which often weigh less than a pound at birth—incredible given their eventual size!

NATIVE STYLE BLACK BEAR (JOKE)

4 lb. bear meat (any cut sufficing top round beast)
1 medium stone
4 large onions

6 large carrots
2 bunches celery
2 cloves garlic
1 tsp. rosemary

In a large stock pot, place a thoroughly cleaned stone, about the size of a softball. Add bear meat, cut into 1 inch cubes, roughly chopped vegetables, rosemary, and garlic. Fill the pot 9/10 full with cold water and set over a high flame. Allow the pot to reach boiling and immediately reduce heat. Simmer for 3 days, topping the pot off with cold water as needed. At the end of the third day, strain pot, setting aside the stone. Discard bear meat, vegetables, and water. At this point, the stone should be tender enough to eat and vastly more appealing than anything else that was in the pot.

Sous Chef Brett Hagadorn, Friends Lake Inn, Chestertown

Covered bridges are part of the country's charm.

Indian Lake, New York

❧ MISCELLANEOUS ❧

NORTH CREEK BAKED SPAGHETTI

1 lb. spaghetti
1 large container stewed tomatoes
1 small onion

Grated Parmesan cheese as
   needed

Cook spaghetti; drain. In a casserole dish put a layer of spaghetti, some stewed tomatoes, some onion, and cheese. Cover layer with cheese. Then start over with another layer. You should get at least 2 layers, possibly 3. Top layer with a good amount of cheese. Bake at 350° for 35 minutes or until top is golden brown.

Betty Tyrel, North Creek, New York

SARATOGA PASTA

8 locally grown tomatoes
6 sprigs locally grown basil,
   roughly chopped
2 cloves garlic, minced

1 Tbs. lite olive oil
1 lb. angel hair pasta
½ c. robust red wine (Chianti,
   burgundy, etc.)

Remove skin from tomatoes (dip into boiling water for 15 to 20 seconds, then peel). Hand crush and set aside. Saute garlic in oil; add wine, tomatoes, and half of the basil. Simmer for ½ hour. Cook pasta in salted water until al dente. Drain; add sauce and top with remaining basil. Serve immediately with crusty Italian bread.

Lee James, Kings Park, New York

ETTA'S LAMB STEW

3 lb. of lamb, cut up for stewing
4 Tbs. cinnamon
Carrots
Broccoli
Cauliflower

Asparagus
Peas
Corn
¼ oz. pepper
1 Tbs. nutmeg

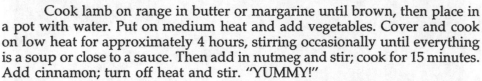

Cook lamb on range in butter or margarine until brown, then place in a pot with water. Put on medium heat and add vegetables. Cover and cook on low heat for approximately 4 hours, stirring occasionally until everything is a soup or close to a sauce. Then add in nutmeg and stir; cook for 15 minutes. Add cinnamon; turn off heat and stir. "YUMMY!"

Henrietta Ellen Birkel, Corinth, New York

SWORDFISH SAUTE

1 lb. swordfish steak
3 large celery stalks
1 yellow pepper, medium size
Salad oil
16 oz. tomatoes
1 Tbs. lemon juice

½ tsp. dried thyme leaves
¼ tsp. salt
¼ tsp. pepper
½ c. pimiento-stuffed olives
Fresh thyme for garnish

Remove skin from swordfish and cut into large pieces. Slice celery and cut yellow pepper. In skillet add 1 tablespoon salad oil on high heat. Cook fish until golden brown on undersides. Turn fish; reduce to medium heat and cook until fish flakes easily. Remove and cover. In same skillet add 1 teaspoon salad oil. Over medium high heat, cook celery and yellow pepper until tender crisp. Add tomatoes with their liquid, lemon juice, thyme, salt, and pepper. Heat to boiling. Stir in chopped olives and gently stir in cooked swordfish; heat through. Garnish with fresh thyme. Serves 4.

Bob Birkel, Corinth, New York

HOT AUGUST GARLIC SHRIMP

3 lb. jumbo shrimp in shells
⅓ c. fresh lime juice
2 tsp. garlic, minced
2 tsp. minced fresh ginger
½ tsp. fennel seeds, lightly
    crushed
½ c. plain yogurt
4 tsp. cumin

4 tsp. coriander
1 tsp. paprika
1 tsp. black pepper
½ tsp. cayenne pepper
½ tsp. salt
Corn oil
Fresh coriander
Lime wedges

Cut legs off shrimp; slit each shell down the back and pull out intestinal vein. Rinse shrimp and pat dry. In large bowl, toss shrimp with lime juice, garlic, ginger, and fennel seeds. Marinate at room temperature for 30 minutes, stirring once. In a small bowl, combine yogurt, cumin, coriander, paprika, black pepper, cayenne, and salt. Add half of the seasoned yogurt to shrimp, coating evenly. Cover and refrigerate shrimp and remaining yogurt for 1½ hours. Drain shrimp, reserving marinade, and arrange on skewers. Brush with oil. Grill or broil for 3 minutes. Turn, oil and grill 2 to 3 minutes. On serving platter, pour remaining yogurt over shrimp and toss. Garnish with fresh coriander and serve with lime wedges.

Bob Birkel, Corinth, New York

ADIRONDACK TROUT

Trout
Salt

Swamp Mass.
Butter

Catch them. Remove innards, pack in fine salt to slime, 2 ounces to each pound of fish. Let them remain the slime for twelve hours, then clean thoroughly and pack in broken ice. Add swamp mass. Keep in a cool place until used.

To fry put in a piece of butter the size of an egg in a pan. Heat as hot as possible without burning. Drain them and lay in pan. Salt lightly. Cook on one side. Remove from pan, and fire turn the trout. Replace in pan and cook to taste. Serve a la Woods.

June S. Shone, Holcomb, New York

151

When You Hug A Tree

Indians say that
When you hug a tree
You gain courage and strength
From its life force
And it gains life strength
From the force of your courage.

The pulse of your heart bonds
With its living fluid to reach
The leafy branches and exchanges
Breath with your breath.
Longing for courage and strength
I search to find a tree to hug.

Deep in the woods there is a tall
    pine,
Grandfather to all the others.
Slipping cautious arms around its
    trunk
I wait quietly to feel the bonding.
Rough bark kisses the side of my
    face
As I press closer and close my eyes
    to listen.

A sapsucker is tapping for insects.
A spider scurried along the
    branches
Looking for a place to spin a lacy
    web.
Leaves rustle, quivering in the
    breeze
While a robin watches over her
    nestlings
In the boughs above my head.

Grandfather tree is full of joy and
    life
And is giving comfort to all who
    shelter here.
I do feel the courage and strength,
    its peace,
Surging through my limbs and
    trunk.
I go now to hug the tree every day
Because it's true, what the Indians
    say.

June Clow

Breads and Pastries

Common Baking Dishes and Pans

Spring Form Pan

Layer Cake or Pie Pan

Ring Mold

Baking or Square Pan

Loaf Pan

Brioche Pan

Angel Cake Pan

Bundt Tube

Equivalent Dishes

4-CUP BAKING DISH
= 9″ pie plate
= 8″ x $1^1 4$″ layer cake pan
= $7^3 8$″ x $3^5 8$″ x $2^1 4$″ loaf pan

6-CUP BAKING DISH
= 8″ or 9″ x $1^1 2$″ layer cake pan
= 10″ pie pan
= $8^1 2$″ x $3^5 8$″ x $2^5 8$″ loaf pan

8-CUP BAKING DISH
= 8″ x 8″ x 2″ square pan
= 11″ x 7″ x $1^1 2$″ baking pan
= 9″ x 5″ x 3″ loaf pan

10-CUP BAKING DISH
= 9″ x 9″ x 2″ square pan
= $11^3 4$″ x $7^1 2$″ x $1^3 4$″ baking pan
= 15″ x 10″ x 1″ flat jelly roll pan

12-CUP BAKING DISH OR MORE
= $13^1 2$″ x $8^1 2$″ x 2″ glass baking dish
= 13″ x 9″ x 2″ metal baking pan
= 14″ x $10^1 2$″ x $2^1 2$″ roasting pan

Total Volume of Pans

TUBE PANS
$7^1 2$″ x 3″ Bundt tube	6 cups
9″ x $3^1 2$″ fancy or Bundt tube	9 cups
9″ x $3^1 2$″ angel cake pan	12 cups
10″ x $3^3 4$″ Bundt tube	12 cups
9″ x $3^1 2$″ fancy tube mold	12 cups
10″ x 4″ fancy tube mold	16 cups
10″ x 4″ angel cake pan	18 cups

SPRING FORM PANS
8″ x 3″ pan	12 cups
9″ x 3″ pan	16 cups

RING MOLDS
$8^1 2$″ x $2^1 4$″ mold	$4^1 2$ cups
$9^1 4$″ x $2^3 4$″ mold	8 cups

BRIOCHE PAN
$9^1 2$″ x $3^1 4$″ pan	8 cups

BREADS AND PASTRIES 🍎

EGGPLANT BREAD

3 eggs
4 tsp. fresh lemon juice
2 Tbs. lemon peel
3 Tbs. vanilla
1 c. vegetable oil
1½ c. sugar
2 c. unpeeled eggplant, shredded
3 c. flour

4½ tsp. baking powder
2 tsp. allspice
2 tsp. cinnamon
½ tsp. salt
1 c. nuts, chopped
1 c. raisins, chopped
¼ c. warm water

Preheat oven to 325°. Grease and flour two 9"x5" loaf pans. In large mixer bowl beat eggs until light and fluffy. Gradually add lemon juice, peel, vanilla, and oil. Gradually add sugar, beating constantly. Stir in eggplant. Sift together the flour, baking powder, spices, and salt. Add to eggplant mixture and mix well. Stir in nuts, raisins, and warm water, mixing well. Divide batter between the pans. Bake in 325° oven for 1 hour or until bread tests done. Cool in pans 15 minutes before inverting on wire racks.

Lynn Paska, Schenectady, New York

153

HEALTHY BANANA BREAD

3 large very ripe bananas, mashed
2 eggs, beaten
½ c. dark brown sugar, packed
¼ c. canola oil
1 c. quick oats

1 c. whole wheat flour
1 tsp. baking soda
1 tsp. cinnamon
6 oz. semi-sweet chocolate chips

Mix first 4 ingredients together, then add remaining ingredients. Mix all together gently and bake 1 hour at 350° in greased and floured loaf pans.

Evelyn Harrington, Glens Falls, New York

BANANA NUT BREAD

½ c. shortening
1 c. sugar
2 eggs
3 ripe bananas, mashed
2 c. flour

1 tsp. baking soda
⅓ c. milk
½ tsp. salt
1 tsp. vanilla
½ c. walnuts, chopped

Cream shortening and sugar together. Add eggs and bananas; beat well. Add sifted dry ingredients, milk, and vanilla; mix well. Stir in nuts. Pour in greased pan. Bake at 350° for 1 hour 10 minutes. Makes 1 loaf or 3 mini loaves.

Karen Graff, Clifton Park, New York

JOHN W. DODSON'S BANANA BREAD

¼ c. butter
1⅓ c. sugar
2 eggs
1 tsp. vanilla
2 c. flour
1 tsp. baking powder

1 tsp. baking soda
¾ tsp. salt
1 c. sour cream
1 c. ripe bananas, mashed
½ c. nuts, chopped

Cream butter and sugar until light and fluffy. Add eggs and vanilla, blending thoroughly. Sift together flour, baking powder, soda, and salt. Add alternately with sour cream to creamed mixture beginning and ending with dry ingredients. Add bananas and nuts, mixing until blended. Bake in loaf pans at 350° for 35 to 40 minutes. Makes 2 large loaves or 3 small loaves.

John W. Dodson, Burnt Hills, New York

TROY CRANBERRY BREAD

2 c. whole wheat flour
1½ tsp. baking powder
½ tsp. salt
¼ c. milk powder
¼ c. orange juice, freshly
    squeezed
2 Tbs. oil
Hot water

2 Tbs. brown sugar
½ c. honey
1 egg, beaten
½ c. broken walnuts
½ c. broken pecans
1 c. raw cranberries
½ c. apple, diced
1 Tbs. orange rind, grated

Combine flour, baking powder, salt, and milk powder in large glass bowl; set aside. Mix orange juice, oil, sugar, and water. Add honey and eggs to liquid. Stir liquid ingredients into dry mixture. Add the nuts, apple, cranberries, and rind; fold carefully together with rubber spatula. Pour mixture into a greased loaf pan. Bake at 325° for 50 minutes. If wooden pick comes out dry, bread is done. Let cool on rack before serving.

Chef Armand Vanderstigchel

CHRISTMAS EGGNOG BREAD

3 c. flour
¾ c. sugar
1 Tbs. baking powder
1 tsp. salt
½ tsp. nutmeg
1½ c. eggnog

1 egg, beaten
¼ c. butter, softened
1 c. white raisins
½ c. green cherries, drained
½ c. red cherries, drained
¾ c. walnuts, chopped

In a large bowl put together the dry ingredients. In separate bowl, mix eggnog, egg, and butter. Add to dry ingredients. Add nuts and fruit. Bake at 350° for 60 minutes. Cool for 10 to 15 minutes.

Esther M. Garback, Gloversville, New York

AUNT VICKI'S MONKEY BREAD

3 cans of biscuits
1 stick butter

1 c. sugar
2 tsp. cinnamon

Cut biscuits into quarters. Put into sugar and cinnamon mixture. Place in bundt pan, one can of biscuits at a time. Pour a little butter on each layer. After third can, pour on remaining butter and sugar mixture. Bake at 350° for 35 minutes.

Kaitlin Graff, Clifton Park, New York

PUMPKIN MAPLE RAISIN NUT BREAD

3 c. flour
2 tsp. baking powder
1¼ tsp. salt
1 tsp. baking soda
1 tsp. cinnamon
½ tsp. nutmeg
2 eggs

1 (16 oz.) can pumpkin
1 c. brown sugar, packed
½ c. real maple syrup
¼ c. oil
½ c. dark raisins
½ c. pecans, chopped

Grease 9"x5" loaf pan. In a large bowl mix first 6 ingredients. In medium bowl, beat eggs with pumpkin, brown sugar, maple syrup, and oil. Stir into flour mixture until flour is moistened. Stir in raisins and nuts; spoon into loaf. Bake in a 350° oven for 1¼ hours. Cool bread in pan on wire rack for 10 to 15 minutes; remove from pan. To serve sprinkle with confectioners sugar. Makes 16 servings.

Esther M. Garback, Gloversville, New York

Esther Garback is a devotee of cooking and baking. Her mother was a cateress for 25 years. Esther inherited her culinary talent, which shows in her proud achievements of 2 awards from BETTER HOMES & GARDENS, 3 from rice success company, 1 from USA contests, and many from county contests. Great recipes, Esther!!!!!

OLD STOVE INSTANT ROLLS

1 c. self-rising flour
3 Tbs. sugar

½ c. milk
1 Tbs. mayonnaise

Mix all together. Drop in greased muffin tins. Bake at 450° until brown.
Karen Graff, Clifton Park, New York

LAKE LUZERNE APPLE ROLLS

¼ c. butter
2 pkg. active dry yeast
1¾ c. hot water
½ c. buttermilk
8 Tbs. sugar
2 tsp. ground cinnamon

1 egg
1 c. whole wheat flour
4 c. all-purpose flour
4 to 6 apples
1 egg, beaten
2 Tbs. sesame seed

Melt butter. In a bowl, dissolve yeast in warm water. Add buttermilk, butter, 6 tablespoons sugar, 1 teaspoon cinnamon, egg, and whole wheat flour. Stir to blend. Add the flour. Knead dough until smooth and elastic. Let rise in a warm place for about 40 minutes. Punch down. Peel apples; cut into wedges. On a floured board, knead dough until satiny. Divide into 3 parts. Roll each out to a rectangle. Cut each rectangle into 10 squares. Place 1 apple wedge in the middle of each square. Combine remaining sugar and cinnamon. Sprinkle mixture over apple wedges. Fold dough over apples to cover completely. Place on a greased baking sheet, seam-side down. Brush with beaten egg. Sprinkle with sesame seed. Bake at 400° for about 8 minutes. Increase temperature to 425° and bake for another 4 minutes until golden brown. Cool, covered, on wire rack.

Tip: These rolls are perfect for freezing. Wrap well in small batches. Thaw and reheat at 350°. Makes 30 rolls.

Chef Armand Vanderstigchel

ELLIE'S SARATOGA BISCUITS

2 c. flour
1 Tbs. baking powder
2 Tbs. sugar

1 tsp. salt
½ c. butter
⅔ c. sweet or regular milk

Sift dry ingredients into mixing bowl. Measure shortening and cut into flour mixture with pastry blender, 2 knives, or blending fork, until mixture looks like "meal". Stir in almost all the milk. If dough does not seem pliable, add remaining milk. Use enough milk to make a soft puffy dough easy to roll out. Knead on a lightly floured board. Too much handling makes tough biscuits. Roll out ¼ inch thick for thin crusty biscuits and ½ inch for thick soft biscuits. Place on ungreased cookie sheet close together for soft sided, an inch apart for crusty sided biscuits. Bake 10 to 12 minutes at 450°. Makes about twenty 2-inch biscuits.

Patricia Stanley, Saratoga Springs, New York

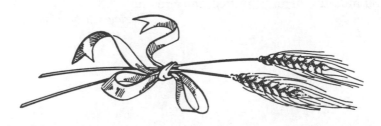

POTTER BISCUITS WITH CHIVES

2 c. flour
2 tsp. baking powder
¼ tsp. baking soda

4½ Tbs. chives, minced
¼ c. margarine or butter
¾ c. buttermilk

Mix together flour, baking powder, and baking soda. Add shortening, buttermilk, and chives. Knead on a lightly floured board for three minutes. Pull apart pieces of dough and put close together in lightly greased pan. Bake at 425° for 12 minutes. Pull apart to eat!

Ruth Potter, Wells, New York

Ruth Potter and her family owned and ran "Potters Lodge" on Lake Algonquin in Wells for 16 years. As the cook, she often made these baking goods by popular demand. Now retired, they spend the winters in Florida and the summers in the Adirondacks. (We call it . . . the best of both worlds.) Good for you Ruth!!!

KAITLIN POPOVERS

2 eggs
1 c. milk

1 c. flour, sifted
½ tsp. salad oil

Preheat oven to 475°. Place eggs in mixing bowl; add milk, flour, and salt. Beat 1½ minutes with beater. Add oil and beat 30 seconds more. Don't overbeat. Fill 6 to 8 well-greased custard cups half full. Bake in very hot oven for 15 minutes. Reduce oven to 350° and bake 25 to 30 minutes longer or until brown and firm. A few minutes before removing from oven, prick with fork to let steam escape. If you like popovers dry and crisp, turn off oven and leave in for 30 minutes with door ajar. Serve hot. Makes 6 to 8.

Karen Graff, Clifton Park, New York

POTATO PUFFS

4 to 6 potatoes, peeled and cooked
in water, mashed
2 egg yolks, well beaten
2 egg whites, beaten until stiff
peaks form

1 small onion, cut into tiny pieces
1 clove of garlic, cut in tiny pieces
1 Tbs. butter or margarine

Fold 2 stiffly beaten egg whites into stiffly mashed potatoes. Put aside. Saute onion and garlic until tender, but not brown. Then add to mashed potatoes with egg yolks; mix together. Put into a greased casserole. Bake at 350° for 30 minutes, or until puffed and brown.

Shirley Fahey, Hadley, New York

MARIA'S DESSERT

1⅓ c. flour
¼ c. ground walnuts
⅓ c. sugar
1 tsp. baking powder
1 stick of butter

1 egg
1 egg yolk
1 (8 oz.) jar of apricot jam
Confectioners sugar

Combine flour, walnuts, sugar, baking powder, butter, and eggs. Place in a pan. Spread the apricot jam over it and sprinkle with confectioners sugar. Bake at 375° until golden brown. About 30 to 35 minutes.

Maria King, Blue Mountain Lake, New York

Adirondack Museum Manager Victoria Verner submitted a recipe from employee Maria King, who has made this dish frequently for the staff. Maria King has been with the staff of The Adirondack Museum for a number of years. She is a sweet woman who lives in Indian Lake. "Maria's Dessert" actually came from Austria, where Maria was born and raised, but she has conquered the Adirondack ovens of the area with this recipe. Stop at the Museum in Blue Mountain Lake for a slice (kidding!).

Blue Moutain Lake, New York

ADIRONDACK STRAWBERRY PASTRIES

6 sheets frozen puff pastry dough,
   thawed

4 Tbs. powdered sugar
2 pints strawberries

Roll each sheet of dough out to about 12"x6". If desired, sift powdered sugar over counter before rolling. Cut each sheet into 4 even pieces. Cover baking sheets with waxed paper. Place dough on prepared sheet. Prick with a fork. Sift powdered sugar over dough. Refrigerate for 30 minutes. Bake dough at 425° for 5 minutes. Increase temperature to 450° and bake for another 3 to 5 minutes until pastries are light, golden, and puffed. Let cool on wire rack.

Spread Vanilla Custard (recipe follows) over half of the baked pastries. Cover with sliced strawberries. Top with second half of pastries. Dust with powdered sugar. Serve. Makes 12 pastries.

VANILLA CUSTARD:

1 vanilla bean
1 c. half and half
3 egg yolks

3 Tbs. granulated sugar
½ c. whipping cream

Split vanilla bean open lengthwise. Place in a heavy saucepan. Add half and half. Bring to a boil. Cook over medium-low heat for 10 minutes. Remove vanilla bean. In a bowl, beat egg yolks and sugar until smooth and creamy. Add a little hot half and half, whisking. Pour this mixture back into saucepan. Bring to a boil, whisking constantly until thick and creamy. Do not boil or custard will curdle. Remove custard sauce from heat. Beat until cool. Whip cream until soft peaks form. Add to vanilla custard.

Bob Birkel, Corinth, New York

NORTH CREEK LEMON MUFFINS

⅓ c. butter or margarine
1 c. granulated sugar
3 eggs
1½ c. flour, sifted

3 tsp. baking powder
⅓ tsp. salt
⅔ c. milk
1 tsp. lemon extract

In large mixing bowl, combine eggs, milk, and extract. Set aside. Stir together butter, sugar, flour, baking powder, and salt. Add to egg mixture. Fill ⅔ full greased or paper-baking-cup-lined muffin cups. Bake at 400° oven for 15 to 20 minutes or until done. Makes at least 12 big muffins.

Betty Tyrel, North Creek, New York

LAKE ALGONQUIN OAT BRAN MUFFINS

1 c. oat bran flour
1 c. white flour
¼ c. sugar (or sugar substitute)
2 tsp. baking powder
¼ tsp. baking soda
¼ c. soft margarine
1 egg
1 c. buttermilk

Sift together all dry ingredients; add shortening, egg, and buttermilk. Bake at 375° for 20 minutes. Makes 12 muffins.

Ruth Potter, Wells, New York

Coffee Grinder at Uncommon Grounds
Saratoga Springs, New York

MARY'S GINGERBREAD MUFFINS

½ c. light molasses
½ c. oil
2 eggs, well beaten
2 c. flour
1 c. sugar
1 c. boiling water

¼ tsp. salt
1 tsp. ginger
1 tsp. baking soda
½ tsp. nutmeg
½ tsp. cinnamon

Mix together eggs, oil, molasses, and sugar. Add hot water and flour mixture alternately. Bake at 350°.

Mary Dodson, Burnt Hills, New York

ADIRONDACK WAFFLES

4 eggs
1 c. sugar
½ stick butter, melted
1 c. milk

2 c. flour
2 tsp. baking powder
1 tsp. vanilla
1 c. sour cream

Mix ingredients all together. For waffles, cook according to waffle iron directions. Can also use as batter for pancakes. Just drop on pan approximately 2 inches apart.

Laura Roberts, Clifton Park, New York

ADIRONDACK FLAPJACKS

4 egg yolks, beaten
4 egg whites, beaten stiff
2 Tbs. sugar
½ tsp. salt

2 c. milk
6 Tbs. butter, melted
2 c. flour
2 tsp. baking powder

Beat all ingredients together thoroughly and add egg whites last. Fry on hot griddle. Serve well-buttered with hot maple syrup or shaved maple sugar and top with whipped cream.

Vivienne Perrier Malaguerra, Lexington, Massachusetts

Viv Malaguerra used to ski out to "Lambs" camp (early 1930s) and eat her fill of Adirondack Flapjacks, covered with heavy cream. She would burn off the calories on the way home, moonlight skiing on the Lake Placid Club golf courses where you could go into an unseen dip and go completely out of sight! "What a flapjack can do to you!!!"

SHEILA'S MORNING COFFEE CAKE

1 tsp. cinnamon
½ c. sugar
1 c. sugar
½ c. butter
2 c. flour

8 oz. sour cream
2 eggs
1 tsp. baking powder
1 tsp. baking soda
1 tsp. vanilla

Place first 2 ingredients in jar and shake. This will be used for the topping. Melt butter in small saucepan and add 1 cup sugar. In a bowl add flour, eggs, baking powder, baking soda, and vanilla. Add melted butter with sugar and mix. The batter will be very dry. Grease pan and pour half the batter in pan and shake half the topping in. Pour rest of batter and shake rest of topping mix on top. Bake in 350° oven for about 40 minutes; this could be more or less baking time, depending on the type of pan used.

Mary Gennusa, Roslyn Heights, New York

RACCOONS are nocturnal and inquisitive, vocal, and sometimes very pesky animals that have a long black-ringed tail. Civilization has not interfered much with his way of life. They are thriving in suburban bakcyards as well as the wild.

Raccoons don't hibernate, but are usually torpid in cold weather; in the North they start denning up in November or December. If they can't find a natural tree cavity to sack out in they don't mind sharing a burrow with a woodchuck.

Most of us can't help enjoying the antics of raccoons even if their actions are annoying. You can't be mad long at a critter that, when you're scolding it, will put its paws over its eyes.

Cakes, Cookies, Desserts

TEMPERATURE TESTS
FOR CANDY MAKING

There are two different methods of determining when candy has been cooked to the proper consistency. One is by using a candy thermometer in order to record degrees, the other is by using the cold water test. The chart below will prove useful in helping to follow candy recipes:

TYPE OF CANDY	DEGREES	COLD WATER
Fondant, Fudge	234 - 238°	Soft Ball
Divinity, Caramels	245 - 248°	Firm Ball
Taffy	265 - 270°	Hard Ball
Butterscotch	275 - 280°	Light Crack
Peanut Brittle	285 - 290°	Hard Crack
Caramelized Sugar	310 - 321°	Caramelized

In using the cold water test, use a fresh cupful of cold water for each test. When testing, remove the candy from the fire and pour about ½ teaspoon of candy into the cold water. Pick the candy up in the fingers and roll into a ball if possible.

In the SOFT BALL TEST the candy will roll into a soft ball which quickly loses its shape when removed from the water.

In the FIRM BALL TEST the candy will roll into a firm, but not hard ball. It will flatten out a few minutes after being removed from the water.

In the HARD BALL TEST the candy will roll into a hard ball which has lost almost all plasticity and will roll around on a plate on removal from the water.

In the LIGHT CRACK TEST the candy will form brittle threads which will soften on removal from the water.

In the HARD CRACK TEST the candy will form brittle threads in the water which will remain brittle after being removed from the water.

In CARAMELIZING the sugar first melts then becomes a golden brown. It will form a hard brittle ball in cold water.

CAKES, COOKIES, DESSERTS 🍒
🍂 CAKES AND ICINGS 🍂

APPLE CAKE

4 c. apples, chopped
2 c. sugar
2 eggs
2 tsp. baking soda
1 tsp. salt

3 c. flour
1 c. oil
1½ c. nutmeats, cut up
1 tsp. baking powder
2 tsp. vanilla

Put sugar over apples and nutmeats; let stand 1 hour. Add oil, eggs, and vanilla; mix well. Add flour, soda, baking powder, and salt. Bake in well-greased 13"x9" dish for 1 hour at 350°. You may make a thin white frosting for the top.

Claire R. Cook, Bloomingdale, New York

APPLE CAKE

2 eggs
½ lb. butter
2 to 3 apples, peeled, cored, and
    sliced
1 c. sugar

2 c. flour
Pinch of salt
⅔ c. milk
Cinnamon and sugar

Mix all ingredients except apples. Pour into small greased roasting pan. Top with sliced apples, placing them in rows. Sprinkle with cinnamon and sugar. Bake at 400° for 45 minutes.

Marilyn Mauro, Clifton Park, New York

FRESH APPLE CAKE

2 c. unsifted flour
2 c. sugar
½ tsp. nutmeg
4 c. raw apples, pared and finely
    diced
½ c. pecans, chopped

2 eggs
2 tsp. baking soda
1 tsp. cinnamon
½ tsp. salt
½ c. soft butter
Confectioners sugar

Preheat oven to 325°. Grease a 9"x13" pan. In large bowl sift flour with sugar, soda, cinnamon, nutmeg, and salt. Add apple, pecans, butter, and eggs. Beat until just combined. It will be thick. Turn into prepared pan. Bake 1 hour or until top springs back when lightly pressed with fingertips. Cool on wire rack. Sprinkle with confectioners sugar. Serve warm, cut into squares. Top with whipped cream or ice cream, if desired.

Carol M. Miller, Northumberland, New York

MARY'S RAW APPLE CAKE

1 stick butter
2 c. sugar
3 eggs
2 c. apples, diced
1 c. nuts, chopped

2 c. flour
1 tsp. baking soda
1 tsp. salt
1 tsp. cinnamon

Cream butter and sugar, then add eggs. Add apples and nuts, then add flour mixture. Bake at 350° for 40 minutes in floured and greased loaf pan.

Mary Dodson, Burnt Hills, New York

TUBE APPLE CAKE

8 large apples, sliced thin
3 tsp. cinnamon
5 Tbs. sugar
3 c. flour
3 tsp. baking powder
1 tsp. salt

1 c. butter, melted
¼ c. orange juice
2 c. sugar
4 eggs
2½ tsp. vanilla

Mix first 3 ingredients together and set aside. In large mixer bowl add rest of ingredients and beat until smooth. Pour half the batter into a greased and floured tube pan. Spread half the apple mixture over batter and pour in remaining batter; top with rest of apple mixture. Bake at 350° for 1½ hours. Cool 15 minutes before removing from pan.

Karen Graff, Clifton Park, New York

AUTUMN CAKE

2 c. apples, cored, peeled, and
   chopped
1 c. sugar
1½ c. flour
1 tsp. baking soda
½ tsp. salt
½ tsp. cinnamon

1 tsp. vanilla
1 egg, beaten
½ c. vegetable oil
½ c. pecans or walnuts, chopped
5 Tbs. brown sugar
3 Tbs. butter
3 Tbs. cream

Combine apples and sugar in large bowl. Let stand until juice forms. Sift together flour, baking soda, and salt. Add to apple-sugar mixture. Add cinnamon, vanilla, egg, vegetable oil, and nuts. Mix well. Bake at 325° for 40 to 45 minutes in an 8"x10" pan or 2 loaf pans.

Bring brown sugar, butter, and cream to a boil in a non-stick saucepan, stirring constantly. Pour on cake; bake 10 to 15 minutes longer.

Carol M. Miller, Northumberland, New York

UPSTATE CHOCOLATE CAKE

4 eggs
¾ c. granulated sugar
6 Tbs. all-purpose flour

3 tsp. cornstarch
1 tsp. baking soda

In a bowl beat eggs and sugar until light and fluffy. In another bowl combine flour, cornstarch, and baking soda. Sift into egg mixture; stir to blend. Line a 9-inch round baking pan greased with wax paper (do not grease sides of pan). Pour batter into pan. Bake at 375° for about 30 minutes. Let cake cool in pan. Loosen around edges with knife. Carefully turn cake out onto rack; peel off paper. Cut cake into 3 layers. Place the Chocolate Filling (recipe follows) between the layers. Frost the top and sides with Glaze (recipe follows) and garnish with grapes and candied flowers.

CHOCOLATE FILLING:

¾ c. butter
1½ c. powdered sugar
3 egg yolks

5 tsp. unsweetened cocoa
4 tsp. orange marmalade

Filling: Beat together the butter and sugar until creamy. Add egg Yolk, cocoa, and orange marmalade; stir until smooth.3 tsp. butter

GLAZE AND GARNISH:

1 (6 oz.) pkg. semi-sweet
   chocolate

Green grapes
Candied flowers (optional)

Glaze: Melt butter and chocolate in a double boiler.

Bob Birkel, Corinth, New York

JANE'S CHOCOLATE CAKE

1 c. flour
1 c. sugar
½ c. cocoa
½ c. vegetable oil
1 tsp. baking soda

1 tsp. baking powder
1 tsp. vanilla
½ tsp. salt
1 large egg
1 c. boiling water

Preheat oven to 350°. Grease and flour pans. Double the recipe for oblong pan. Put all ingredients, except water, in mixing bowl in order listed. Very gradually add boiling water a little at a time while beating in. Batter will be thin. Pour into pan; bake for 30 to 35 minutes.

Patricia Stanley, Saratoga Springs, New York

DATE CHOCOLATE CHIP CAKE

1 c. dates
1½ c. boiling water
1 tsp. baking soda
2 oz. cream
4 Tbs. butter

1 c. sugar
2 eggs
1½ c. flour, sifted
1 tsp. salt
Topping (recipe follows)

Soak 1 cup of chopped dates in 1½ cups of boiling water. Add 1 teaspoon baking soda; stir several times. Cream 2 ounces of cream with 1 cup of sugar; add 2 eggs and cream until light and fluffy. Add date mixture and blend. Add 1½ cups of sifted flour, 1 teaspoon of salt, ½ teaspoon of baking soda, and beat all ingredients until smooth (electric mixer). Pour into a 9"x13" pan. Sprinkle Topping over top of mixture in pan. Bake at 350° for 20 minutes, then at 325° for 15 minutes. Comes out glazed and ready to eat when cooled. (This is best after it has been refrigerated.)

TOPPING:

½ c. sugar
½ c. brown sugar

3 oz. walnuts, chopped
6 oz. chocolate chips

Mix together and sprinkle over cake batter before baking.

Joan Smith, Saratoga Springs, New York

DISAPPEARING DARK CHOCOLATE CAKE

2 c. sugar
2½ c. flour
2 c. brewed coffee, cooled
1 c. cocoa

1 c. mayonnaise
2 tsp. baking soda
2 eggs

Mix together sugar, flour, and cooled coffee. Add cocoa, mayonnaise, baking soda, and eggs. Beat about 3 minutes. Pour into 2 greased cake pans and bake at 350° for 35 to 45 minutes or until knife comes out clean in center.

Freda Bates, Alabmont, New York

DEEP DARK CHOCOLATE CAKE

1¾ c. flour
2 c. sugar
¾ c. baking cocoa
1½ tsp. baking soda
1½ tsp. baking powder
1 tsp. salt

2 eggs
1 c. milk
½ c. vegetable oil
2 tsp. vanilla
1 c. boiling water

Combine dry ingredients in large mixer bowl. Add eggs, milk, oil, and vanilla. Beat 2 minutes at medium speed. Stir in boiling water (batter will be thin). Pour into greased and floured 13"x9"x2" pan. Bake at 350° for 35 to 40 minutes or until cake tester comes out clean. Cool and frost.

Karen Graff, Clifton Park, New York

WHITE CHOCOLATE FUDGE CAKE
AND FROSTING

¾ c. (3 squares) broken white
   chocolate
½ c. hot water
1 c. butter, softened
1½ c. sugar
3 eggs
1 tsp. vanilla

2½ c. flour
1 tsp. baking soda
1 tsp. baking powder
½ tsp. salt
1 c. buttermilk
¾ c. pecans, finely chopped

Melt white chocolate with hot water in small pan over low heat. In large bowl combine flour, sugar, soda, baking powder, salt, butter, and buttermilk. Blend at low speed for 1 minute, scraping sides of bowl occasionally. Add eggs, one at a time beating at medium speed. Add melted and cooled chocolate and vanilla. Blend well and beat 1 minute. Stir in nuts. Pour into two 9-inch layer pans which have been greased and floured on bottom only. Bake at 350° for 30 to 35 minutes. Cool for 15 minutes. Loosen edges and remove from pans. Cool completely. Frost with WHITE CHOCOLATE FUDGE FROSTING.

WHITE CHOCOLATE FUDGE FROSTING:

¾ c. (3 squares) broken white
   chocolate
1 c. milk
2½ Tbs. flour

1 c. shortening
1 c. sugar
1½ tsp. clear vanilla

In small pan over warm water melt chocolate. In another small fry pan combine milk and flour. Cook over medium heat until mixture is very thick, stirring constantly. Cool and add chocolate. Blend well. In large bowl cream shortening, sugar, and vanilla until light and fluffy, about 3 minutes. Gradually add completely cooled white chocolate mixture. Beat at high speed until consistency of whipped cream. Spread between layers and over cooled cake. Decorate with pecans and dark chocolate slivers.

Helen Witts, Schenectady, New York

Old Fashioned Adirondack Stove

CRANBERRY-DATE CAKE

2¼ c. flour
1 c. sugar
1 tsp. baking soda
¼ tsp. salt
1½ c. fresh cranberries, coarsely
   chopped
1 c. pitted dates, snipped

1 c. walnuts, chopped
2 eggs, beaten
1 c. buttermilk
¾ c. oil
½ c. orange juice
¾ c. sugar

Glaze: In a small saucepan combine the orange juice and the sugar. Cook and stir until sugar dissolves. Set aside.

Cake: Stir together flour, sugar, baking soda, and salt. Add cranberries, dates, and nuts. Combine eggs, buttermilk, oil; add to flour mixture and mix well. Turn the batter into a greased and floured 8-inch fluted tube pan. Bake at 350° for 55 minutes. Cool in pan for 15 minutes. Remove from pan onto a wire rack. While warm, spoon on the glaze.

Esther M. Garback, Gloversville, New York

GRANDMA'S CRAZY CAKE

1½ c. flour
1 c. sugar
3 Tbs. cocoa
1 tsp. baking soda
¼ tsp. salt

¼ tsp. vanilla
6 Tbs. cooking oil
2 Tbs. vinegar
1 c. water

Sift first 5 ingredients together in a square baking pan and make 3 holes. Add vanilla in one hole, cooking oil in another, and vinegar in the other hole. Add water and stir. Bake at 350° for 25 to 30 minutes.

Mary Dodson, Burnt Hills, New York

CRUMB CAKE

2 c. flour
½ c. sugar
¾ c. oil
½ tsp. salt

1 tsp. baking powder
½ c. milk
1 egg
1 tsp. cinnamon

Mix flour, sugar, oil, salt, and baking powder together; take 1 cup of this mixture out for crumbs on top. To the remaining mixture add milk and egg. To cup of crumb mix, add cinnamon. Put cake mixture in greased round pan. Top with crumb mixture. Bake at 350° for 30 minutes.

Marilyn Mauro, Clifton Park, New York

SARATOGA SPRINGS DIRT CAKE

8 oz. cream cheese
2 boxes vanilla pudding
2½ c. milk
16 oz. whipped cream
1 lb. Oreo cookies, mixed in
    blender

1 plastic flower pot
Plastic leaves
1 trowel for serving

Mix milk and pudding until thickened; add cream cheese. Fold in whipped cream. Add one layer of cookie crumble in the bottom of the flower pot, then half of the mixture. Add another layer of cookie crumble and top with remaining mixture. Cover top with cookie crumbs and the artificial flower. Serve with serving trowel.

Natalie J. Smith, Saratoga Springs, New York

COUNTRY UPSIDE DOWN CAKE

5 c. rhubarb, cut into ½-inch
    pieces
1 c. sugar

2 (3 oz.) pkg. red jello
2 c. mini marshmallows
1 pkg. yellow or white cake mix

Grease 9"x13" pan. Spread rhubarb over bottom and sprinkle sugar over it. Now sprinkle jello over it. Scatter marshmallows over jello. Prepare cake batter as instructed on box; pour over mixture in pan. Bake at 350° for 55 minutes. Cool and serve with whipped topping.

Ruth Lebanon, Corinth, New York

NANNY'S HOT MILK CAKE

2 eggs, creamed
1 c. flour
1 tsp. vanilla
Salt
1 c. sugar
1 tsp. baking powder

½ c. milk, heated with 2 Tbs.
    butter (boil)
5 Tbs. brown sugar
3 Tbs. butter
¾ coconut
3 Tbs. milk

Mix eggs, flour, vanilla, salt, sugar, power powder, and milk/butter mixture together and bake about 30 minutes at 375° in greased 13"x9"x2" pan.

Topping: Melt butter. Add sugar, milk, and coconut. Let boil up, then spread on cake. Place cake with Topping under the broiler until the Topping bubbles.

Marilyn Mauro, Clifton Park, New York

HUMMINGBIRD CAKE

3 c. flour
2 c. sugar
1 tsp. baking soda
1 tsp. salt
1 tsp. cinnamon
3 eggs, beaten

1 c. oil
1½ tsp. vanilla
8 oz. crushed pineapple, drained
1 c. pecans, chopped
2 c. bananas, chopped

Combine first 5 ingredients; add egg and oil. Add dry ingredients and stir until moistened. Spoon batter into 3 greased and floured 9-inch round cake pans. Bake at 350° for 25 to 30 minutes or until toothpick inserted in center comes out clean. Cool in pans for 10 minutes. Remove and cool completely.

Ruth Lebanon, Corinth, New York

MARBLE CAKE

2 c. flour
2 tsp. baking powder
¼ tsp. salt
1 c. milk
1 tsp. vanilla

½ c. shortening
1 c. sugar
2 eggs
4 Tbs. cocoa

Cream shortening until soft and creamy. Add sugar; gradually add eggs and beat until creamy. Add dry ingredients. Measure milk and add vanilla to it. To one-half of batter add cocoa. Spoon alternately in loaf pan. Bake at 350° for 1 hour.

Marilyn Mauro, Clifton Park, New York

MAYO CAKE

3 c. flour
1½ c. sugar
⅔ c. cocoa
1½ tsp. baking soda

2¼ tsp. baking powder
1½ c. mayonnaise
1½ c. warm water
1½ tsp. vanilla extract

Mix dry ingredients together. Add remaining ingredients. Beat well and bake in greased and floured layer pans at 350° for 35 minutes until done.

Evelyn Harrington, Glens Falls, New York

MOLASSES CAKE

1 c. shortening (bacon fat is
  better)
½ c. sugar
1 egg
1 c. molasses
¼ tsp. salt

1 Tbs. ginger
1 c. warm with 1 tsp. baking
  powder added
3 c. flour
Raisins (optional)

Bake in slow oven (not too fast — 325°) in a 13"x9" pan until done. When cake is done, the top of cake will spring back when touched. Serve with whipped cream, ice cream, or cream cheese frosting with a touch of nutmeg.

Sylvia Klausen, Johnston, New York

Sylvia's recipe for "Molasses Cake" was given to her children's great-grandmother Grace Cole. She was half American Indian and passed away in her 80s, approximately 20 years ago. She left us a great recipe. Thank you, Grace!

NORTH CREEK WAR-TIME CAKE

1 c. sugar
1 c. water
½ c. raisins
½ c. shortening
2 c. flour

1 tsp. baking soda
Salt
1 tsp. ground cloves
1 tsp. cinnamon
1 tsp. nutmeg

Combine first 4 ingredients. Put this on the stove. Boil 3 minutes, then set out to cool. Add rest of ingredients. Stir all ingredients together into a large bowl, beating well. Bake at 350° in a medium size pan until done.

Betty Tyrel, North Creek, New York

ROCKY MOUNTAIN CAKE AND FROSTING

2 c. sifted flour
1½ c. sugar
1 Tbs. baking powder
1 tsp. salt
1 tsp. cinnamon
½ tsp. nutmeg
½ tsp. allspice

½ tsp. ground cloves
7 eggs, separated
2 Tbs. caraway seeds
½ c. oil
¾ c. ice cold water
½ tsp. cream of tartar

Sift flour, sugar, baking powder, salt, and spices together several times. Combine egg yolks, caraway seeds, oil, and water in large bowl. Beat about ½ minute at low speed. Add cream of tartar to egg whites. Beat until stiff peaks form. Gradually pour egg yolk mixture over beaten egg whites. Gently fold in. Pour in an ungreased tube pan. Bake in slow oven at 325° for 55 minutes, then at 350° for 10 to 15 minutes. Invert to cool.

ROCKY MOUNTAIN FROSTING:

½ c. butter
2½ Tbs. flour
¼ tsp. salt
½ c. milk

½ c. brown sugar, firmly packed
2 c. confectioners sugar, sifted
1 tsp. vanilla
1 c. walnuts

In saucepan blend butter with flour and salt. Cook 1 minute; do not brown. Add milk and cook until thick. While hot, add brown sugar; beat well. Add confectioners sugar; beat until thick and creamy. Add vanilla and walnuts. Spread over top and sides of cake.

Sylvia Klausen, Johnston, New York

Sylvia Klausen from Johnstown submitted this 35-year-old recipe. Sylvia received this recipe from an older woman who lived in Fulton County her whole life. Back in the early part of the 1900s, desserts were an important part of the day. This cake is a little time consuming, but worth the effort!

SWEET MOUNTAIN CAKE

1¾ c. sugar
½ c. butter, softened
3 eggs, separated
1 c. milk

1½ tsp. baking powder
2 c. flour
2 tsp. vanilla
Salt

Blend butter, eggs, and sugar, then add dry ingredients. Bake in loaf pan for 30 minutes at 350° or until done.

Karen Graff, Clifton Park, New York

TOMATO SOUP CAKE

1 c. sugar
2 Tbs. shortening
1 tsp. cinnamon
1 tsp. cloves
1 can tomato soup

2 c. flour
1 tsp. baking soda dissolved in
warm water
1 c. raisins, floured
¾ c. nutmeats, chopped

Cream together all ingredients. Bake for 45 minutes at 350°. Reduce oven temperature to 325° and bake another 15 minutes. Cool, then frost cake.

ICING:

1 pkg. cream cheese
2 c. confectioners sugar

6 tsp. vanilla

Soften cream cheese to room temperature. While mixing, gradually add confectioners sugar and vanilla to cream cheese; cream until smooth.

Freda Bates, Alabmont, New York

Now is the calm, but soon they will be here. The stores are all stocked, and full with their gear. The town is all anxious, the streets are all clear. The restaurants are all loaded, and bars have their beers. It won't be long now, people are coming from all over, the day is so bright, it's summer in Saratoga!!

Robert E. Birkel, Jr.

WILHELMENA CAKE AND
MINNEHAHA FROSTING

⅓ c. fat
1 c. sugar
3 egg yolks
⅔ c. milk
2 c. flour

3 tsp. baking powder
⅛ tsp. salt
3 egg whites
1 tsp. vanilla

Cream the fat; add sugar gradually and continue to cream until the mixture is creamy. Sift flour, baking powder, and salt together. Set aside. To the fat and sugar mixture, add the well-beaten egg yolks, milk, and the flour mixture alternately, beating mixture thoroughly. Fold in the stiffly beaten whites and vanilla. Bake in a loaf or layers.

MINNEHAHA FROSTING:

Raisins, chopped and seeded
1 c. water
½ c. water

1/16 tsp. cream of tartar
1 or 2 egg whites
½ tsp. vanilla

Dissolve the sugar and the cream of tartar in the water. Cover the saucepan the first 5 minutes of cooking to prevent the formation of crystals on the sides of the saucepan. If 1 beaten egg is used, boil the sugar solution to the softball stage, until it forms 2-inch threads when dropped from a spoon or a fork. If 2 egg whites are used, boil to the firm ball stage. The syrup should not be stirred during the process of cooking, nor the saucepan moved. If crystals do form on the sides of the saucepan, remove them with a wet cloth or a wet brush. When the sugar solution has boiled to the right temperature, pour it gradually into the stiffly beaten egg whites, beating continually while pouring, and continue beating, until the right consistency to spread on the cakes. Add flavoring; add chopped seeded raisins to cream frosting.

Wilhelmena Birkel, Corinth, New York

YOU NAME IT ICING

½ c. margarine
1 c. sugar
2 Tbs. flour

½ c. shortening
1 c. milk
1 tsp. vanilla extract

Mix flour and milk together. Cook over low heat until very thick. Let mixture cool. Combine shortening, margarine, and sugar. Beat until light and fluffy. Add cooled flour mixture. Beat well again. Add vanilla and mix well again. Frost cooled cake. Frosts 1-layer cake.

Freda Bates, Alabmont, New York

BUTTER FROSTING

¼ c. butter
¾ c. milk
3 Tbs. flour

1½ tsp. vanilla
½ c. butter
¾ c. confectioners sugar

Melt ¼ cup butter in saucepan. Blend in flour. Gradually stir in milk; cook, stirring constantly, until mixture boils and thickens. Let cool by refrigerating one-half hour. Take out and add vanilla. Cream remaining butter with confectioners sugar until fluffy. Gradually add refrigerated mixture, beating until frosting is fluffy, about 5 minutes. Spread on cake.

Note: In hot weather, chill frosting before spreading.

Karen Graff, Clifton Park, New York

GRANDMA'S TOPPING

2 c. milk
½ c. sugar
2 tsp. cornstarch
Water

1 tsp. vanilla extract
½ tsp. cinnamon
1 tsp. butter

Bring milk and sugar to boiling point. Thicken to the desired consistency with cornstarch. (Mix cornstarch with water for paste.) Remove from heat and add vanilla, cinnamon, and butter. Mix all together. Pour over servings of dessert.

Gram Harris, Ballston Spa, New York

MOUNTAIN FROSTING

4 Tbs. butter
2 oz. chocolate
⅔ c. milk
3 Tbs. flour

1½ tsp. vanilla
½ c. butter
¾ c. granulated sugar

Melt 4 tablespoons and chocolate together. Add milk and flour. Cook, mixing until thick. Cool; add vanilla. Cream ½ cup butter with sugar until fluffy. Beat into cooked mixture until light and fluffy. Frost cake.

Lynn Paska, Schenectady, New York

PORCUPINE actually means "pig with spines" although he is a rodent with large chisel-like front teeth. He can do considerable damage with those teeth to forest trees by girdling the bark, which eventually kills the tree.

He is a clumsy animal that averages 34 inches in length and 15 pounds in weight. His lethal defense mechanism consists of quills about 4 inches long with a band of 1,000 microscopic barbs at the tip. An adult male can have 36,000 barbed quills covering his head, cheeks, legs, feet, and tail.

Although he is slow-moving, he is an excellent climber and swimmer, the hollow quills providing buoyancy. He dens up in rocks or holes underground and breeds in the fall. A single youngster is born with soft spines in May or June and weighs in at a pound, measuring an incredible 12 inches, and has a life-expectancy of about ten years.

❧ COOKIES ❧

EGG YOLK COOKIES

1 c. butter
½ c. sugar
2 c. flour

1 tsp. lemon juice
4 hard-boiled egg yolks

Cream first 3 ingredients together, then add remaining 2. Drop by teaspoonful on cookie sheet. Decorate with maraschino cherries. Bake for 10 minutes at 325°.

Marilyn Mauro, Clifton Park, New York

OLD FASHIONED FORGOTTEN COOKIES

2 egg whites
⅔ c. sugar

1 c. chocolate chips
1 c. nuts

Beat egg whites until stiff. Add sugar slowly to egg whites. Add chocolate chips and nuts to mixture. Preheat oven to 350°. Drop mixture by spoonfuls onto baking sheet and place in oven. Turn off oven and leave cookies in oven overnight.

Mary Dodson, Burnt Hills, New York

GINGER SNAPS

¾ c. shortening
¼ c. molasses
1 c. sugar
1 egg, beaten
¼ tsp. salt

2 tsp. baking soda
1 tsp. cinnamon
2 tsp. ginger
2 c. flour

Cream shortening, molasses, and sugar. Add egg and dry ingredients. Make into small balls and roll in sugar. Bake 10 minutes at 350°. Makes 4 dozen.

Karen Graff, Clifton Park, New York

MOLASSES COOKIES

1 heaping c. sugar
3 eggs
½ c. margarine
½ c. Crisco
1½ c. black molasses
5 c. flour

1 c. cold strong coffee
2 tsp. baking soda
2 tsp. ginger
½ tsp. ground cloves
2 Tbs. orange rind, grated
2 tsp. cinnamon

Add spices to flour. Set aside. Mix eggs, sugar, margarine, and Crisco together until fluffy. Mix baking soda in coffee. Alternately add flour, molasses, and coffee to egg and sugar mixture. Mix well. Refrigerate 2 hours or overnight. Roll out ⅓ at a time after kneading with flour. Best if cut thick. Sprinkle on sugar. Bake at 400° for 10 minutes.

June Shone, Holcomb, New York

CAMP MOSS ROCK MOLASSES COOKIES

¾ c. shortening
1 c. sugar
¼ c. molasses
1 egg
2 c. flour
2 tsp. baking soda
½ tsp. cloves

½ tsp. ginger
½ tsp. cinnamon
½ tsp. salt
½ c. raisins (optional)
½ c. nuts, chopped (optional)
1 (6 oz.) pkg. chocolate chips
  (optional)

Melt shortening in saucepan over low heat. Let cool. Add sugar, molasses, and egg. Beat well. Combine dry ingredients and add to first mixture. Mix well. Chill 2 hours or overnight. Form into 1-inch balls; roll in sugar. Bake 8 to 10 minutes in 375° oven. May add ½ cup raisins, ½ cup chopped nuts, or a 6-ounce package of chocolate chips.

Emma Purdy, Clifton Park, New York

Emma Purdy enclosed a recipe given to her by a camp cook on Upper Sranac Lake. She hopes it will become a favorite like it has been for her family. Thank you, Emma!!!

MOLASSES SUGAR COOKIES

¾ c. shortening, melted
1 c. sugar
¼ c. molasses
1 egg
½ tsp. cloves

½ tsp. ginger
1 tsp. cinnamon
½ tsp. baking soda
½ tsp. salt
2 c. flour, sifted

Cream together shortening, sugar, molasses, and egg. Add flour, soda, spices, and salt. Mix all ingredients together and chill for at least 1 hour. After chilling, shape into balls, roll in sugar and place on greased cookie sheet 2 inches apart. Bake in a preheated 375° oven for 10 minutes.

Meribeth Henzler, Saratoga Springs, New York

PUMPKIN COOKIES

2 c. shortening
2 eggs
6 c. flour
2 tsp. cloves
1 tsp. baking powder
3 c. sugar

2 c. pumpkin (NOT the pie
   filling)
2 tsp. baking soda
Walnuts (optional)
2 large pkg. chocolate chips

Cream everything together and bake cookies on greased cookie sheets. Drop by tablespoons onto cookie sheets and bake at 350° for about 10 minutes. Can be put in the freezer. Much better when they stand a few days. Makes about 10 dozen.

Claire R. Cook, Bloomingdale, New York

SARATOGA SNOWBALLS

2 sticks margarine, slightly
   softened
1 c. nuts, chopped

2 c. flour
½ c. confectioners sugar
1 tsp. vanilla

Mix all ingredients except sugar and make into balls. Bake at 325° for 30 minutes. Roll in sugar while hot.

Karen Graff, Clifton Park, New York

June m clow
1989

THE WOODCHUCK is a memeber of a group of burrowing and hibernating marmots also called a ground hog. His Algonquin Indian name is WEJACK and his Cree/Chippewa name is OTCHEK.

A tree hibernator, it is said that if he wakes up and comes out of his den on February 2nd and sees his shadow he will return to his hole for another six weeks of winter weather.

When he does emerge in February it is not to look for his shadow, but to look for a mate. He will move in with her for the rest of the winter until she drives him out just before the kits are born.

❧ DESSERTS ❧

APPLE CRISP

5 to 6 c. apples, sliced
1 c. flour
½ c. sugar
1 tsp. baking powder

¾ tsp. salt
1 egg
⅓ c. butter, melted
½ tsp. cinnamon

Place apples in pie pan. Mix flour, sugar, baking powder, salt, and egg until crumbly. Arrange over apples. Melt butter and cinnamon and pour over crumbs. Bake for 30 minutes at 375°.

Karen Graff, Clifton Park, New York

GRANDMA'S APPLE DESSERT

8 medium apples, pared and
   sliced
Cinnamon and sugar

¼ c. flour
White cake dough

Place apples in a bowl. Add cinnamon and sugar to desired taste and ¼ cup flour. Set aside. Make a white cake dough. Into large casserole, layer apples and cake dough ending with cake on top. Bake in a 350° oven until center of cake is done and apples are tender. Can top with whipped cream or Grandma's Topping.

Gram Harris, Ballston Spa, New York

WHIPPED CREAM APPLE DESSERT

2½ c. flour, sifted
2 tsp. baking powder
1 tsp. salt
2 Tbs. sugar
1 c. butter
1 egg, slightly beaten
1 tsp. vanilla

6 medium cooking apples,
  peeled, cored, and sliced
1½ c. sugar
2½ Tbs. flour
¼ tsp. salt
¼ c. butter
1 tsp. cinnamon

Sift flour, baking powder, salt, and sugar into bowl. Cut in butter until crumbly. Blend egg and vanilla; add to first mixture. Turn into a shallow 10"x15" pan and press evenly against sides and bottom. Arrange sliced apples evenly on top. Combine sugar, flour, salt, cinnamon, and butter. Sprinkle on top of apples. Bake in a 350° oven for 45 minutes. Serve with whipped cream.

Carol M. Miller, Northumberland, New York

PATTIE ANN'S APPLE CRUNCH

6 to 8 apples, peeled and sliced
2 tsp. baking powder
2 tsp. cinnamon or nutmeg
¼ c. flour
¾ c. oatmeal

1 egg
¼ c. butter or margarine
¼ tsp. salt
½ c. white sugar
½ c. brown sugar

Line baking dish greased with margarine with apple slices. (Sprinkle with a little extra cinnamon.) Mix remaining ingredients and sprinkle over apples. Bake at 375° for 30 minutes or until apples are tender and topping well browned.

Patricia Stanley, Saratoga Springs, New York

BLUEBERRIES IN LEMON MOUSSE

4 egg yolks
½ c. sugar
¼ c. lemon juice
2 tsp. lemon peel, grated

2 egg whites, beaten stiff
½ c. heavy cream, whipped
1 c. fresh blueberries, washed

Beat egg yolks until thick and pale. Gradually beat in sugar. Beat in lemon juice and peel. Cook in top of double boiler over hot water stirring constantly until thick. Cool. Fold in egg whites, whipped cream, and blueberries. Spoon into parfait glasses; garnish with a few more blueberries. Chill 4 hours. Yields 4 servings.

Carol M. Miller, Northumberland, New York

CHEESECAKE

1¼ c. graham cracker crumbs
¼ c. sugar
¾ c. butter, melted
2 (8 oz.) pkg. cream cheese,
   softened
1 lb. creamed cottage cheese
1½ c. sugar
4 eggs, slightly beaten

3 Tbs. cornstarch
3 Tbs. flour
1½ Tbs. lemon juice
2 tsp. vanilla extract
1 pint dairy sour cream
Chocolate mini-chips (optional)
2 oz. Amaretto (optional)

Preheat oven to 325°. Grease a 9" or 10" spring-form pan. Mix crumbs, sugar, and ¼ cup melted butter together with fork. Press crumbs evenly over bottom of pan and partially up the sides. Set aside.

In a large bowl, beat at high speed the cream cheese with cottage cheese until creamy and well-combined, at least 10 to 12 minutes. Gradually beat in sugar, then eggs until well blended. At low speed beat in cornstarch, flour, lemon juice, and vanilla. Add ½ cup melted butter and sour cream. Beat just until blended and smooth. Pour into prepared pan with crumb mixture. Bake 1 hour and 10 minutes or until firm around the edges. Cake need not brown. Turn oven off. Let cake stand in oven for 2 hours. Remove from oven and let cool completely. Run spatula around the side of the cake to loosen it. Remove side of spring-form pan, leaving bottom of pan in place. Refrigerate. Add your favorite topping if you like. Can also mix in 1 cup of chocolate mini-chips or 2 ounces Amaretto before putting in pan.

William J. Davis, Clifton Park, New York

THANKSGIVING PUMPKIN WALNUT TORTE

½ c. walnuts, chopped
1 c. flour
½ c. light brown sugar
⅓ c. butter
1 (3 oz.) pkg. cream cheese
1 large egg

1 (16 oz.) can pumpkin
14 oz. sweetened condensed milk
1 tsp. nutmeg
1 tsp. cinnamon
½ tsp. salt
½ c. hot water

Chop walnuts medium fine. Combine flour and brown sugar. Cut in butter until mixture resembles coarse meal. Add walnuts. Press firmly in an even layer over bottom of 6"x10" baking dish. Bake at 350° for about 20 minutes.

Filling: Soften cream cheese; beat in egg. Add pumpkin, condensed milk, spices, and salt. Beat until smooth. Stir in hot water.

Pour Filling into crust and return to oven. Bake 50 minutes longer or until the filling is set in center. Cool well before cutting.

Esther M. Garback, Gloversville, New York

DOUBLE DECADENT BROWNIE TORTE

½ c. butter
½ c. light corn syrup
1 c. semi-sweet chocolate chips
½ c. sugar
3 eggs

1 tsp. vanilla
1 c. flour
1 c. walnuts or pecans, chopped
Chocolate Glaze (recipe follows)

Butter and flour a 9-inch round cake pan. In a saucepan, heat butter and corn syrup until butter is melted. Stir in chocolate chips. Stir until melted. Add sugar and eggs. Stir until well blended. Stir in vanilla, flour, and nuts. Pour batter into pan. Bake at 350° for 30 minutes, until center springs back when touched. Cool in pan for 10 minutes. Turn out of pan onto a rack. After completely cooled, frost top and sides of torte with Chocolate Glaze. Chill until set. Garnish with sliced strawberries; cut into wedges.

CHOCOLATE GLAZE:

½ c. chocolate chips
2 Tbs. butter
1 Tbs. corn syrup

1 tsp. vanilla
Slicing strawberries

Combine chocolate chips, butter, and corn syrup in saucepan. Stir over low heat until chocolate is melted. Remove from heat; add vanilla.

Bob Birkel, Corinth, New York

THE ORIGINAL SARATOGA BROWNIES

2 boxes Brownie Supreme Mix
1 c. walnuts, chopped
1 c. pecans, chopped
1 can black cherries (check for pits)

½ c. sugared pitless dates (optional)

Make brownies according to package; mix well. Combine all ingredients. Pour into 9"x13" buttered and floured pan. Bake at 350° for 40 minutes, checking until done.

Al Retzlaff, Saratoga Springs, New York

MOIST AMSTERDAM GINGERBREAD

1 c. butter
1 c. brown sugar
2 eggs, beaten
¾ c. molasses
½ c. buttermilk
3 c. flour
2 tsp. ground ginger
1 tsp. ground cinnamon

½ tsp. ground cloves
½ tsp. ground anise
½ c. roasted almond slivers,
    chopped
¼ tsp. salt
2 tsp. baking soda
¾ c. boiling water

Cream butter; gradually add sugar, beating at medium speed of an electric mixer until light and fluffy. Beat in eggs, molasses, and buttermilk. Combine flour, spices, and salt; dissolve soda in boiling water separately.

Pour batter into a greased and floured 13"x9"x2" pan. Bake at 350° for approximately 35 minutes or until a wooden pick inserted comes out clean. Cut into squares. Yield: 12 servings.

Chef Armand Vanderstigchel

You're in your car, and you're going somewhere, you're anxious with desire, you're nearly there. The sound of the crowds, the colors around you. The grounds are so huge, that everything astounds you. The action is so high, there's people all over, isn't it great just being in Saratoga.

Robert E. Birkel, Jr.

THE BEAVER is an aquatic rodent with webbed hind feet and a scaly tail that is almost a foot long. He has four orange colored incisor teeth—two up and two down—that continually grow throughout his lifetime and only constant gnawing keeps them filed down.

His fur is waterproofed by an oily section and he can remain as long as fifteen minutes under water. The autumn is his busiest time of year as he cuts and collects enough food to supply his family all winter.

The mating season is during January or February and the youngsters that are born in April or May are little balls of soft furry fluff. When they reach their second year they move on to establish homes of their own.

Pies
and Puddings

EQUIVALENT CHART

3 tsp.	1 Tbsp.	¼ lb. crumbled Bleu cheese	1 c.
2 Tbsp.	⅛ c.	1 lemon	3 Tbsp. juice
4 Tbsp.	¼ c.	1 orange	⅓ c. juice
8 Tbsp.	½ c.	1 lb. unshelled walnuts	1½ to 1¾ c. shelled
16 Tbsp.	1 c.	2 c. fat	1 lb.
5 Tbsp. + 1 tsp.	⅓ c.	1 lb. butter	2 c. or 4 sticks
12 Tbsp.	¾ c.	2 c. granulated sugar	1 lb.
4 oz.	½ c.	3½-4 c. unsifted powdered sugar	1 lb.
8 oz.	1 c.	2¼ c. packed brown sugar	1 lb.
16 oz.	1 lb.	4 c. sifted flour	1 lb.
1 oz.	2 Tbsp. fat or liquid	4½ c. cake flour	1 lb.
2 c.	1 pt.	3½ c. unsifted whole wheat flour	1 lb.
2 pt.	1 qt.	4 oz. (1 to 1¼ c.) uncooked	
1 qt.	4 c.	macaroni	2¼ c. cooked
⅝ c.	½ c. + 2 Tbsp.	7 oz. spaghetti	4 c. cooked
⅞ c.	¾ c. + 2 Tbsp.	4 oz. (1½ to 2 c.) uncooked	
1 jigger	1½ fl. oz. (3 Tbsp.)	noodles	2 c. cooked
8 to 10 egg whites	1 c.	28 saltine crackers	1 c. crumbs
12 to 14 egg yolks	1 c.	4 slices bread	1 c. crumbs
1 c. unwhipped cream	2 c. whipped	14 square graham crackers	1 c. crumbs
1 lb. shredded American cheese	4 c.	22 vanilla wafers	1 c. crumbs

SUBSTITUTIONS FOR A MISSING INGREDIENT

1 square **chocolate** (1 ounce) = 3 or 4 tablespoons cocoa plus ½ tablespoon fat
1 tablespoon **cornstarch** (for thickening) = 2 tablespoons flour
1 cup sifted **all-purpose flour** = 1 cup plus 2 tablespoons sifted cake flour
1 cup sifted **cake flour** = 1 cup minus 2 tablespoons sifted all-purpose flour
1 teaspoon **baking powder** = ¼ teaspoon baking soda plus ½ teaspoon cream of tartar
1 cup **sour milk** = 1 cup sweet milk into which 1 tablespoon vinegar or lemon juice has been
    stirred
1 cup **sweet milk** = 1 cup sour milk or buttermilk plus ½ teaspoon baking soda
¾ cup **cracker crumbs** = 1 cup bread crumbs
1 cup **cream, sour, heavy** = ⅓ cup butter and ⅔ cup milk in any sour milk recipe
1 teaspoon **dried herbs** = 1 tablespoon fresh herbs
1 cup **whole milk** = ½ cup evaporated milk and ½ cup water or 1 cup reconstituted nonfat dry
    milk and 1 tablespoon butter
2 ounces **compressed yeast** = 3 (¼ ounce) packets of dry yeast
1 tablespoon **instant minced onion, rehydrated** = 1 small fresh onion
1 tablespoon **prepared mustard** = 1 teaspoon dry mustard
⅛ teaspoon **garlic powder** = 1 small pressed clove of garlic
1 lb. **whole dates** = 1½ cups, pitted and cut
3 medium **bananas** = 1 cup mashed
3 cups **dry corn flakes** = 1 cup crushed
10 **miniature marshmallows** = 1 large marshmallow

GENERAL OVEN CHART

Very slow oven	250° to 300°F.
Slow oven	300° to 325°F.
Moderate oven	325° to 375°F.
Medium hot oven	375° to 400°F.
Hot oven	400° to 450°F.
Very hot oven	450° to 500°F.

CONTENTS OF CANS

Of the different sizes of cans used by commercial canners, the most common are:

Size:	Average Contents
8 oz.	1 cup
Picnic	1¼ cups
No. 300	1¾ cups
No. 1 tall	2 cups
No. 303	2 cups
No. 2	2½ cups
No. 2½	3½ cups
No. 3	4 cups
No. 10	12 to 13 cups

PIES AND PUDDINGS 🍎

🍂 PIES 🍂

DEEP DISH APPLE PIE

1½ c. sugar
½ c. flour
1 tsp. nutmeg
1 tsp. cinnamon

¼ tsp. salt
12 c. (ten) apples, thinly sliced
Pie crust mix

Stir together dry ingredients; mix with apples. Turn into ungreased square glass pan. Heat oven to 425°. Prepare pie crust as directed e; roll into 10-inch square. Fold pastry in half; cut slits near center. Unfold over fruit in pan. Fold edges under just inside edge of pan. Bake 1 hour or until juice begins to bubble through slits in crust. Best served warm.

Marilyn Mauro, Clifton Park, New York

BLUEBERRY CRUNCH PIE

3 c. whole blueberries, washed
¾ c. sugar
½ c. pecans, chopped
1 stick margarine

1 c. sugar
2 eggs, beaten
1 c. flour

Spread blueberries in greased 9-inch pie pan; cover with ¾ cup sugar and pecans. Melt margarine; mix with sugar, eggs, and flour. Beat until batter is smooth. Pour over blueberry mixture and bake 1 hour at 325°. Turn upside down and serve warm with vanilla ice cream or whipped cream. Recipe freezes well. Serves 8.

Note: Can substitute fresh raspberries and strawberries when they are in season. Can also use sliced, peeled apples in the fall and whole cranberries all winter.

Carol M. Miller, Northumberland, New York

CRANBERRY CRUNCH PIE

3 c. whole cranberries, washed
¾ c. sugar
½ c. pecans, chopped
½ c. margarine (1 stick)

1 c. sugar
2 eggs, beaten
1 c. flour

Spread cranberries in greased 9-inch pie pan. Cover with ¾ cup sugar and pecans. melt margarine, mix in 1 cup sugar, eggs, and flour. Beat until batter is smooth. Pour over cranberry mixture and bake 1 hour at 325°. Turn upside down and serve warm with vanilla ice cream or whipped cream. Recipe freezes well. Serves 8.

Carol M. Miller, Northumberland, New York

GERMAN CHOCOLATE PIE

4 oz. German sweet chocolate
¼ stick butter
1⅔ c. evaporated milk
1½ c. sugar
⅛ tsp. salt
3 Tbs. cornstarch

1 tsp. vanilla
½ c. pecans, chopped
2 eggs
1⅓ c. flaked coconut
10" pie shell

Melt butter with chocolate over low heat; stir until blended. Remove from heat. Gradually add milk. Mix cornstarch and salt with sugar. Add to chocolate mixture. Beat in eggs and vanilla. Pour into pie shell. Sprinkle coconut and pecans over filling. Bake at 375° for 45 minutes or until top is ruffed. Filling will be soft but will set while cooling. Cool a few hours before serving.

Karen Graff, Clifton Park, New York

HEAVENLY MOCHA PIE

MERINGUE PIE SHELL:

Non-stick cooking spray
2 large egg whites, at room
    temperature
⅛ tsp. cream of tartar

½ c. sugar
¾ tsp. vanilla extract
1½ tsp. unsweetened cocoa
    powder

Preheat oven to 275°. Spray 9-inch pie plate. In medium bowl, at low speed, beat egg whites until frothy. Add cream of tartar and increase to medium high speed. Beat until whites form peaks. Add sugar, one teaspoon at a time, and beat until a stiff glossy meringue forms. Beat in vanilla. Spread over pie plate. Lightly dust border with cocoa powder. Bake 1 hour. Turn off oven and leave pie shell in oven for 30 minutes. Cool on wire rack.

MOCHA FILLING:

6 oz. Swiss dark chocolate,
    chopped
1 Tbs. and 1 tsp. espresso powder
1 Tbs. vanilla extract

1¼ c. heavy whipping cream
5 large egg yolks
¼ c. and 1 Tbs. sugar
¼ c. water

In double boiler over hot water, melt chocolate. Remove top of double boiler and cool chocolate for 5 to 10 minutes. In small cup, stir together espresso powder and vanilla until dissolved. In a chilled medium bowl, using mixer set at medium speed, beat cream until soft peaks form. Cover and refrigerate. Beat egg yolks at medium speed until blended. Beat at medium high speed for 10 to 12 minutes. In a heavy small saucepan over medium low heat, combine sugar and water and stir until crystals are dissolved. Bring mixture to a boil. Cook sugar syrup until it reaches 248° (firm ball stage). Remove from hat. Using hand-held mixer on medium speed, beat syrup into whipped egg yolks. Increase speed to medium high and beat egg yolks for 8 to 10 minutes. Beat in espresso/vanilla mixture. Beat in chocolate. Fold whipped cream into chocolate mixture. Cover and refrigerate for 2 hours.

TOPPING:

¾ c. heavy whipping cream
1 Tbs. sugar
1 Tbs. coffee liqueur

Chocolate coffee beans for
    garnish

In a chilled bowl, beat heavy cream with sugar until soft peaks form. Beat in the coffee liqueur. No more than 1½ hours before serving, spread whipped cream over center of pie, making swirls and peaks. Garnish with chocolate coffee beans. Refrigerate until ready to serve.

Bob Birkel, Corinth, New York

PEANUT BUTTER PIE A LA POTTER

Grape nut cereal
8 oz. cream cheese (soft)
½ c. crunchy peanut butter
¾ c. powdered sugar

½ c. milk
8 oz. frozen whipped dairy
   topping (thawed)

Place 1 cup of grape nuts cereal in the bottom of a 9-inch pie plate. With a mixer combine cream cheese, peanut butter, powdered sugar, and milk. Mix until smooth, then fold in unfrozen whipped topping. Pour into the grape nuts; some cereal will go up the sides, but it is not necessary to have it on the top. Freeze for 2 hours. Take out of freezer 10 minutes before cutting pie.

Ruth Potter, Wells, New York

PEANUT BUTTER PIE

8 oz. cream cheese
½ c. peanut butter
½ c. milk
½ c. 4x sugar

Graham cracker pie crust
1 (9 oz.) container Cool Whip
⅓ c. melted margarine
3 Tbs. sugar

Combine cream cheese, peanut butter, milk, and 4x sugar. Cream thoroughly until smooth. Fold in the Cool Whip. Pour into a graham cracker crust. Combine melted margarine and sugar, stirring until all sugar is dissolved. Add topping to pie and freeze. To serve thaw a little before serving.

Freda Bates, Alabmont, New York

SARATOGA PEANUT BUTTER PIE

1 (4 oz.) pkg. cream cheese
⅓ c. peanut butter
1 (8 oz.) container whipped
   topping

1 c. powdered sugar
Crushed peanuts
1 (9-inch) graham cracker or
   chocolate crumb crust

Combine cream cheese and peanut butter. Blend in whipped topping and sugar. Pour into 9-inch graham cracker crust or chocolate crumb crust. Refrigerate until firm. The "trick" is to let it get firm at least 4 hours. It is good as is, but better with at least ½ cup crushed peanuts sprinkled over the top before refrigerating. It's a sort of peanut cheesecake with a subtle peanut flavor.

Joan Smith, Saratoga Springs, New York

PECAN PIE

1 c. sugar
1¼ c. dark corn syrup
4 eggs

¼ c. butter or margarine
1 tsp. vanilla
1¼ c. broken pecans

Preheat oven to 350°. In saucepan, boil sugar and syrup for 2 to 3 minutes. Beat eggs, not too stiff. Slowly pour hot syrup into beaten eggs, stirring as you pour. Add butter, vanilla, and pecans. Turn into unbaked lard pie crust and bake for 45 minutes.

William J. Davis, Clifton Park, New York

PUMPKIN PIE

16 oz. sold pack pumpkin
3 eggs
1 c. sugar
½ tsp. salt
1 tsp. cinnamon

¼ tsp. ground cloves
¼ tsp. nutmeg
¼ tsp. ginger
1½ c. milk

Mix all ingredients and pour into unbaked pie shell. Bake at 450° for 10 minutes and then at 350° for 1 hour.

Marilyn Mauro, Clifton Park, New York

THE LYNX is no longer missing in the high peaks area of the Adirondacks. Three females and two males were reintroduced to the area in January of 1989.

This original inhabitant of the north country is well adapted to living at high elevations of more than 2,500 feet above sea level. The cat's large, furry paws are perfect for traveling over deep snow. Not an endangered species, the lynx is a game animal that is off-limits to hunters and trappers in New York State.

❧ PUDDINGS ❧

DUTCH APPLE PUDDING

2 c. flour
4 tsp. baking powder
½ tsp. salt
1 c. milk
1 egg

2 Tbs. butter
3 apples
¼ c. sugar
¼ tsp. ground cinnamon
Lemon Sauce (recipe follows)

Cream butter and sugar, then add egg and beat well. Mix and sift flour, salt, and baking powder and add to the first mixture alternately with milk. Beat well and pour into well-buttered baking dish (approximately 7"x11"). Pare, quarter, core, and slice apples and place in rows on top of cake mixture in pan. Sprinkle with sugar and cinnamon; bake at 350° for about 30 minutes. Serve with Lemon Sauce.

LEMON SAUCE:

½ c. sugar
1 Tbs. flour

1 c. boiling water
Lemon flavoring

Mix sugar and flour; add to boiling water. Reduce to low heat, stirring constantly until thickened to desired consistency. Add lemon flavoring to taste.

Carol M. Miller, Northumberland, New York

BISCUIT PUDDING

2½ c. stale biscuits, crumbled fine
1 c. milk
1 c. margarine, melted

2 c. sugar
4 eggs, slightly beaten
½ tsp. vanilla

Combine ingredients in baking dish; stir well. Bake at 325°. Pudding is done when knife inserted in center is clean. Remove and serve warm.

Laura Roberts, Clifton Park, New York

MINNIE'S BREAD PUDDING

4 loaves white bread
½ lb. raisins
3 qt. milk

Cinnamon
3 c. sugar
6 eggs

Combine in a roasting pan 2 quarts of milk with sugar. Sprinkle with cinnamon. Add eggs and stir. Break up the loaves of bread and put in pan. Be sure to submerge bread; add raisins. Add 1 quart of milk and mix until all is yellow. Bake at 375° for 1 hour or until done. Center should not be gooey, just cakey moist.

Wilhelmina Birkel, Corinth, New York

PUMPERNICKEL RAISIN BREAD PUDDING

1 loaf pumpernickel raisin bread
1 c. raisins
2 c. sugar
2 tsp. vanilla
¼ c. brandy

2 tsp. cinnamon
2 tsp. nutmeg
4 eggs
1 qt. milk

Cut bread into 1-inch pieces. Place into bowl. Pour milk over bread; let soak for 1 hour. Whip sugar and eggs together in separate bowl. When blended, add vanilla and brandy. Add cinnamon and nutmeg. Stir in raisins. Fold this mixture in with bread after soaking period. Bake at 350° for 30 to 40 minutes.

Tip: Cooking pan in water bath will prevent the bottom from burning.

Pastry Chef Edward Castro

SETTLERS RICE PUDDING

1 c. rice
1 qt. water
1 qt. milk
Raisins

3 eggs
1½ c. sugar
1 Tbs. vanilla
½ c. heavy cream

Add rice to 1 qt. water; cook until water is almost gone. Add 1 qt. milk and raisins; cook until thick, approximately 45 minutes. In separate bowl mix rest of ingredients. Pour into pot and stir. When thick, pour into pan.

Karen Graff, Clifton Park, New York

MINNIE'S RICE PUDDING

1 lb. rice
½ lb. raisins
3 qt. milk

Cinnamon
3 c. sugar
6 eggs

Boil one pound of rice; lay in pan and add 2 quarts of milk with sugar. Sprinkle with cinnamon. Add eggs and stir. Be sure to submerge rice. Add raisins. Add 1 quart milk and mix until all is yellow. Bake at 375° for one hour or until done. Should look pasty and crusty and should be an even tan in color. Refrigerate and serve.

Minnie Birkel, Corinth, New York

NEE'S SUET PUDDING

1 c. chopped suet (fat)
1 c. molasses
1 c. sweet milk
1 cup plus 1 Tbs. flour
1 tsp. baking soda dissolved in
    milk

1 tsp. cinnamon
½ tsp. ground cloves
1 c. raisins
Salt

Whip ingredients together until smooth. Steam 2 hours in the top of a double boiler. Serve hot with whipped cream.

June Shone, Holcomb, New York

June Shone of Holcomb sent her grandmother's recipes, from a time she was a cook in a logging camp. After trying June's recipes, we agreed the lumberjacks were lucky to have her around as the cook. The "Suet Pudding" was her famous Christmas dessert!

"Jeremy"
As Tall as an Adirondack Tree

    He was a young soul, as I was told. A bright young lad, sometimes good, sometimes bad. He was young and very fair. With a spirit so alive, like pure Adirondack air. Then his time took a fall, and as the trees he stood tall. As God whispers . . . so young! so fair through the warm breeze in the evening air. He lived to play on the court. He loved his school and all that he was taught. I thought I heard God whisper down the hall, and as I remember, he loved his mom, his dad, his brother, and his game of basketball!!

Robert E. Birkel, Jr.

THE BABY BOX TURTLE, if he escapes all his predators, can expect to live 60 to 80 years in the wild.

A cold-blooded, dry-land turtle, he has a colorful, high, dome-shaped shell with a hinged plastron which, when he gets older, will enable him to slam shut as tight as a "box." He probably will not travel more than 400 feet from his home during his lifetime.

Hibernating in winter, he will use his webbed hind feet to dig down into the soil about 2 feet. Backfilling to cover himself, he will not come up again until the warmer weather.

Miscellaneous

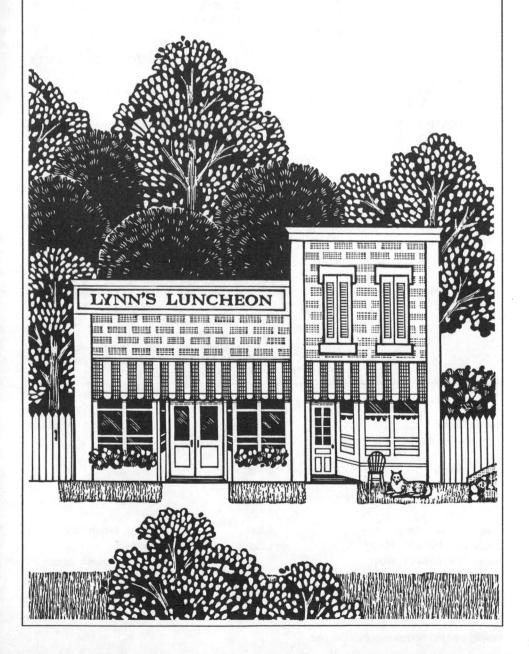

HEART HEALTHY TIPS
Substitutions, Modifications and Equivalents

Instead of	Use	Instead of	Use
1 c. butter 498 mg cholesterol	⅞ c. polyunsaturated oil-0 mg cholesterol 1 c. tub margarine-0 mg cholesterol 2 stks margarine-0 mg cholesterol	1 c. whole milk yogurt, plain-250 calories	1 c. part skim milk yogurt, plain-125-145 calories
		1 c. sour cream-416 calories	1 c. blended low-fat cottage cheese-208 calories
1 c. heavy cream-832 calories, 296 mg cholesterol	1 c. evap. skim milk-176 calories 8 mg cholesterol	1 oz. baking chocolate 8.4 gm sat. fat	3 Tbsp. cocoa powder-1.7 gm sat. fat PLUS
1 md whole egg-274 mg cholesterol	¼ c. egg sub-0 mg cholesterol*		1 Tbsp. polyunsaturated oil - 1.1 gm sat. fat TOTAL: 2.8 gm sat. fat

*Some egg substitutes do contain cholesterol. Check label to be sure.

To Reduce Cholesterol or Saturated Fats:

1. Select lean cuts of meat.
2. Serve moderate portions.
3. Replace animal fats with appropriate substitutes.

Examples

Instead of	Use
Butter, lard, bacon or bacon fat, and chicken fat	Polyunsaturated margarine or oil
Sour cream	Low-fat yogurt
Whole milk	Skim milk
Whole milk cheeses	Low-fat cheeses
Whole eggs	Egg whites or egg substitutes

To Reduce Calories or Fats:

1. Brown meat by broiling or cooking in non-stick pans with little or no oil.
2. Chill soups, stews, sauces, and broths. Lift off congealed fat (saves 100 calories per Tbsp. of fat removed).
3. Trim fat from meat. Also remove skin from poultry.
4. Use water-packed canned products (canned fish, canned fruits).
5. In recipes for baked products, the sugar can often be reduced ¼ to ⅓ without harming the final product. Cinnamon and vanilla also give the impression of sweetness.
6. Use fresh fruit whenever possible. If canned fruit must be used, select water-packed varieties, fruit in own juice, or drain heavy syrup from canned fruit.
7. For sauces and dressings, use low-calorie bases (vinegar, mustard, tomato juice, fat-free bouillon) instead of high calorie ones (creams, fats, oils, mayonnaise).

Equivalents for Sugar Substitutes

Brand Name	Amount	Substitution for Sugar
Adolph's Powder	1 tsp. 4 tsp.	= ¼ c. = 1 c.
Equal Powder	1 pkt.	= 2 tsp.
Sweet N'Low Powder	1 pkt. 1 tsp. 4 tsp.	= 2 tsp. = ¼ c. = 1 c.
Sweet N'Low Brown	4 tsp.	= 1 c. brown sugar
Sugar Twin Powder	1 tsp.	= 1 tsp.
Sugar Twin Brown Powder	1 tsp.	= 1 tsp. brown sugar
Sweet-10 Liquid	10 drops 2 Tbsp.	= 1 tsp. = 1 c.

MISCELLANEOUS ❦

PIQUANT BARBECUE SAUCE

8 oz. tomato sauce
2 Tbs. onion, minced
2 Tbs. Worcestershire sauce

2 Tbs. vinegar
½ tsp. garlic salt

Combine all ingredients together and use to baste pork, ham, chicken, or beef. Makes 1½ cups.

Lynn Paska, Schenectady, New York

GRACE SAUCE

1 bushel ripe tomatoes
6 large onions
2 c. celery
¾ c. salt
2 lb. brown sugar

5 c. strong vinegar (may dilute to taste)
5 green peppers, chopped
2 tsp. white mustard seed

Chop tomatoes in a wooden bowl and drain for 2 hours. Chop onions and celery; add to tomatoes. Mix all ingredients together and pack COLD in jars. (Use Bell wide-mouth jars with metal tops. Will take about ten 1-quart jars.)

Place filled jars in a large pot of boiling water. The water should just cover the jar tops. Boil about 20 minutes. Remove jars and allow them to cool. Jar tops should pop down when cool. This recipe can be halved.

Araxie Dunn, Lake Placid, New York

Araxie Dunn's stepfather, Willis O. Heald, was an Adirondack guide during the 1920s and 1930s. He spent most of his life in the woods and could make a meal out of almost everything. Try his Grace Sauce, an original Keene, New York recipe named after Grace Heald. The Healds were one of the original settler families in this area.

MOUNTAIN RESERVE CATSUP

1 qt. tomato juice
1 c. vinegar
1 c. sugar

1 tsp. black pepper
1 tsp. cinnamon
1 Tbs. salt

The drained tomato juice mentioned in GRACE SAUCE can be made into this old style catsup. Combine all ingredients and cook until thick, then bottle.

Araxie Dunn, Lake Placid, New York

AWARD-WINNING STEAK MARINADE

1 qt. Gravy Master
¼ c. soy sauce
1 c. teriyaki
1 c. brown sugar
2 onions, ground up

1 tsp. allspice
1 tsp. oil
1 tsp. garlic, minced
1 c. white vinegar
1 pineapple, cut up

Bring all ingredients to a quick boil. Let cool down for 2 hours. Place steak in marinade at room temperature for 3 hours. Drain meat. Grill and enjoy.

Chef Tommy Dimonti

SARATOGIAN SALSA

4 red tomatoes, cored and
   chopped
1 small can yellow or green chiles,
   chopped
4 cloves garlic, crushed
5 scallions, chopped
1 large yellow onion, chopped

2 Tbs. cilantro, chopped
3 fresh or canned tomatillos
   (green tomatoes), chopped
Salt and pepper
4 jalapeno peppers, deseeded,
   sliced julienne and sliced
   again

Combine all ingredients and mix well. Great for everything — meat sandwiches, scrambled eggs, hot dogs, burgers — anything you want.

Al Retzlaff, Saratoga Springs, New York

GREEN MOUNTAIN ONION DRESSING

1 tsp. garlic, minced
2 tsp. white pepper
1 tsp. cayenne pepper
2 tsp. Lea Perrins Worcestershire
   sauce
1 tsp. salt
2 tsp. sugar

2 tsp. grain mustard
3 whole eggs
2 yolks
6 bunches green onions
½ c. white vinegar
1 c. oil

Add all ingredients into a food processor, except the oil. Liquefy all ingredients in blender; slowly add oil until smooth. Great over salads and grilled meats.

Chef Tommy Dimonti

BAKED APPLE RELISH

6 small baking apples
2 Tbs. butter or margarine
1 large onion, finely chopped
1 tomato, peeled and chopped (1 cup)
¼ c. raisins

1 Tbs. preserved ginger, finely chopped
¼ tsp. red pepper, crushed
¼ tsp. dry mustard
4 Tbs. red currant jelly
4 Tbs. cider vinegar

Cut a slice from top of each apple. Remove core with apple corer or small knife. Scoop out apples with the tip of a small spoon, leaving a shell about ½ to ¾ inch thick. Chop the scooped out apple (about 1 cup). Heat butter in a large skillet; add onion and saute for 5 minutes. Stir in chopped apple, tomato, raisin, ginger, crushed red pepper, mustard, 1 tablespoon of the currant jelly, and 1 tablespoon of the vinegar. Cook, stirring often, 5 minutes longer or until slightly thick. Spoon cooked mixture into hollowed-out apples. Arrange apples in shallow baking pan. Add remaining jelly and vinegar to skillet; heat just until melted. Spoon over and around apples. Bake uncovered, basting once or twice, in a moderate oven (350°) for 25 minutes or until apples are glazed and tender. Let cool, basting with juices in pan, for 15 minutes before serving.

Carol M. Miller, Northumberland, New York

GEISLER PICCALILLI RELISH

4 qt. tomatoes, peeled and chopped (approximately 32 tomatoes)
2 qt. cabbage, chopped (1 head)
2 c. sweet red peppers, chopped
1 c. onions, chopped

4½ c. vinegar
½ c. salt
1½ c. brown sugar
2 Tbs. mustard seed
1 Tbs. horseradish

Place vegetables in crock; sprinkle salt over mix. Let stand 3 to 4 hours. Drain well. Add sugar, horseradish, spices, and vinegar in saucepan. Simmer 15 minutes. Add vegetables; heat to boiling. Pack, boiling hot, into clean sterilized pint or quart jars. Leave ¼" space. Process 10 minutes in hot water bath. Makes 5 pints/3 quarts.

Hope Geisler, Ballston Spa, New York

3-VEGGIE DILL PICKLES

1 lb. green peppers, sliced long
1¼ lb. carrots, sliced long
1 medium head cauliflower
    florets
4 cloves garlic

4 tsp. dillweed
4 tsp. crushed red pepper
2 c. vinegar
2 c. water
¼ c. salt

Arrange slices of peppers on bottom of each canning jar, cauliflower florets in middle of each, and carrot slices on top. Combine vinegar, water, and salt. Bring to a boil. Turn off heat. Stir in the dillweed and red pepper. Pour this hot brine into each jar. Seal tightly. Does not need hot water bath. Makes 4 pints. If you want 7 quarts, triple recipe.

Hope Geisler, Ballston Spa, New York

ADIRONDACKS BLOSSOMS

Squash or pumpkin blossoms
1 c. flour
4 tsp. baking powder

Salt and pepper
Favorite wine

Pick the squash or pumpkin blossoms just before they open. Clean blossoms; snap off little green nubs. Open blossoms carefully and run water through them. Drain well. For batter, sift together the flour, baking powder, salt, and pepper. Add enough water to make a thin batter. Dip flowers into the batter, covering the base, and fry quickly in hot lard until they are a deep golden color. Drain on paper towels in a warm oven until all flowers are fried. Serve immediately with salt and pepper. These make fine hors d'oeuvres, served with your favorite wine.

Mrs. Nancy Lucas, Gloversville, New York

Although this is a seasonal dish, Nancy's family has enjoyed it for many years. It is a delectable way to utilize blossoms that would otherwise be discarded. Surprise your guests with this different hors d'oeuvre.

NORTHERN SHRIMP DIP

1 large pkg. cream cheese,
    softened at room
    temperature
1 can shrimp, drained, whole or
    cut up

1 Tbs. mayonnaise
1 Tbs. wine vinegar
1 tsp. onion, grated
Salt and pepper
Dash of Tabasco sauce

Cream together until smooth the cream cheese, mayonnaise, vinegar, onion, and salt and pepper. Fold in the shrimp. To thin down, add more mayonnaise or milk.

Freda Bates, Alabmont, New York

CLIFTON DEVILED EGGS

12 hard-boiled eggs, cooled   ¼ c. mayonnaise
Salt and pepper to taste   Paprika
1 Tbs. mustard

Remove shells from hard-boiled eggs; cut lengthwise through egg. Remove yolks. Mash yolks and mix with seasonings and mayonnaise to form a smooth paste. Fill egg whites lightly with mixture. Sprinkle with paprika.

Marilyn Mauro, Clifton Park, New York

Adirondack picnics in the old days at the great camps

As the cool waters glimmer, and the day grows on and dimmer, the trees move within the air, as wildlife stirs somewhere. You start to feel so fine, in a land that's so divine, where people can just relax, "that's right," you're in the Adirondacks!!

Robert E. Birkel, Jr.

June Clow
Covered Bridge at Jay, New York

Hints

Kitchen Hints for Kids

Children under 10 should cook with supervision nearby. Older children can be supervised according to their experience and ability.

1. If you have long hair, tie it back so it won't get into the food or in the way as you work.

2. Don't wear loose fitting clothing that could drag in the food or on the stove burners.

3. Always wash your hands before you handle the food.

4. Read the recipe through to the end. Make sure you have all the ingredients and utensils that you'll need. Be sure you know how to do everything.

5. Use dry pot holders or mitts for hot pans and pot handles. Damp pot holders carry heat.

6. Keep pot handles facing the back of the stove to avoid pots being knocked off stove top.

7. Use wooden spoons to stir hot liquids. Metal spoons get hot and burn your fingers.

8. Pick up knives by handles only.

9. When cutting or peeling food, cut away from your hands.

10. Cut food on a wooden cutting board to avoid cutting into counter top. Cool hot pots on a rack so counter tops are not burned.

11. Clean up as you go. Clean up spills immediately, especially those on the floor that could cause someone to slip and fall.

12. Do not put knives in clean-up water to avoid cutting your hand on sharp blade.

Adults should help -

1. Turn burners or oven on.

2. Open cans.

3. Place or remove food in the oven.

4. Handle hot liquids or drain foods cooked in hot liquids.

5. Handle electrical appliances for the young cook.

Cleaning up the kitchen -

1. Wash utensils in warm, soapy water. Rinse, dry and put away.

2. Wash counter tops and stove.

3. Be sure stove and oven are turned off and refrigerator door and drawers are shut.

Suggestions for Lowering Fat Content in Your Diet

FOOD CATEGORY	CHOOSE	DECREASE
Meat Fish Poultry	Lean cuts of meat with fat trimmed, such as: beef-round, sirloin, rump steak, loin Poultry without skin Pork tenderloin	"Prime" grade meats Fatty cuts, like: corned beef, brisket, short ribs, spareribs Goose, duck, organ meats, sausage, bacon, hot dogs, regular luncheon meats
Dairy Products	Skim milk, lowfat buttermilk, lowfat evaporated or nonfat milk Lowfat or nonfat yogurts and cheeses	Whole milk, cream, half & half, nondairy creamers, real or nondairy whipped cream, cream cheese, sour cream, ice cream, custard-style yogurt High-fat cheese, like: Brie, Swiss, American, Cheddar
Eggs	Egg whites, cholesterol and fat-free egg substitutes	Egg yolks (substitute 2 egg whites for 1 egg)
Fats Oils	Unsaturated vegetable oils (in limited quantities): corn, olive, peanut, canola, safflower, sesame, soybean Fat-free mayonnaise, cream cheese, and salad dressings Mustard and flavored vinegars (when cooking, use spray oils or nonstick pans and decrease amount of fat in recipe by ⅓ or substitute applesauce for fat)	Butter, coconut oil, palm kernel oil, palm oil, lard, bacon fat
Breads Cereals Pasta	Breads like whole wheat, pumpernickel, rye, pita, bagels, English muffins, rice cakes Lowfat crackers and bread sticks Plain cereals (hot and cold) Spaghetti and macaroni Any grain Dried peas and beans	Croissants, butter rolls, sweet rolls, pastries, doughnuts, most snack crackers, granola-type cereals made with saturated fats, egg noodles, pasta and rice prepared with cream, butter, or cheese sauces
Vegetables Fruits	Fresh, frozen, canned (no salt added)	Vegetables prepared in butter, cream, or sauce Fruits served in glazes

Fat Facts

Reducing fat in the diet is a major focus in America today, and for good reason. A high fat diet can contribute to elevated blood cholesterol levels, a risk factor for heart disease. Excess dietary fat has also been linked to obesity and cancer. As a result, lower fat intake has become a priority for many.

Cholesterol is a fat-type substance found in all animal tissues. In adults, a blood cholesterol level below 200 milligrams per deciliter is desirable. A level above 240 milligrams is considered high. Blood cholesterol can also be broken into two categories: "good" and "bad" cholesterol. High density lipoproteins (HDL) are known as "good" cholesterol because of their high protein content and low cholesterol content, and because people with higher HDL levels have a lower incidence of heart disease. Low density lipoproteins (LDL) contain more cholesterol than HDL and are responsible for cholesterol build-up on artery walls, thus earning the label "bad" cholesterol. A lowfat, low cholesterol diet, as well as exercise and being at a desirable weight, can help lower blood cholesterol levels and raise HDL levels.

Dietary fat can be divided into three different types: saturated, poly-unsaturated, and monounsaturated. Foods we eat contain a mixture of these fats.

- **SATURATED FATS** are generally solid at room temperature. They have been shown to increase blood cholesterol levels. Saturated fats are primarily found in animal products such as butter, milk, cream, and lard. Some plant foods, such as palm oil, coconut oil, vegetable shortening, and some peanut butters also contain large amounts of saturated fats.

- **POLYUNSATURATED FATS** tend to lower blood cholesterol levels. These fats are found in high concentrations in vegetable oils, and are usually liquid at room temperature. Fats such as sunflower oil, corn oil, and soft margarines have large amounts of polyunsaturated fats.

- **MONOUNSATURATED FATS** have also been shown to decrease cholesterol levels in the blood. They can be liquid or solid at room temperature, and can be from plant or animal sources. Olive, peanut, and canola oils are high in monounsaturated fats.

- **DIETARY CHOLESTEROL** comes from animal sources such as meat, poultry, fish and other seafood, and dairy products. Egg yolks and organ meats contain high amounts of dietary cholesterol.

- **HYDROGENATION** is a chemical process in which hydrogen is added to unsaturated oils to make them firmer at room temperature. Hydrogenated fats such as shortening or margarine are more saturated than the oil from which they are made. When choosing a margarine, pick one with 2 grams or less saturated fat per tablespoon.

Heart Healthy guidelines include: (1) Limit total fat intake to 30% or less of total calories. (2) Of these calories, up to one-third can be saturated fat, and the remaining two-thirds should come from polyunsaturated and monounsaturated sources. (3) Limit daily cholesterol intake to 300 milligrams or less.

Calculating Percent Fat

To achieve a desirable percentage of total calories from fat, it is helpful to know how much fat is in individual foods. To determine the percentage of a food's total calories that come from fat, you can use the following formula. In order to calculate this percentage, you need to know the total calories and the grams of fat per serving, both of which are usually listed on the food label.

$$\frac{\text{grams of fat x 9*}}{\text{total calories}} \quad \text{x} \quad 100 \quad = \quad \% \text{ of total calories from fat}$$

* Each gram of fat contains 9 calories. Multiplying grams of fat by 9 gives the total calories from fat. On food labels, this number has already been calculated, and is listed on the same line as total calories.

When reading a food package, the front of the label may not tell the whole story. For instance, a package of boiled ham might claim to be 96% fat free. From this information, the consumer might assume that the food contains 4% fat, which is well within the recommended guideline of eating foods with 30% or less of total calories from fat. Although the 96% fat free claim is truthful, it refers to the amount of fat by weight rather than by the food's total calories. To get a clearer picture, use the above calculation. The label of the boiled ham shows 60 calories and 2.5 grams of fat per serving.

$$\frac{\text{2.5 grams of fat x 9}}{\text{60 total calories}} \quad \text{x} \quad 100 \quad = \quad 37\% \text{ of total calories from fat}$$

By calculating the percentage of total calories from fat, you can make more informed decisions about the nutritional qualities of foods. In this case, the ham may be lower in fat than other ham products, but it is still above the 30% guideline. If you are trying to follow a lowfat diet, you should eat this food in moderation.

"Heart Healthy" Recipe Substitutions

ORIGINAL INGREDIENT	ALTERNATIVE	REDUCES:		
		TF	SF	C
1 pound ground beef	• 1 pound ground turkey	✔	✔	✔
1 ounce Cheddar, Swiss, or American cheese	• 1 ounce lowfat cheese • 1 ounce part-skim cheese (Mozzarella)	✔ ✔	✔ ✔	✔ ✔
1 egg	• 2 egg whites • ¼ c. low cholesterol egg substitute	✔ ✔	✔ ✔	✔ ✔
1 c. whole milk	• 1 c. skim milk	✔	✔	✔
1 c. cream	• 1 c. evaporated skim milk	✔	✔	✔
1 c. sour cream	• 1 c. nonfat sour cream • 1 c. plain nonfat yogurt • 1 c. lowfat cottage cheese plus 1 to 2 tsp. lemon juice, blended smooth	✔ ✔ ✔	✔ ✔ ✔	✔ ✔ ✔
1 ounce cream cheese	• 1 ounce nonfat cream cheese • 1 ounce Neufchatel cheese	✔ ✔	✔ ✔	✔ ✔
1 c. butter	• 1 c. margarine • 1 c. vegetable oil		✔ ✔	✔ ✔
1 c. shortening	• 7 oz. vegetable oil		✔	
1 ounce baking chocolate	• 3 Tbsp. cocoa powder plus 1 Tbsp. vegetable oil		✔	
roux: 1 part fat 1 part starch	• ½ part fat to 1 part starch	✔		
1 can condensed cream soup	• Mix together: ½ c. nonfat dry milk 2 Tbsp. cornstarch 2 tsp. low sodium chicken bouillon ¼ tsp. onion powder ⅛ tsp. garlic powder ¼ tsp. basil ¼ tsp. thyme ¼ tsp. white pepper 9 oz. cold water Add the following if desired: ¼ c. chopped celery or ½ c. sliced mushrooms Heat to a boil; stir frequently. Per "can": 215 calories, 1g fat, 8mg cholesterol, 200mg sodium	✔	✔	✔

KEY:
TF = total fat
SF = saturated fat
C = cholesterol

Food Labeling Definitions

Government regulations give specific guidelines as to what words can be used on a food label to describe the product. Here is a list of these descriptive terms.

FREE A product must contain no amount or only an insignificant amount of one or more of the following: fat, saturated fat, cholesterol, sodium, sugar, and calories. The terms *no, without,* and *zero* can also be used.

Calorie-free: less than 5 calories per serving
Sugar-free or Fat-free: less than 0.5g per serving
Sodium-free: less than 5mg per serving

LOW This term can be used when referring to one or more of the following: fat, cholesterol, sodium, and calories. The terms *little, few,* and *low source of* can also be used.

Low calorie: 40 calories or less per serving
Lowfat: 3g or less per serving
Low saturated fat: 1g or less per serving
Low cholesterol: less than 20mg per serving
Low sodium: less than 140mg per serving
Very low sodium: less than 35mg per serving

LEAN Meat, poultry, and seafood containing less than 10g of fat, less than 4g saturated fat, and less than 95g of cholesterol per 3.5 oz. serving.

EXTRA LEAN Meat, poultry, and seafood containing less than 5g of fat, less than 2g saturated fat, and less than 95g of cholesterol per 3.5 oz. serving.

HIGH One serving of a product must contain 20% or more of the *Daily Value* (recommended daily intake of a nutrient).

GOOD SOURCE One serving must contain 10% to 19% of the Daily Value.

REDUCED A nutritionally altered product containing 25% less of a nutrient or of calories than the regular product. If the regular product already meets the criteria for *low, a reduced* claim cannot be made.

LESS A food that contains 25% less of a nutrient or of calories than a similar food. Cream cheeses that have 25% less fat than butter could use the term *less* or *fewer.*

LIGHT This term can still be used to describe food characteristics such as color and texture if the label makes the meaning clear; for example, *light brown sugar.*
The term also carries two other meanings:

✦ A nutritionally altered product that contains one-third less calories or half the fat of the original food
✦ A food's sodium content has been cut by 50% or more

MORE A food using this claim must contain 10% more of the Daily Value of a nutrient than the reference food. To use the words *fortified, enriched,* or *added,* this standard must also be met.

UNSALTED, NO SALT ADDED, or WITHOUT ADDED SALT The sodium naturally found in the product is still there, but it has been prepared without the salt that is normally added.

Sodium

Sodium is a mineral used by the body to maintain a proper balance of water in the blood. Although it is a vital nutrient, the body needs very little sodium to stay healthy. Because it is found naturally in some foods and is added to many other foods, getting too little sodium is usually not a problem. A high sodium diet, on the other hand, can contribute to high blood pressure in some people. Reducing sodium intake in the diet may help prevent or control high blood pressure. It is hard to know who will develop high blood pressure, or who might benefit from eating less sodium. For these reasons, and because most individuals consume much more sodium than needed, it is generally suggested that we reduce sodium intake.

Table salt is the major source of sodium in our diet. It is made up of about half sodium and half chloride. An adult diet containing between 1,100mg and 3,300 mg of sodium per day is considered adequate. One teaspoon of salt contains 2,000 mg of sodium.

WAYS TO REDUCE DIETARY SODIUM

✦ Taste food before salting. Salt food only sparingly at the table.

✦ Cut back on sodium slowly to give the body time to adjust to less salty flavors. *Salt-craving* taste buds will eventually be replaced by new ones that do not have an affinity for salt.

✦ Choose foods that have little or no sodium added. In general, the more processed the food, the more sodium it contains. For example, processed turkey breast purchased at a deli has considerably more sodium than fresh turkey breast.

✦ In many recipes, the salt can be cut back or even eliminated without greatly affecting the taste. Experiment with recipes at home, using less salt each time and using low sodium substitutes for high sodium ingredients.

✦ Read labels on food packages. Compare the sodium content to similar items and to the recommended sodium intake for an entire day.

✦ Limit intake of high sodium foods such as cheeses, processed meats, soups, broths, snack foods, canned vegetables and vegetable juices, pickled vegetables, gravies, sauces, commercial casserole mixes, frozen dinners, and condiments. In many cases, lower sodium alternatives are available.

✦ When eating in restaurants, ask for foods to be prepared without added salt and request to have sauces, gravies, dressings, and condiments served on the side.

✦ Use herbs and spices instead of salt to enhance the flavor of foods. Check the label of seasonings to be sure they do not contain sodium. Use onion powder rather than onion salt, garlic powder instead of garlic salt. In place of seasoning salt, try commercially prepared herb and spice blends or make your own.

Low Sodium Seasoning Suggestions

	Allspice	Basil	Bay Leaves	Caraway Seed	Celery Seed	Chives	Curry Powder	Dill	Garlic	Ginger	Dry Mustard	Onion Powder	Oregano	Rosemary	Sage	Tarragon	Thyme
Beef	✔								✔	✔				✔	✔		
Pork				✔					✔					✔			✔
Veal			✔			✔			✔				✔				✔
Ground Meat	✔	✔			✔				✔		✔						
Poultry			✔			✔				✔				✔		✔	
Fish						✔	✔	✔							✔		
Eggs					✔	✔							✔	✔			
Soups/Stews	✔	✔	✔	✔	✔				✔			✔					✔
Sauces		✔												✔		✔	
Pasta				✔													
Rice		✔				✔						✔					
Popcorn									✔								
Asparagus				✔													
Beets				✔													
Broccoli											✔		✔				
Cabbage				✔					✔								
Carrots			✔	✔													
Cauliflower						✔										✔	
Green Beans									✔		✔						
Lima Beans						✔	✔								✔		
Potatoes											✔				✔		✔
Tomatoes		✔				✔			✔				✔				
Salads				✔		✔						✔					

Try this low sodium spice blend in your shaker instead of salt:

1 Tbsp. dry mustard	1 tsp. sage
1 tsp. garlic powder	½ tsp. marjoram, crushed
1½ Tbsp. onion powder	1 Tbsp. paprika
½ Tbsp. ground pepper	½ tsp. basil, crushed
½ Tbsp. thyme, crushed	½ tsp. ground oregano

Food Safety Guidelines

Food safety is an important part of food preparation. Bacteria that cause food-borne illnesses are present in many foods. Fortunately, with proper handling and cooking of foods, the danger from these bacteria and the toxins they may produce can be greatly reduced.

Follow these safety guidelines to help protect against food-borne illnesses:

Keep the temperature in the refrigerator between 35° F. and 40° F. A freezer should be at 0° F. or below.

Thaw all meat, fish, or poultry in the refrigerator. Do not thaw on the kitchen counter. For faster thawing, a microwave can be used, but meat should be cooked immediately after thawing.

Cook all meat and poultry thoroughly. The following chart is a guide.

FOOD	MINIMAL INTERNAL TEMPERATURE
Ground Meat	160°
Ground Poultry	165°
Beef, Veal, Lamb	145°
Pork	160°
Poultry	170°

Cook fish until it is opaque, firm, and flakes easily with a fork.

Cook eggs until the white is set and the yolk is starting to thicken. Do not eat raw eggs or those with cracks in the shell. Separate the egg white from the yolk by using an egg separator or a slotted spoon rather than by using the shell.

Once cooked, hold food at temperature below 40° F. or above 140° F. Do not allow perishable food to sit between these temperatures for more than two hours. This is considered the *danger zone* at which bacteria can readily grow or produce toxins.

Cool foods such as soups, sauces, and gravies in shallow pans no more than two inches deep.

Keep raw animal products and their juices separate from other foods.

✦ Place raw meat on a plate or pan in the refrigerator to keep juices from dripping on other foods.
✦ Wash kitchen surfaces, utensils, and hands after they have been exposed to raw meat, poultry, fish, and eggs.
✦ Thoroughly clean cutting boards used for rawmeat before using them for cooked foods or foods to be eaten raw, such as salad greens.
✦ Use a clean container to hold cooked meat. Do not reuse the container that held the raw meat without cleaning it first.

When roasting a turkey or chicken with stuffing, it is best to cook the stuffing in a separate pan instead of in the cavity of the bird. If you choose to stuff the bird, however, do so just prior to putting it in the oven. When checking for doneness, make sure a thermometer placed into the center of the stuffing reads at least 165° F.

Basic Guidelines for Losing Weight

There are many diets and weight loss products available for those struggling to lose weight. The sad reality, however, is that most diets do not work. In the long run, people often regain even more weight than they originally lost. There is hope for those who want to shed some extra pounds. The key to long-term weight reduction is gradual and permanent changes in lifestyle habits.

Decrease the amount of total fat eaten. Fat has more than twice the calories of carbohydrates or protein. Thus, even small amounts of high fat items such as butter, margarine, oil, sauces, and gravies can contain large amounts of calories. Dietary fat is also the nutrient most easily converted into body fat. Much of the carbohydrates and protein we eat are burned up before they can be stored as fat.

Eat a variety of foods and do not restrict certain foods from the diet. In general, it is not the occasional food that keeps someone from achieving a desirable weight; it is what is eaten on a daily basis. For example, limit dessert to one or two times per week instead of after each meal. Forbidding foods often makes them more desirable, and may undermine weight loss efforts.

Eat breakfast. People who eat breakfast are generally more successful at losing weight.

Try not to eat before going to bed. Food eaten at this time of day is often not burned up and is more likely to be stored as fat.

Eat single portions of food and give the body time to signal that it is full. Often we eat so fast that the second portion of food is almost gone before the body can signal that it was satisfied after the first.

Eat foods high in complex carbohydrates. This includes breads, cereals, pasta, rice and other grains, fruits, and vegetables. Although many weight loss diets in the past have limited starchy foods, it is the high fat items that often accompany these foods that inhibit weight loss efforts, not the starchy foods themselves.

Exercise. Aerobic excercise is an excellent way to achieve and maintain a desirable weight. Walking, jogging, biking, and rowing are examples of aerobic activities. Before beginning any exercise program, it is a good idea to consult a physician.

Do not starve yourself. Low calorie diets may slow a body's metabolism, making weight loss more difficult.

Lose weight slowly, 1 to 2 pounds per week is desirable. Most people who need to lose weight need to lose excess fat. The body cannot burn off more than a few pounds of fat per week. Faster weight loss is probably due to muscle breakdown.

Set reasonable weight goals. Despite our society's obsession with thinness, it is not practical for most of us to expect to have the body of a model. Instead, setting a goal which is achievable and maintainable may, over time, result in greater physical and psychological health benefits.

Understanding the
Nutrition Facts Food Label

The *Nutrition Facts* food label is designed to help the consumer make nutritious choices when selecting foods. It can be found on most packaged products in the grocery store. Information about serving size, calories, and several nutrients help to give an overall picture of the nutritional qualities of each food. The label on the following page is a typical example, although some labels list additional nutrients.

Serving Sizes have been set at an amount that people would typically eat. If your normal serving is smaller or larger, adjust the nutrient values accordingly. Serving sizes are in standard household and metric measures. Metric abbreviations used on the label include:

g: grams - 28g = 1 ounce
mg: milligrams - 1,000mg = 1g
ml: milliliters - 30ml = 1 fluid ounce

Nutrients listed are those considered to be important to today's health conscious consumer. These include total fat, saturated fat, cholesterol, sodium, and fiber.

The *Percent of Daily Value* tells you if the food is high or low in a particular nutrient. It also shows how that food fits into an entire day's diet. Percent of Daily Values are based on a 2,000 calorie diet and on current dietary guidelines. An individual's daily values may be higher or lower depending on calorie needs. As a rule of thumb, if the Daily Value is 5% or less, the food contains only a small amount of that nutrient. For total fat, saturated fat, cholesterol, and sodium, foods with a low Percent of Daily Value are good choices.

Terms used on the label to describe the food's nutritional content have strict definitions set by the government. Eleven *Descriptive Terms* have been identified: *free, low, lean, extra lean, less, reduced, light, fewer, high, more, and good source.* Because precise guidelines must be met for a food to use one of these terms, you can be assured that the claim is believable. For example, if a food claims to be sodium free, it must have less than 5ml of sodium per serving.

Claims regarding a food's relationship to various health-related conditions must also meet specific guidelines. To make a health claim about fats and heart disease, a food must be low in total fat, saturated fat, and cholesterol. A food making a statement regarding blood pressure and sodium must be low in sodium.

The *Ingredients List* is located in a separate location on the label. Ingredients are listed in descending order by weight; thus, if the first ingredient is sugar, there is more sugar in that product than anything else.

———————— ❦ ————————

*See the
following page
for an example of the
Nutritional Facts Food Label.*

The Nutrition Facts Food Label

Nutrition Facts

Serving Size 1 cup (228g)
Servings Per Container 2

Amount Per Serving

Calories 260 Calories from Fat 120

% Daily Value*

Total Fat 13g	**20%**
Saturated Fat 5g	**25%**
Cholesterol 30mg	**10%**
Sodium 660mg	**28%**
Total Carbohydrate 31g	**10%**
Dietary Fiber 0g	**0%**
Sugars 5g	
Protein 5g	

Vitamin A 4%	•	Vitamin C 2%	
Calcium 15%	•	Iron 4%	

* Percent Daily Values are based on a 2,000 calorie diet. Your daily values may be higher or lower depending on your calorie needs:

	Calories:	2,000	2,500
Total Fat	Less than	65g	80g
Sat Fat	Less than	20g	25g
Cholesterol	Less than	300mg	300mg
Sodium	Less than	2,400mg	2,400mg
Total Carbohydrate		300g	375g
Dietary Fiber		25g	30g

Calories per gram:
Fat 9 • Carbohydrate 4 • Protein 4

FOOD GUIDE PYRAMID
A Guide to Daily Food Choices

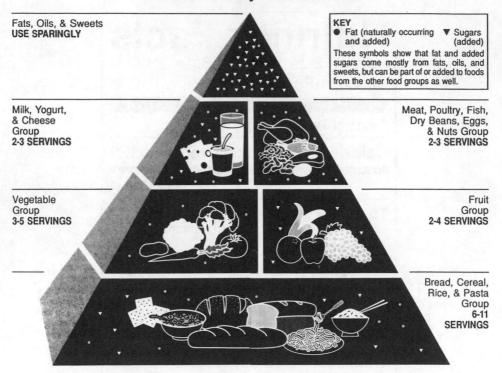

Fats, Oils, & Sweets
USE SPARINGLY

KEY
● Fat (naturally occurring   ▼ Sugars
   and added)   (added)

These symbols show that fat and added sugars come mostly from fats, oils, and sweets, but can be part of or added to foods from the other food groups as well.

Milk, Yogurt,
& Cheese
Group
2-3 SERVINGS

Meat, Poultry, Fish,
Dry Beans, Eggs,
& Nuts Group
2-3 SERVINGS

Vegetable
Group
3-5 SERVINGS

Fruit
Group
2-4 SERVINGS

Bread, Cereal,
Rice, & Pasta
Group
**6-11
SERVINGS**

SOURCE: U.S. Department of Agriculture/U.S. Department of Health and Human Services

Use the Food Guide Pyramid to help you eat better every day . . . the Dietary Guidelines way. Start with plenty of Breads, Cereal, Rice, and Pasta; Vegetables; and Fruits. Add two to three servings from the Milk group and two to three servings from the Meat group.

Each of these food groups provides some, but not all, of the nutrients you need. No one food group is more important than another—for good health you need them all. Go easy on fats, oils, and sweets, the foods in the small tip of the Pyramid.

A HANDY SPICE AND HERB GUIDE

ALLSPICE-a pea-sized fruit that grows in Mexico, Jamaica, Central and South America. Its delicate flavor resembles a blend of cloves, cinnamon, and nutmeg. USES: (Whole) Pickles, meats, boiled fish, gravies; (Ground) Puddings, relishes, fruit preserves, baking.

BASIL-the dried leaves and stems of an herb grown in the United States and North Mediterranean area. Has an aromatic, leafy flavor. USES: For flavoring tomato dishes and tomato paste, turtle soup; also use in cooked peas, squash, snap beans; sprinkle chopped over lamb chops and poultry.

BAY LEAVES-the dried leaves of an evergreen grown in the eastern Mediterranean countries. Has a sweet, herbaceous floral spice note. USES: For pickling, stews, for spicing sauces and soup. Also use with a variety of meats and fish.

CARAWAY-the seed of a plant grown in the Netherlands. Flavor that combines the tastes of anise and dill. USES: For the cordial Kummel, baking breads; often added to sauerkraut, noodles, cheese spreads. Also adds zest to French fried potatoes, liver, canned asparagus.

CURRY POWDER-a ground blend of ginger, turmeric, fenugreek seed, as many as 16 to 20 spices. USES: For all Indian curry recipes such as lamb, chicken, and rice, eggs, vegetables, and curry puffs.

DILL-the small, dark seed of the dill plant grown in India, having a clean, aromatic taste. USES: Dill is a predominant seasoning in pickling recipes; also adds pleasing flavor to sauerkraut, potato salad, cooked macaroni, and green apple pie.

MACE-the dried covering around the nutmeg seed. Its flavor is similar to nutmeg, but with a fragrant, delicate difference. USES: (Whole) For pickling, fish, fish sauce, stewed fruit. (Ground) Delicious in baked goods, pastries, and doughnuts, adds unusual flavor to chocolate desserts.

MARJORAM-an herb of the mint family, grown in France and Chile. Has a minty-sweet flavor. USES: In beverages, jellies, and to flavor soups, stews, fish, sauces. Also excellent to sprinkle on lamb while roasting.

MSG (MONOSODIUM GLUTAMATE)-a vegetable protein derivative for raising the effectiveness of natural food flavors. USES: Small amounts, adjusted to individual taste, can be added to steaks, roasts, chops, seafoods, stews, soups, chowder, chop suey, and cooked vegetables.

OREGANO-a plant of the mint family and a species of marjoram of which the dried leaves are used to make an herb seasoning. USES: An excellent flavoring for any tomato dish, especially pizza, chili con carne, and Italian specialties.

PAPRIKA-a mild, sweet red pepper growing in Spain, Central Europe, and the United States. Slightly aromatic and prized for brilliant red color. USES: A colorful garnish for pale foods, and for seasoning Chicken Paprika, Hungarian Goulash, salad dressings.

POPPY-the seed of a flower grown in Holland. Has a rich fragrance and crunchy, nut-like flavor. USES: Excellent as a topping for breads, rolls, and cookies. Also delicious in buttered noodles.

ROSEMARY-an herb (like a curved pine needle) grown in France, Spain, and Portugal, and having a sweet fresh taste. USES: In lamb dishes, in soups, stews, and to sprinkle on beef before roasting.

SAGE-the leaf of a shrub grown in Greece, Yugoslavia, and Albania. Flavor is camphoraceous and minty. USES: For meat and poultry stuffing, sausages, meat loaf, hamburgers, stews, and salads.

THYME-the leaves and stems of a shrub grown in France and Spain. Has a strong, distinctive flavor. USES: For poultry seasoning, croquettes, fricassees, and fish dishes. Also tasty on fresh sliced tomatoes.

TURMERIC-a root of the ginger family, grown in India, Haiti, Jamaica, and Peru, having a mild, ginger-pepper flavor. USES: As a flavoring and coloring in prepared mustard and in combination with mustard as a flavoring for meats, dressings, salads.

RULES FOR USING HERBS

1. Use with a light hand - the aromatic oils are strong and objectionable if too much is used.

2. Blend or heat with butter, margarine, or oil to draw out and extend the flavor. Unsalted butter is best. When using herbs in French dressing, have the oil tepid.

3. Cut or chop leaves very fine. The more cut surface exposed, the more completely the aromatic oil is absorbed.

4. Dried herbs are two to four times stronger than fresh herbs, so that if you substitute dried for fresh herbs use ¼ to ½ the amount. Experimentation is the best guide.

5. The flavor of herbs is lost by extended cooking.

6. To taste the true flavor of an herb you have not used before, mix ½ teaspoon crushed herb with 1 tablespoon cream cheese or sweet butter, let stand 10-15 minutes. Taste on a cracker.

7. The beginner should err on the side of too little rather than too much. It is easy to overseason, and one flavor should never be allowed to overpower another. A person should not be able to recognize the presence of an herb or what accounts for the delicious flavor. More of an herb can be added, but it cannot be taken out.

8. Herbs are used in addition to salt and pepper.

9. For **herb butters,** 1 tablespoon of the minced fresh herb is mixed into ¼ pound softened butter or margarine. Let stand at room temperature for at least one hour, preferably more. After flavor has been absorbed into butter, it should be chilled in the refrigerator. This will keep for several days if covered tightly so it does not absorb odors from the refrigerator.

UNUSUAL HERBS

Angelica-bienniel, homegrown herb. Leaves, seeds, and root used.

Bergamots-used in recipes are the orange-scented mint and Napaka (Monarda austromonta) or mountain oregano.

Borage-hairy annual, self-seeds, leaves and flowers used, cucumber flavor.

Burdock-root vegetable or pot herb; in Japanese produce section known as "Gobo."

Burnet-pretty leafy perennial; leaves have cucumber flavor.

Chervil-annual; taste similar to parsley, but milder with slight anise taste.

Chia-the seed of a sage; high in protein.

Cilantro-Mexican name for fresh leaf of coriander. Also called Chinese Parsley.

Chuchupate-root of a celery flavored plant. Robust in flavor. Use sparingly.

Coltsfoot-used in Japanese cooking; bought in cans; grows wild all over England.

Damiana (Turnera diffusa)-aphrodisiac herb used by Aztecs in their rites.

Epasote-Mexican herb (Chenopodium ambrosidies) used with pork and fish.

Jamica Roselle Hibiscus (Hibiscus Sabdariffa)-makes a pink lemonade tea.

Lemon Balm-perennial; lemon flavored used for flavoring.

Lemon Grass-lemon flavored grass; used in cooking and teas.

Lemon Eucalyptus (Eucalyptus citriodora)-30 foot tree with lemon scented leaves.

Lemon Thyme-very fragrant; lemon scented.

Mate-a South American tea containing large amount of caffeine.

Mints-orange, apple, pineapple scented; use interchangeably in any mint recipe.

Oriental Garlic-looks like a wide leaf chive. Just leaves are used.

Perilla-annual, called "Sisho" by Japanese. Resembles purple coleus. Perilla can be used in salads.

Pineapple Sage-pineapple fragrance; much used with fruit recipes.

Purslane-fleshy weed common in gardens; good cooked or raw; high in Vitamin C.

Quelites (Chenopodium album)-Indian pot herb; a variety of lamb's-quarters.

Saffron-stamens of Corcus Sativus; most expensive spice in the world.

Shallots-bulbs are small, lavender; mild onion flavor.

Skirret-roots and leaves used in salad, also good cooked; green leafy plant.

Tarragon-mild licorice taste. Do not start from seed, get divisons from nursery.

Woodruff-coumarin scented when dry; good in wine or jelly.

Yerbanis (Pericon, Tagetes Lucida)-marigold leaves, tarragon-type flavor-Mexico.

VEGETABLE CANNING OUTLINE

Name	Preparation	Time for Blanching	Boiling Water Plus: *	The Waterless Cooker, Mary Dunbar Model	Pressure Cooker	
					Min.	Lb.
ASPARAGUS	Wash, trim, cut.	4 min.	1 tsp. salt	3 hours	40	15
BEANS (STRING OR WAX)	Wash, string, break.	7 min.	1 tsp. salt	2 hours	60	10
BEANS (LIMA)	Shell.	4 min.	1 tsp. salt 2 tsp. sugar	4 hours	60	15
BEETS	Cut stems, but not roots. When blanched, cold dip 2 min.; remove skins.	10 min.	boiling water	2 hours	40	10
BRUSSELS SPROUTS	Wash.	7 min.	1 tsp. salt	2 hours	40	10
CABBAGE	Wash.	7 min.	1 tsp. salt	2 hours	40	10
CARROTS	Scrape, split lengthwise.	none	1 tsp. salt	2 hours	40	15
CAULI-FLOWER	Wash, break apart; soak 30 min. in cold salted water.	4 min.	1 tsp. salt	1½ hours	40	15
CORN (ON COB)	Remove husks and silk.	10 min.	1 tsp. salt	3 hours	90	10
CORN (OFF COB)	Husk, clean, cut from cob.	6 min.	1 tsp. salt	3 hours	90	10
GREENS (ANY TYPE)	Clean thoroughly; stem	4 min.	1 tsp. salt	3 hours	50	15
PEAS	Shell, rinse in cold water.	5 min.	2 tsp. sugar 1 tsp. salt	4 hours	60	15
PEPPERS (BELL)	Wash, remove seed-pod after blanching; flatten.	3 min.	1 tsp. salt	45 min.	35	10
PUMPKIN	Peel, cut in small pieces.	3 min.	boiling water	2 hours	40	15
SAUER-KRAUT	Pack.	none	none	1 hour	40	10
SUCCOTASH BEANS CORN	Cut corn from cob after blanching.	5 min. each	1 tsp. salt	3½ hours	90	10
TOMATOES	Blanch, cold dip, skin.	2 min.	1 tsp. salt	25 min.	10	10

If water does not completely cover jars, fold cloth over the jars permitting corners
to dip into the boiling water.

* Salt or sugar quantities per quart jar.
Keep boiling vigorously during processing.

FRUIT CANNING OUTLINE

Name	Preparation	Time for Blanching	Type of Boiling Syrup	Processing Time		
				The Waterless Cooker, Mary Dunbar Model	Pressure Cooker	
					Min.	Lb.
APPLES	Core and peel, cut in halves or quarters.	2 min.	thin	20 min.	10	5
APPLESAUCE	Cook in usual manner.	none	none	20 min.	10	5
APRICOTS	Wash, peel, halve and remove stones after blanching.	2 min.	medium	20 min.	10	5
BERRIES	Sort, hull.	none	thin	20 min.	10	5
CHERRIES	Wash, stone.	¼ min.	medium	25 min.	10	5
CURRANTS	Stem, wash.	none	medium	20 min.	10	5
FIGS	Wash, place in soda bath; drain, rinse.	none	medium	20 min.	10	5
GOOSE- BERRIES	Stem, wash.	none	medium	25 min.	10	5
GRAPES	Stem, wash.	none	medium	20 min.	10	5
PEACHES	Blanch, cold dip, peel, halve and stone.	1 min.	medium	25 min.	10	5
PEARS	Wash, peel, core and slice. Cook 6 minutes in syrup.	none	thin	25 min.	10	5
PINEAPPLE	Peel, remove eyes, cut, slice, or shred.	none	thin	30 min.	12	5
PLUMS	Wash, peel or prick skin.	none	medium	30 min.	12	5
RHUBARB	Wash, trim, cut.	none	medium	25 min.	15	5

The 10-quart pot for the Waterless Cooker, Mary Dunbar Model, is particularly recommended for canning. The 7-quart pot will take care of pints and half pints. The 10-quart pot and rack may be used with the same cover and base as the 7-quart cooker.

SYRUPS USED FOR CANNING FRUITS

With fruits, a boiling hot syrup instead of water or brine is used to fill the jar. This is made by dissolving sugar in water and bringing to a boil.

The Proportions are:

Thin Syrup: 1 part sugar to 2 parts water.

Medium Syrup: 3 parts sugar to 2 parts water.

Thick Syrup: 2 parts sugar to 1 part water.

APPLE VARIETIES

NAME	SEASON	COLOR	FLAVOR/ TEXTURE	EATING	PIE
Astrachan	July-Aug	Yellow/ Greenish Red	Sweet	Good	Good
Baldwin	Oct-Jan	Red/ Yellowish	Mellow	Fair	Fair
Cortland	Oct-Jan	Green/ Purple	Mild, tender	Excel.	Excel.
Delicious, Red	Sept-June	Scarlet	Sweet, crunchy	Excel.	Good
Delicious, Golden	Sept-May	Yellow	Sweet, semifirm	Excel.	Excel.
Empire	Sept-Nov	Red	Sweet, crisp	Excel.	Good
Fameuse	Sept-Nov	Red	Mild, crisp	Excel.	Fair
Granny Smith	Apr-Jul	Green	Tart, crisp	V. Good	V. Good
Gravenstein	July-Sept	Green w/red stripes	Tart, crisp	Good	Good
Ida Red	Oct	Red	Rich	Good	Good
Jonathan	Sept-Jan	Brilliant red	Tart, tender, crisp	V. Good	V. Good
Macoun	Oct-Nov	Dark red	Tart, juicy, crisp	Excel.	Good
McIntosh	Sept-June	Green to red	Slightly tart, tender, juicy	Excel.	Excel.
Newtown Pippin	Sept-June	Green to red	Slightly tart, firm	V. Good	Excel.
Northern Spy	Oct	Red	Crisp, tart	V. Good	V. Good
Rhode Island Greening	Sept-Nov	Green	Very tart, firm	Poor	Excel.
Rome Beauty	Oct-June	Red	Tart, firm, slightly dry	Good	V. Good
Stayman-Winesap	Oct-Mar	Red	Semifirm, sweet, spicy	V. Good	Good
Winesap	Oct-June	Red	Slightly tart, firm, spicy	Excel.	Good
Yellow Transparent	July-Aug	Yellow	Tart, soft	Poor	Excel.

IRON FROM SOME COMMON FOOD SOURCES

Food	Amount	Iron (mg.)
Egg	1	1.1
Meat, lean	3 oz.	(approx.) 3.0
Mature beans and peas (legumes), nuts		
Almonds, Brazil nuts, cashew nuts, walnuts	¼ cup	(approx.) 1.5
Beans, common varieties, cooked, drained	1 cup	4.9
Lentils, cooked	1 cup	3.2
Peas, dry, cooked	1 cup	4.2
Vegetables		
Lima beans, immature, cooked	1 cup	4.3
Carrots, cauliflower, sweet corn	1 cup	(approx.) 1.0
Greens, cooked	1 cup	(approx.) 2.5
Peas, green, cooked	1 cup	2.9
Sweet potato	1 med. lg.	1.0
Tomato, cooked	1 cup	1.2
Fruits		
Apricots and peaches, dried, cooked	1 cup	5.1
Berries, fresh	1 cup	(approx.) 1.5
Dates, dry, cut	½ cup	2.6
Grape juice	1 cup	0.8
Prunes, dried, softened	4 medium	1.1
Prune juice, canned	1 cup	10.5
Raisins, dried	½ cup	2.8
Watermelon	Wedge 4x8 inch	2.1
Grain Products		
Bread, enriched	1 slice	(approx.) 0.6
Flour and meal, whole or enriched, dry	¼ cup	(approx.) 1.0
Spaghetti and macaroni, enriched, dry	⅓ cup	(approx.) 1.0
Wheat germ	¼ cup	1.8
Syrup, dark	1 Tbsp.	(approx.) 1.0
Sugar, brown	1 Tbsp.	.5

GRILLING TIPS

1. To clean the grilling surface, heat grill for five minutes, then brush with a wire brush to loosen debris.
2. When cooking meats without sauce, oil the grill with one to two tablespoons of vegetable or olive oil to prevent meat from sticking.
3. Trim cuts of meat of all excess fat before grilling, leaving ¼ inch around the edges.
4. Ribs will cook better when simmered for approximately one hour in water before grilling. This process removes fat from the ribs, and will prevent flare-ups on the grill.
5. Cuts of beef and lamb for outdoor grilling should be a minimum of 1½ inches thick, but not more than three inches thick, to retain pink inside after the surface sears.
6. When marinating small cuts of meat, allow three hours per inch of thickness in refrigerator. For larger cuts of meat, allow one to two days in the refrigerator, depending on the size of the cut. Turn the meat occasionally to distribute the marinade.
7. Always marinate in a noncorrosive container, such as glass, porcelain, glazed earthenware or stainless steel.
8. Use tongs to turn meat and fish. Piercing the food will let the juices escape.
9. When using bamboo skewers for kabobs, soak them in water for at least 30 minutes before use to prevent them from burning.
10. Cutting into meat to check for doneness will let the juices escape. Instead of cutting, touch the meat. If it is firm to the touch, then it is well done. If it feels very soft, it is still raw. If it feels soft to the touch but springs back, it is medium rare. (Be careful not to burn yourself.)
11. Chicken with bones can be baked in an oven for 15 to 20 minutes, covered, at 300° before grilling. Alternatively, parboil for about five minutes (with or without skin). This keeps grilling time down and prevents chicken from drying out.
12. Remove skin, clean and parboil chicken. Cover with barbecue sauce or other marinade and freeze in an appropriate quantity for your meal. This gets the mess and work behind you and allows the marinade to be absorbed. Thaw when you are ready to grill.
13. Chicken cutlets can be grilled quickly over high heat. Do not overcook! Use a grilling basket if pieces are small.
14. To test chicken for doneness, light meat should be white and the juice translucent, not pink; dark meat juices should be clear.
15. It is difficult to keep fish from sticking to the grill. Thicker cuts and fish steaks work best. The easiest solution is a grilling basket, sprayed with Pam.
16. Fish is done if opaque throughout. Do not overcook!
17. Hard vegetables, such as cauliflower, broccoli, and small onions, should be parboiled approximately 1½ minutes before putting on skewers. Soft vegetables, such as cherry tomatoes and mushrooms, can be boiled for 30-45 seconds.
18. One inch cross sections of corn on the cob make a nice addition to kabobs.
19. Marinate sliced eggplant or zucchini in Italian dressing overnight then grill as desired.
20. Do not mix items on a kabob that require different cooking times, such as steak and mushrooms. Segregate items on separate skewers to adjust times. It is not as pretty, but it avoids a cooking disaster.
21. Be creative with marinades, but do not forget old stand-bys such a bottle of Catalina dressing for chicken or a mixture of Italian dressing (one bottle) and tomato paste (large can) for beef kabobs. All you need for fish is some tamari sauce (similar to soy sauce) and a few drops of oil.

FIRST AID IN HOUSEHOLD EMERGENCIES

POISONING: When a poison has been taken internally, start first aid at once. Call doctor immediately.

- Dilute poison with large amounts of liquid — milk or water.
- Wash out by inducing vomiting, when not a strong acid, strong alkali, or petroleum.
- For acid poisons do not induce vomiting, but neutralize with milk of magnesia. Then give milk, olive oil, or egg white. Keep victim warm and lying down.
- For alkali poisons such as lye or ammonia, do not induce vomiting.
- Give lemon juice or vinegar. Then give milk and keep victim warm and lying down.
- If poison is a sleeping drug, induce vomiting and then give strong black coffee frequently. Victim must be kept awake.
- If breathing stops, give artificial respiration.

SHOCK: Shock is brought on by a sudden or severe physical injury or emotional disturbance. In shock, the balance between the nervous system and the blood vessels is upset. The result is faintness, nausea, and a pale and clammy skin. Call ambulance immediately. If not treated the victim may become unconscious and eventually lapse into a coma.

- Keep victim lying down, preferably with head lower than body.
- Don't give fluids unless delayed in getting to doctor, then give only water. (Hot tea, coffee, milk, or broth may be tried if water is not tolerated.)
- Never give liquid to an unconscious person. Patient must be alert.
- Cover victim both under and around his body.
- Do not permit victim to become abnormally hot.
- Reassure victim and avoid letting him see other victims or his own injury.
- Fainting is most common and last form of shock. Patient will respond in 30-60 seconds by merely allowing patient to lie head down, if possible, on floor.

FRACTURES: Pain, deformity, or swelling of injured part usually means a fracture. If fracture is suspected, don't move person unless absolutely necessary, and then only if the suspected area is splinted. Give small amounts of lukewarm fluids and treat for shock.

BURNS: Apply or submerge the burned area in cold water. Apply a protective dry sterile cloth or gauze dry dressing if necessary. Do not apply grease or an antiseptic ointment or spray. Call doctor and keep patient warm (not hot) with severe burns.

- If burn case must be transported any distance, cover burns with clean cloth.
- Don't dress extensive facial burns. (It may hinder early plastic surgery.)

WOUNDS: Minor cuts — Apply pressure with sterile gauze until bleeding stops. Use antiseptic recommended by your doctor. Bandage with sterile gauze. See your doctor. **Puncture Wounds** — Cover with sterile gauze and consult a doctor immediately. Serious infection can arise unless properly treated.

ANIMAL BITES: Wash wounds freely with soap and water. Hold under running tap for several minutes if possible. Apply an antiseptic approved by your doctor and cover with sterile gauze compress. Always see your doctor immediately. So that animal may be held in quarantine, obtain name and address of owner.

HEAT EXHAUSTION: Caused by exposure to heat or sun. Symptoms: Pale face, moist and clammy skin, weak pulse, subnormal temperature, victim usually conscious.
Treatment: Keep victim lying down, legs elevated, victim wrapped in blanket. Give salt water to drink (1 tsp. salt to 1 glass water), ½ glass every 15 minutes. Call doctor.

GENERAL DIRECTIONS FOR FIRST AID

1. Effect a prompt rescue.
2. Maintain an open airway.
3. Control severe bleeding by direct pressure over bleeding site. No tourniquet.
4. Give First Aid for poisoning.
5. Do not move victim unless it is necessary for safety reasons.
6. Protect the victim from unnecessary manipulation.
7. Avoid or overcome chilling by using blankets or covers, if available.
8. Determine the injuries or cause for sudden illness.
9. Examine the victim methodically but be guided by the kind of accident or sudden illness and the need of the situation.
10. Carry out the indicated First Aid.

ENTERTAINING MADE EASY

Nearly everyone is occasionally the host or hostess of an event. Whether it is a family dinner, children's party, or elegant reception, it need not be a time to panic. It is fun and easy to entertain if you plan.

Planning is the key to any successful event. Thinking through your ideas early and writing them all down frees your mind to carry out the tasks and to enjoy the event. Another added benefit of planning is that time and money management will result. You can spread your time and money expense out over a period of time, and you can prioritize so that you do and buy the most important things first.

Where to start planning? Contrary to popular belief, it is NOT with the food. The menu should come much later. Look at these steps.

1. EVALUATION. Evaluate you and what you really want. Consider when the party will be. What space is available? What is your budget?

Part of the evaluation is knowing the reason for giving the party. Sometimes, it is set — like the family's Thanksgiving Dinner or your daughter's birthday. Others center around specific happenings like a bridal shower, anniversary, or new home. Perhaps it is truly wanting to entertain friends.

Decide early if you are giving the event alone or if you need help. Must you reserve a place, rent tables, hire a caterer, arrange help or engage musicians? If so, determine these contracts before going any further.

2. SET THE THEME. Be creative, but remember your evaluation and the reason for the party. The theme is important because the entire event will be based on it, including food, music, decorations, and guest list.

It may be helpful to think of a couple different themes and compare them to your space requirement, budget and other known factors. Then you will be able to choose the one that really fits you and your guests best.

3. INVITATION LIST. Consider the invitation list carefully. There is no need for each one invited to be exactly alike, but they should mix well. Remember, it often shows if you invite someone only because you feel obligated.

4. MENU. What foods go with the theme? Will it be refreshments or a dinner? Will the meal be a sit-down affair or a buffet? What will the budget allow? Again consider your space, the type of service, your dishes and seating. A buffet is easy to serve, but if seating is limited, you may have to restrict the menu to finger foods.

Whatever the food is, it should be simple, attractively served and there should be plenty of it. Think of what foods can be done in advance, and what must be done the day of the party. Generally, the best party menus are ones in which very little must be prepared at the last minute.

5. MAIL INVITATIONS. Invitations should be sent (or guests called) about 2 weeks before the party or up to 1 month before for weddings or other major events. Be sure and include the date, time for the party to begin and end, place, and your own name, address and phone number. An R.S.V.P. (with a phone number noted) will help remind people to call and let you know if they are coming.

Be sure the invitation is clear and complete. For example, are children invited? Is Bob to come alone or bring a guest? Be sure and specify if a special event, like showing slides, or going out dancing is planned.

6. MAKE LISTS. Keep a detailed list of all that is needed. What can be done in advance and what must be done the day of the party?

7. DECORATIONS AND ARRANGEMENTS. What can be done to make it festive? What decorations will carry out the theme the best? Remember to plan serving bowls, napkins, garnishes and centerpieces as part of the decorations.

Think of your guests in all arrangements. It is usually best to clear away the rare and breakable. Clear off tables and provide coasters so guests can set drinks. Where will the pet stay? Are there fresh towels, soaps, and ashtrays. Is there plenty of ice?

8. ENJOY. The best parties are those that are given for fun and relaxation. The comfort of the guests is considered and all is done in a true spirit of friendship. Planning helps to make it possible and will add to the fun.

226

THE BEST USE OF YOUR FREEZER
MAY MAKE MEALTIME EASIER

Is your freezer a mystery? Is it an empty, dark cave, filled with the unknown, or is it so full you can't see what is there?

Whatever its state, the fact that you have one can mean a real difference in meal planning. If you are interested in convenience, quality, and food variety, the freezer may hold the key.

These tips will help you use your freezer correctly.

FREEZE AT THE PEAK OF FRESHNESS. If you have a garden, this means freezing vegetables very quickly after picking. If it is your casserole, or the appetizers for next week's party, freeze it soon after preparing. Remember, the freezer will preserve food — not refresh it.

FREEZE FOOD QUICKLY. Quick freezing means that ice crystals are smaller and flavor and texture will be the best. Slower freezing means larger ice crystals and even more opportunity to reduce flavor and texture. Chill the food first in the refrigerator. Then, place the food to be frozen right on the shelf.

WRAP CAREFULLY. Wrapping must be moisture-proof and air-proof to prevent drying or freezer burn. The freezer is not a cold, still world; rather it is a constant motion of air currents and food must be protected. Select freezer wrap, heavy duty aluminum foil or specially marked plastic wrap. Many plastics (like store wraps or sandwich bags) are not moisture or air-proof.

KEEP THE FREEZER AT ZERO. Check this with a thermometer, not the hardness of food. It is possible for the food to "feel hard" but not be solidly frozen. If the food is not solidly frozen, the quality will decline.

FREEZE FOOD ONCE. Thawing food, then refreezing may destroy moisture, flavor, texture and nutrition.

LABEL THE FOOD. Contrary to what you might think, you will not remember what that funny shaped package is. Include the contents, and the date. If you note the cooking or heating instructions right on the label, others will know how to heat it.

KEEP FREEZER FULL. A freezer kept 75%-85% full will operate most efficiently.

USE THE FOOD - don't just save it. Plan to restock at least twice a year for optimum food flavor.

FOLLOW THE RULE OF FIRST IN - FIRST OUT. Rotate the food and use the oldest items first.

THAW FOOD PROPERLY - if at all. Some foods need no thawing before cooking. If thawing is required, thaw it slowly in the refrigerator or in a water-proof container in cold water.

BUY FROZEN FOOD WISELY. Be sure that the packages are solidly frozen and not heavily frosted. If it is frosted or misshapen, you will know that thawing has occurred and some quality was lost.

REFREEZE CAREFULLY. Refreezing may not cause a health hazard if the food is cold and some ice crystals remain. Discard any food that has an off odor or has an off color. If in doubt, do not refreeze. Do not refreeze ice cream, fish, shell fish or prepared dishes. Remember, quality will have deteriorated when any food is refrozen.

SOME FOODS ARE BEST NOT FROZEN — or, will change somewhat. For example, potatoes may become mushy. Fried foods may become soggy and stale. Lettuce and greens wilt. Milk or cheese sauce may curdle.

HOW LONG CAN FOOD STAY FROZEN? This is a general idea, based on optimum quality and flavor for foods held at 0° F.

Ice Cream	1 month
Fruits, Vegetables	Up to 1 year
Butter or Margarine	1 month
Ground Beef	2-3 months
Pork	4-6 months
Beef steak, Roast	Up to 1 year
Cooked meat, Poultry	1-6 months
Turkey	6-8 months
Lean Fish	6-9 months
Shell Fish	Up to 4 months
Baked Cakes	3-4 months
Baked Pies	1-2 months

GIFTS FROM THE KITCHEN

The kitchen is generally used for preparing nourishing family meals. But more and more, the kitchen is becoming an art and craft studio or workshop for gifts.

Home spun items, homemade foods and other "kitchen-crafts" are really popular today. Perhaps there is no gift more desired than something made "especially for you" from the kitchen.

WHAT FOODS MAKE PERFECT GIFTS?

Any food item that you make especially well, is unique, or represents your cultural background is a wonderful gift.

Some ideas include:

Bread	Rolls	Muffins
Cakes	Cookies	Pies
Jams	Jelly	Candy
Flavored vinegars	Soup mix	Drink mixes
Relish	Pickles	Syrup
A favorite seasoning blend	Flavored nuts	

MAKE IT LOOK FESTIVE

Food will look extra festive and special if attractively presented. Try the stenciling idea, which follows, or look to pretty boxes, baskets, tins or other containers to give a special look.

Sometimes the container is really a part of the gift and will serve double duty. A set of glasses or mugs could each hold a different relish, jam or jelly. One coffee mug filled with candy, cookies, or nuts, and tied with ribbon might make the perfect gift for a child to give to the teacher. Fill a decorative cannister with a soup mix, and tie a soup ladle in with the bow. Fill a salad dressing cruet with an herb-flavored vinegar.

The wrap itself might also be functional as well as pretty. For example, a kitchen towel might wrap a bread, or napkins might wrap the jars filled with tea mix.

SPECIAL INSTRUCTIONS AND GIFT CARDS

Always tell the person how to serve the gift and include special information about storing. For example, specify if jam is to be refrigerated or frozen or note if the torte is filled with cream or cream cheese and must be refrigerated.

For a special touch, write the history of the dish, some serving ideas, how to store it and even the recipe on a decorative card and tie it to the package.

SOME GIFTS DO NOT REQUIRE COOKING

Gifts from the kitchen do not have to be the finished food. Try tying the ingredients for your favorite dish and the recipe together in a decorative basket. Or assemble some special ingredients for a certain type of cooking together on a tray or cutting board.

STENCILED OR PAINTED FOOD

Stencil or paint food to give a special look that is perfect for any holiday or party. It is also fun to personalize a food when giving it to a friend.

To make an edible paint, lightly beat together egg yolks. Blend in food coloring until the desired color is reached. Apply using a new, clean brush.

If desired, find a pattern or use a clean, new art stencil. Children's coloring books are also good sources of large pictures that can be traced.

Yeast bread and double crust pies are perfect for stenciling. Note these tips:

Bread — Yeast breads have a smooth crust that is easily painted. Paint or stencil after bread has baked and cooled.

Pie — Double-crust fruit pies are pretty stenciled with a holiday design or pictures of the fruit inside. Paint the crust after positioning on the pie, but before baking.

Seasoning know-how

More and more, you are told to use herbs or spices instead of salt, sugar, or fats.

They really do add flavor to the food and they are simple to use.

Is it an herb or a spice? Actually the word doesn't make much difference since both add wonderful flavor. The difference is that spices come from the roots, buds, flowers, fruits, bark or seeds, while herbs come from the leaves of plants.

Herbs come fresh or dried, in whole leaf, seed or ground form. Spices are available whole or ground.

Herbs and spices should be carefully stored as they will become stale or lose their flavor easily. Store them tightly covered, in a cool, dry place, away from the range. The flavor of herbs naturally weaken with age so buy small bottles and replace them often.

Dry herbs are more concentrated than fresh. If substituting fresh herbs for dried herbs, use 2 to 3 times more fresh herbs than dried.

Whole leaf herbs and whole spices will hold their flavor better during long cooking. If tied in cheesecloth, they are easy to remove before serving. Add ground herbs during the last 5-10 minutes of cooking. Ground spices give an almost instant flavor and are best for baking, or quick-cooking food.

Many herbs and seasonings are now available in blends, salts, or powders. A blend is simply a combination of herbs, spices and perhaps other seasonings like salt or sugar. Read the label carefully. Salts are combinations of an herb or spice and salt. Powder is the ground form of the seasoning.

COMMON SEASONINGS AND THEIR USE

ALLSPICE — Use in pickling, on baked ham, in baking cakes, cookies, in tomato sauce or soup.

BASIL — Use in soups, stews, sauces. Also good on eggs or pasta.

BAY — Use in soups, stews, in tomato dishes and in pickles.

CARAWAY — Popular in baking breads, cakes, or cookies. Use also on cabbage or beets.

CHIVES —Excellent on eggs, salads, or potatoes.

CINNAMON — Excellent on baked fruit, in fruit butter, on hot cereal or in baking cakes, cookies, pies, or breads.

CLOVES — Use in fruit dishes, on ham or pork, in baking cakes, cookies, pies, breads, or pastries or in pickling.

CORIANDER — Popular in pickling, in stuffing for poultry, on fresh pork or when making sausage.

DILL — Use in dips, on fish, in pickling or in making soups, stews, or sauces.

GINGER — Use in cakes, cookies, breads, on beef, in stews, on sweet potatoes or carrots.

MACE — Use in pickling or preserves, in cherry pie, in fruit cobblers, or in some sauces.

MARJORAM — Popular on chicken, in cheese or egg dishes, as a poultry seasoning or in salads.

MINT — Use fresh leaves in beverages. Use dried with fruit or in sauces.

NUTMEG — Use in sausages, on ham or pork, in baking cakes, cookies, or in egg-nog.

OREGANO — Use in tomato sauces, in beef stew, in pizza or in pasta dishes. It is an ingredient in chili powder.

PAPRIKA — Use it to season shell fish, salad dressings, and some beef dishes or stews. Its red color gives a finishing touch to many casseroles.

PARSLEY — A popular seasoning for many dishes, including sauces, stews, soups, egg dishes, or salads.

PEPPER — Available in red, black or white forms. It will provide zest for any dish, including salads, meats, soups, stews, casseroles, or fish, and is used in pickling.

SAGE — Use in sausage and in poultry dishes or stuffings.

THYME — Use in soups, stews, or sauces.

ATTRACTIVE FOOD IS FUN AND EASY

How something looks really affects your enjoyment of it. You know that appearances can work against food -- like wilted lettuce or an off-color sauce. So too, the appearance can really enhance food. It can make a plain meal into a festive, special one. It will entice the picky eater to eat. It tells your family you are really glad to share dinner with them.

Appearance is a combined effort of color, texture, and shape. Think not only of the food itself, but also of the linens and dishes that will be used with the meal.

Gone are the days when we could only use white china and linen. Today's table is set with bright colored plastics on vinyl cloths. Or it is pastel stoneware on home-style mats. Colors once never used with food, like purple, or black, are now fine. We can even mix or match china, stoneware and baskets. This really means your creativity can soar. And the beautiful dishes and cloths need more than that old wilted sprig of parsley as a garnish.

Look at some new serving and garnishing ideas that will highlight your cooking, without taking up too much time.

SET THE MOOD. Establish a feeling or select the theme of the meal. Is it formal or informal? What kind of meal is it? What season of the year is it? This will help your creative thoughts plus give you ideas for linens to use, for centerpieces or other decorations, as well as help you select the food itself and how to serve it.

LOOK AT COLOR. Make sure there is a wide variety and that they go together. Most food colors "go together" so it is simply a matter of offering foods that have lots of different colors, then match the colors of the napkins, cloths or garnishes to the colors of the food. Offer pleasing contrasts and accents that make the food stand out and look its best.

LOOK AT STYLE. Some foods and events just naturally call for a certain style of presentation. Holidays are a perfect example.

Halloween seems to be an informal time, while Valentine's Day may fit any style but the presentation could include silver or candlelight.

Tastefully done, you can mix old and new, or silver with less-formal pieces. But do so with caution and a critical eye.

TEXTURES SHOULD ADD VARIETY. Textures can be interesting and really add to your presentation. Interesting mats over cloths, various baskets and other accessories really add to the interest.

SERVING PIECES. Serving pieces can be as varied as your imagination will allow and this is a really easy way to liven up the table. Use a variety of shapes and sizes of containers. Can an old book be gracefully wrapped in a napkin and used to hold an appetizer plate up at a different height? Arrange finger food on a footed cake server. Would old, antique glasses show off parfaits?

FOOD CONTAINERS. Look to food itself for the container. Hollow out a pumpkin and use it to serve a stew or a punch. Hollow out a green or red pepper to hold a dip. Remove the heart of a head of red cabbage and fill with slaw. Serve fruit salad from a melon or cantaloupe boat. Use your imagination, and the season of the year. Just be sure that the food used as a container is fresh, clean and well chilled.

MAKE ALL FOOD LOOK ATTRACTIVE. When preparing any food, look for methods to make the food look extra nice. Make it a habit to look at the food and see if there is a way to add a little color interest -- and see how fast the flavor interest climbs too. These ideas are easy and quick and will turn any good cook into that extraordinary cook.

A quick sprinkle of paprika, herbs, bread crumbs or slivered almonds will liven up a plain casserole.

Leave the peel on fruits if possible to add extra color.

Slice celery or carrots into pieces large enough that they can be identified and can add color to the rest of the dish.

Slice some foods straight across, while others at a diagonal.

Sprinkle toasted coconut over a cake or fruit salad.

Drizzle chocolate over a cake frosted with a white frosting.

Sprinkle croutons and shredded cheese over cups of soup. Thinly slice a lemon, orange, zucchini, tomato or other food that matches the flavor of the soup and float the pieces in the bowl.

Always toss sliced bananas or chopped apples into lemon juice to prevent darkening.

GARNISHES

CHOCOLATE LEAVES. The leaves are beautiful on a cake, or on top of the whipped cream on a chocolate cream pie.

Wash and dry fresh mint leaves. Melt semi-sweet chocolate morsels over hot, not boiling water. Let chocolate cool but not harden. Using a new, clean paint brush, paint chocolate on back (dull-side) of leaves. Place, chocolate side up, on plate covered with wax paper. Freeze about 10 minutes or until firm. Carefully peel off chocolate, starting at stem end. Keep chocolate leaves chilled until ready to serve.

LEMON SPIRALS. Lemon spirals are one of the easiest and most versatile garnishes known. Use them on cakes, lemon meringue pie, nestled in parsley on a lemon-pasta dish, or on poultry or fish.

Select firm, deep yellow lemons. Do not peel. Slice full, thin, slices across center of fruit. On each slice, cut through peel and up just to center of the slice. Twist one half forward and one half backward.

Orange or lime spirals can be made in the same way.

FRUIT CUPS. Use fruit as a cup to hold colorful food accents.

Cut a scalloped pattern around an orange about ⅓ down. Discard top. Cut away fruit pulp from top. Fill with whole-berry cranberry sauce and place next to turkey or ham.

Cut a grapefruit in the same fashion and top with cherries for a breakfast or brunch garnish.

VEGETABLE CUPS. Thin slices of summer vegetables really dress up meat dishes when filled with relish.

Slice a zucchini, yellow squash or cucumber in slices 1-inch thick. Carefully spoon out the pulp, leaving the peel in an attractive ring. Fill with relish.

TOMATO ROSE. This elegant garnish is very popular today in gourmet restaurants, and really is easier than it looks.

With a very sharp knife, thinly peel a tomato in one, continuous strip, about ¾ inch wide. Gently, rewind the peel into a coil, with each coil fanning out a little to resemble a rose. Place on a bed of mint or basil leaves.

FOOD STORAGE CHART

Meat	Refrigerate	Freeze
Beef Steaks	1 to 2 days	6 to 12 months
Beef Roasts	1 to 2 days	6 to 12 months
Pork Chops	1 to 2 days	3 to 4 months
Pork Roast	1 to 2 days	4 to 8 months
Fresh Pork Sausages	1 to 2 days	1 to 2 months
Veal Cutlets	1 to 2 days	6 to 9 months
Veal Steaks	1 to 2 days	6 to 12 months
Lamb Chops, Steaks	1 to 2 days	6 to 9 months
Lamb Roasts	1 to 2 days	6 to 9 months
Stew meat (any type)	1 to 2 days	3 to 4 months
Ground beef, veal, lamb	1 to 2 days	3 to 4 months
Ground pork	1 to 2 days	1 to 3 months
Variety meats (liver, kidney, brains)	1 to 2 days	3 to 4 months

STORE IT RIGHT! Meat keeps best in the refrigerator if it's loosely wrapped in plastic wrap or wax paper. To freeze it, wrap in moisture/vapor-proof wrapping, such as heavy plastic wrap. Always remember to label and date it.

Poultry

	Refrigerate	Freeze
Whole chickens	1 to 2 days	12 months
Cut up chickens	1 to 2 days	9 months
Chicken giblets	1 to 2 days	3 months
Whole turkey	1 to 2 days	12 months
Cut up turkey	1 to 2 days	6 months
Whole ducks or geese	1 to 2 days	6 months

STORE IT RIGHT! In the refrigerator, remove giblets and wrap and store them separately. Store poultry loosely wrapped in the coldest part of the refrigerator. To freeze, wrap in a moisture/vapor-proof wrap. Label and date it.

CAUTION: Never freeze poultry with the stuffing inside. Stuffing may be frozen separately.

FOOD STORAGE CHART (Cont.)

Cooked Meats & Leftovers	Refrigerate	Freeze
Fried chicken	1 to 2 days	4 months
Beef roast	3 to 4 days	2 to 3 months
Beef stew	3 to 4 days	2 to 3 months
Canned/cured ham	4 to 5 days	1 month
Fresh ham or pork	3 to 4 days	2 to 3 months
Gravy or meat broth	1 to 2 days	2 to 3 months
Meat sauce (spaghetti sauce)	3 to 4 days	6 to 8 months
Meat loaf	2 to 3 days	3 months
Cooked pork or lamb	3 to 4 days	2 to 3 months
Cooked chicken, slices or pieces, covered with broth or gravy	1 to 2 days	6 months
Cooked chicken, alone	1 to 2 days	1 month
Chicken or tuna salad	1 to 2 days	do not freeze
Leftover fish	2 to 3 days	1 month
Chicken and turkey pies	1 to 2 days	2 to 3 months

STORE IT RIGHT! Always chill leftovers and cooked meats quickly. Keep covered in the refrigerator. Separate leftover poultry meat from the stuffing when refrigerating. To freeze package and freeze quickly. Meat stuffing should always be frozen separately.

Cured Meats	Refrigerate	Freeze
Ham, whole	1 week	1 to 2 months
half	3 to 5 days	1 to 2 months
Frankfurters	1 week	1 month
Bacon	1 week	2 to 4 months
Canned ham	1 year if unopened	not recommended
Ham slices	3 days	1 to 2 months
Corned beef	7 days	2 weeks
Luncheon meat	3 to 5 days	not recommended
Sausage, smoked	7 days	not recommended

STORE IT RIGHT! Keep meat loosely covered in refrigerator. To freeze, wrap it tightly in moisture/vapor-proof wrapping, pressing out as much air as possible. When freezing smoked meat, wrap extra well so its odors won't permeate other foods. Cured meats don't keep their high quality for long when frozen, because the seasonings that are added in the curing process speed rancidity.

FOOD STORAGE CHART (Cont.)

Fish	Refrigerate	Freeze
Fresh fish	1 to 2 days	6 to 9 months
Shrimp	1 to 2 days	2 months
Lobster, crabs	1 to 2 days	1 to 2 months
Oysters, clams, scallops	1 to 2 days	3 to 6 months

STORE IT RIGHT! Before refrigerating, first rinse fish thoroughly in cold water. Pat dry with paper towels and cover loosely with wax paper. Store in the coldest part of the refrigerator. To freeze fillets, wrap them well in moisture/vapor-proof wrapping. Shrimp keep best if frozen uncooked. To freeze crab or lobster, cook first without any salt, cool in refrigerator and remove meat from shell before freezing. To freeze oysters, clams, or scallops, shell them first and pack in own liquid. Don't forget to label and date your fish.

Dairy Products	Refrigerate	Freeze
Butter, unsalted	2 weeks	6 months
salted		3 months
Eggs, whole	2 to 3 weeks	6 to 8 months
whites	1 week to 10 days	6 to 8 months
yolks	2 to 3 days	6 to 8 months
Milk, cream	1 week	1 month
Cheese spreads	1 to 2 weeks when opened	1 to 2 months
Hard cheese, Parmesan, Swiss or Cheddar	2 to 3 months tightly wrapped	6 months
Soft cheeses, Camembert	2 weeks	2 months
Cottage cheese	5 to 7 days	1 to 2 weeks
Cream cheese	2 weeks	2 weeks

STORE IT RIGHT! In refrigerator, store eggs in their own carton. To freeze, eggs must be removed from their shell first. For whole eggs, stir in 2 tablespoons sugar or 1 teaspoon salt for each pint of lightly beaten eggs. Pack in freezer containers, leaving half an inch of headspace. Label and date. Refrigerate cheese in its original wrapping, if possible; or cover cut surface tightly with plastic wrap or foil. To freeze cheese, wrap in moisture/vapor-proof wrap or store in the original wrap with a foil overlap. Do not freeze in amounts larger than 1 pound.

TERMS USED IN RECIPES

Bake — To cook covered or uncovered in an oven or oven-type appliance. For meats cooked uncovered, it's called roasting.

Baste — To moisten foods during cooking with pan dripings or special sauce to add flavor and prevent drying.

Beat — To make mixture smooth by adding air with a brisk whipping or stirring motion using spoon or electric mixer.

Blend — To thoroughly mix two or more ingredients until smooth and uniform.

Boil — To cook in liquid at boiling temperature (212 degrees at sea level) where bubbles rise to the surface and break. For a full rolling boil, bubbles form rapidly throughout the mixture.

Braise — To cook slowly with a small amount of liquid in tightly covered pan on top of range or in oven.

Broil — To cook by direct heat, usually in broiler or over coals.

Candied — To cook in sugar or syrup when applied to sweet potatoes and carrots. For fruit or fruit peel, to cook in heavy syrup till transparent and well coated.

Chill — To place in refrigerator to reduce temperature.

Chop — To cut in pieces about the size of peas with knife, chopper, or blender.

Cool — To remove from heat and let stand at room temperature.

Cream — To beat with spoon or electric mixer till mixture is soft and smooth. When applied to blending shortening and sugar, mixture is beaten till light and fluffy.

Cut In — To mix shortening with dry ingredients using pastry blender or knives.

Dice — To cut food in small cubes of uniform size and shape.

Dissolve — To disperse a dry substance in a liquid to form a solution.

Glaze — A mixture applied to food which hardens or becomes firm and adds flavor and a glossy appearance.

Grate — To rub on a grater that separates the food into very fine particles.

Marinate — To allow food to stand in a liquid to tenderize or to add flavor.

Mince — To cut or finely chop food into very small pieces.

Mix — To combine ingredients, usually by stirring, till evenly distributed.

Poach — To cook in hot liquid, being careful that food holds its shape while cooking.

Precook — To cook food partially or completely before final cooking or reheating.

Roast — To cook uncovered without water added, usually in an oven.

Saute — To cook brown or cook in a small amount of hot shortening.

Scald — To bring to a temperature just below the boiling point where tiny bubbles form at the edge of the pan.

Scallop — To bake food, usually in a casserole, with sauce or other liquid. Crumbs are often sprinkled atop.

Steam — To cook in steam with or without pressure. A small amount of boiling water is used, more water being added during steaming process if necessary.

Stir — To mix ingredients with a circular motion until well blended or of uniform consistency.

Toss — To mix ingredients lightly.

Truss — To secure fowl or other meat with skewers to hold its shape during cooking.

Whip — To beat rapidly to incorporate air and produce expansion, as in heavy cream or egg whites.

CHEESE GUIDE

Cheese	How it looks and tastes	How to serve
American, Cheddar	Favorite all-around cheeses. Flavor varies from mild to sharp. Color ranges from natural to yellow-orange; texture firm to crumbly.	In sandwiches, casseroles, souffles, and creamy sauces. With fruit pie or crisp crackers; on a snack or dessert tray with fruit.
Blue, Gorgonzola, Roquefort	Compact, creamy cheeses veined with blue or blue-green mold. Sometimes crumbly. Mild to sharp salty flavor. (Stilton is similar, but like a blue-veined Cheddar.)	Crumble in salads, salad dressings, dips. Delicious with fresh pears or apples for dessert. Blend with butter for steak topper. Spread on crackers or crusty French or Italian bread.
Brick	Medium firm; creamy yellow color, tiny holes. Flavor very mild to medium sharp.	Good for appetizers, sandwiches, or desserts. Great with fresh peaches, cherries, or melons.
Brie *(bree)*	Similar to Camembert, but slightly firmer. Distinctive sharp flavor, pronounced odor.	Serve as dessert with fresh fruit. Be sure to eat the thin brown and white crust.
Camembert *(kam' em bear)*	Creamy yellow with thin gray-white crust. When ripe, it softens to the consistency of thick cream. Full, rich, mildly pungent.	Classic dessert cheese—serve at room temperature with fresh peaches, pears, or apples, or with toasted walnuts and crackers.
Cottage	Soft, mild, unripened cheese; large or small curd. May have cream added.	Used in salads, dips, main dishes. Popular with fresh and canned fruits.
Cream	Very mild-flavored soft cheese with buttery texture. Rich and smooth. Available whipped and in flavored spreads.	Adds richness and body to molded and frozen salads, cheesecake, dips, frostings, sandwich spreads. Serve whipped with dessert.
Edam, Gouda	Round, red-coated cheeses; creamy yellow to yellow-orange inside; firm and smooth. Mild nutlike flavor.	Bright hub for dessert or snack tray. Good in sandwiches or crunchy salads, or with crackers. Great with grapes and oranges.
Liederkranz, Limburger	Robust flavor and highly aromatic. Soft and smooth when ripe. Liederkranz is milder in flavor and golden yellow in color. Limburger is creamy white.	Spread on pumpernickel, rye, or crackers. Team with apples, pears, and Tokay grapes. Serve as snack with salty pretzels and coffee.

Cheese	How it looks and tastes	How to serve
Mozzarella, Scamorze	Unripened. Mild-flavored and slightly frim. Creamy white to pale yellow.	Cooking cheese. A "must" for pizza, lasagne; good in toasted sandwiches, hot snacks.
Muenster *(mun' stir)*	Between Brick and Limburger. Mild to mellow flavor, creamy white. Medium hard, tiny holes.	Use in sandwiches or on snack or dessert tray. Good with fresh sweet cherries and melon wedges.
Parmesan, Romano	Sharp, piquant, very hard cheese. Come in shakers grated. (Parmesan is also available shredded.) Or grate your own.	Sprinkle on pizza, main dishes, breads, salads, soups. Shake over buttered popcorn!
Port du Salut *(por du sa lu')*	Semisoft, smooth, and buttery. Mellow to robust flavor between Cheddar and Limburger.	Dessert cheese—delicious with fresh fruit; great with apple pie. Good for snack tray.
Provolone *(pro vo lo' nee)*	Usually smoked; mild to sharp flavor. Hard, compact and flaky. Pear or sausage shaped.	Use in Italian dishes, in sandwiches, on snack and appetizer trays.
Swiss	Firm pale yellow cheese, with large round holes. Sweet nutlike flavor.	First choice for ham-cheese sandwiches, fondue. Good in salads, sauces, as a snack.
Process cheeses	A blend of fresh and aged natural cheeses, pasteurized and packaged. Smooth and creamy, melts easily. May be flavored.	Ideal for cheese sauces, souffles, grilled cheese sandwiches, in casseroles. Handy for the snack tray, too.

HOW TO OPEN A CLAM

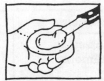

1. Wash clams thoroughly, discarding any that have broken shells or that do not close with handling. Wearing a heavy glove for safety, hold the clam in your palm and force the blade of a clam knife between the shell halves.

2. Run the knife around the edge of the shell to cut through the muscles holding it together.

3. Open clam and remove top shell. Use knife to loosen clam from the bottom shell. Check for shell fragments before serving.

HOW TO CRACK A CRAB

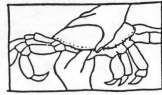

1. To remove back, hold the crab in one hand and pry off the shell with the other.

2. Using a small, heavy knife, cut away the gills. Wash away the intestines and spongy matter.

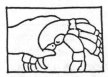

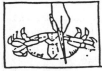

3. Break off the claws and crack them with the knife's handle, a mallet, or the back of a cleaver. Use a knife to pry meat out if necessary. Twist legs loose from the body, crack them, remove meat.

4. Cut the body down the middle, then cut halves into several parts. Use the point of the knife to remove the lump of meat from each side of the rear portion of the body.

5. Remove the remainder of the meat by prying upward with the knife.

HOW TO CLEAN A SHRIMP

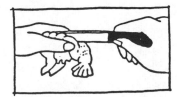

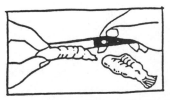

1. With a sharp knife, make a shallow cut along the back of the shrimp, from head to tail. Peel off shell and legs, leaving the shell on the tail, if desired. To devein, hold shrimp under cold running water. The water will help rinse out the vein.

2. To "butterfly," cut along the back of the shrimp, but not all the way through. Spread the halves open.

INDEX OF RECIPES

BED & BREAKFAST

THE CORNERSTONE VICTORIAN
CORNERSTONE'S SWEET SOUFFLES......... 4
SAVORY EGGS IN BAKED CROUSTADES 3

ALYNN'S BUTTERFLY INN BED & BREAKFAST
ALYNN'S BUTTERFLY INN CARAMEL FRENCH
     TOAST 6

THE BARK EATER
BARK EATER GRANOLA 11
CHILLED TOMATO BISQUE............... 10

1852 INN
SEPTEMBER FRIED GREEN TOMATOES AND
     PUFFBALL MUSHROOMS............... 15

COUNTRY ROAD LODGE
COUNTRY ROAD LODGE OATMEAL 20
HERBERT HOEGER'S APPLE RAISIN
     CAKE................................ 20

PINE TREE INN
OATMEAL APPLE RAISIN MUFFINS 23
OVERNIGHT SWEET ROLLS 23

HIGH PEAKS INN
HIGH PEAKS INN CLOVE MUFFINS 26

THE LAMPLIGHT INN
CINNAMON BUTTERMILK
     COFFEECAKE......................... 31
LAMPLIGHT APPLE OATMEAL CRISP 32
LAMPLIGHT PEAR AND CRANBERRY
     CRISP 31
LINDA'S STRAWBERRY BREAD............ 30
MOM'S CHEESECAKE.................... 32

THE INN AT SARATOGA
GRILLED BREAST OF DUCK WITH
     STRAWBERRY RHUBARB CHUTNEY 37

FO'CASTLE FARMS
HARVEST MAPLE PUMPKIN SOUP 38

THE FRIENDS LAKE INN
APPLE CIDER SAUCE 46
PAN SEARED DUCK BREAST WITH SHERRY
     MAPLE SAUCE........................ 44
SNAPPING TURTLE SOUP 42
VEGETARIAN CHILI 43
WILD BOAR CHOPS WITH APPLE CIDER
     SAUCE 45

THE BOOK & BLANKET BED & BREAKFAST
NON-DAIRY (AKA VEGAN) BANANA
     BREAD.............................. 49

THE POINT
PEPPERED SEA BASS WITH RED WINE
     SAUCE 58

**OSCAR'S ADIRONDACK MOUNTAIN
SMOKEHOUSE**
ARMAND & BOB'S FAMOUS TAILGATE
     SMOKED LIVERWURST SANDWICH 60

THE LODGE ON LAKE CLEAR
GERMAN APPLE CAKE 65
OVEN OMELET 67
PORK TENDERLOIN SAUTE 65

THE CHESTER INN
ADIRONDACK BAKED FRENCH BREAD 73
CHESTER INN STRAWBERRY CREAM
     DRESSING 73
TOMATO MUSHROOM AND BASIL
     SOUP 72

THE STAGECOACH INN
ORANGE BUTTER 77
STAGECOACH INN PANCAKES 77

GOOSE POND INN
BRANDIED FRENCH TOAST WITH SAUTEED
     APPLES 82
CARROT-WALNUT PANCAKES............ 82

MOOSE RIVER HOUSE
APPLE MUFFINS 85

MIRROR LAKE INN
VENISON SIRLOIN WITH CHERRY & MELON
     COMPOTE............................ 88

VEGETABLES

ASPARAGUS AU RASPBERRY 101
AUSABLE BEANS........................ 102
CARROTS PIEDMONTESE 104
CORN SOUFFLE 104
DEVILED GREEN BEANS................. 106
DODSON POTATO CAKES............... 107
EGGPLANT CORLEONE.................. 105
FRESH CORN FRITTERS................. 104
GRANDMA HARRIS' HOME FRIES........ 107
HENRIETTA'S KARTOFFOGLAZE......... 106
HIKER'S BAKED BEANS................. 103
IMPOSSIBLE GARDEN PIE.............. 109
MAPLEWOOD BAKED POTATOES 106
MATUMBLA BAKED BEANS 102
NORTHERN RED CABBAGE 103
POTATO PUFFS 108
SLICED BAKED POTATOES 108
SQUASH DELIGHT 108
SWEET POTATOES AND APPLES 109
TWICE-TASTY POTATOES 107
VEGETABLE QUICHE 109

SOUPS AND CHOWDERS

ADIRONDACK HOT DOG SOUP........... 111
BAVARIAN LENTIL SOUP 112
CAMP CHILI.......................... 111
FISH CHOWDER 114
FISHERMAN'S CHOWDER............... 114
LUZERNE CHEESE AND CHEDDAR
     CHOWDER.......................... 113
NORTHWAY ONION SOUP 112
ORANGE CARROT SOUP................ 113
POLISH POTATOES AND SAUSAGE
     SOUP 113

ENTREES

BEEF

BILLY'S GOLF BALLS 119
CHRISTMAS EVE MEAT PIE 122
FRENCH CANADIAN MEAT PIE 118
HAYDEN STEW 116
HENRIETTA'S SAURBRATEN.............. 117
HENRIETTA'S STUFFED PEPPERS......... 117
LEAFY STUFFED CABBAGE.............. 122
MEATLOAF BAKE 120
NORTHERN MEATLOAF WITH CHEESE.... 116
OLD FASHIONED PUMPKIN
    MEATLOAF 119
ONIONY STEAK AND POTATOES 121
POOR MAN'S STEW 118
SAUTEED BEEF AND WILD
    MUSHROOMS WITH BALSALMIC
    VINEGAR.......................... 115
SCHENECTADY CON CARNE............. 118
SPICED POT ROAST 119
UNCLE BUCK'S JUICY RIB STEAKS 121
WARRENSBURG BEEF PROVENCALE 116

POULTRY

ADIRONDACK WILDBERRY CHICKEN..... 123
APPLE HERB STUFFING FOR CHICKEN OR
    PORK 132
BIRCHTON TURKEY DIVAN 131
CHICKEN A LA QUEENSBURY 125
CHICKEN CASSEROLE 125
CHICKEN D'EBLEE 126
GLAZED CHICKEN WITH GRAPE
    SAUCE 126
GLOVERVILLE CHICKEN BAKE 127
GRILLED ADIRONDACK SWEET POTATO
    CHICKEN 123
HENZLER CHICKEN BAKE 128
OUTDOOR CHICKEN 129
PEPPERCORN CHICKEN BREASTS....... 129
ROB'S HOT CHICKEN AND RICE......... 129
SARATOGA HONEY-CURRIED
    CHICKEN 130
SWISS CHICKEN CUTLETS 130
TUPPER LAKE CHICKEN SQUASH
    SOUFFLE 131
TURKEY A LA CHRISTOPHER............ 132
WATERVLIET CHICKEN CACCIATORE 131

PORK

ADIRONDACK PORK 135
BAKED PORK CHOPS WITH FRESH
    FRUIT. 139
GLENS FALLS HARVEST STEW........... 137
HAM NOODLE CASSEROLE 137
LAKE PLACID BOILED DINNER.......... 138
NORTH CHURCH FRIED DUMPLINGS 138
SPARERIBS AND KRAUT 139

WILD GAME

BERTH GOOSE WITH VENISON-WILD RICE
    STUFFING 141
NATIVE STYLE BLACK BEAR (JOKE)....... 147
RACQUETTE RIVER RABBIT 142
SECOND OF SEPTEMBER VENISON 143
VENISON CHILI....................... 143
VENISON MAGGIE 144
VENISON STEW....................... 144
WHITETAIL STEW 145
WORKMAN'S NOODLES 146

MISCELLANEOUS

ADIRONDACK TROUT 151
ETTA'S LAMB STEW 150

HOT AUGUST GARLIC SHRIMP 150
NORTH CREEK BAKED SPAGHETTI 149
SARATOGA PASTA 149
SWORDFISH SAUTE 150

BREADS AND PASTRIES

ADIRONDACK FLAPJACKS.............. 162
ADIRONDACK STRAWBERRY PASTRIES.... 159
ADIRONDACK WAFFLES 162
AUNT VICKI'S MONKEY BREAD 155
BANANA NUT BREAD................... 154
CHRISTMAS EGGNOG BREAD 155
EGGPLANT BREAD 153
ELLIE'S SARATOGA BISCUITS........... 157
HEALTHY BANANA BREAD 154
JOHN W. DODSON'S BANANA BREAD..... 154
KAITLIN POPOVERS 158
LAKE ALGONQUIN OAT BRAN
    MUFFINS.......................... 161
LAKE LUZERNE APPLE ROLLS.......... 157
MARIA'S DESSERT. 159
MARY'S GINGERBREAD MUFFINS. 161
NORTH CREEK LEMON MUFFINS 160
OLD STOVE INSTANT ROLLS 156
POTATO PUFFS 158
POTTER BISCUITS WITH CHIVES....... 158
PUMPKIN MAPLE RAISIN NUT BREAD 156
SHEILA'S MORNING COFFEE CAKE 163
TROY CRANBERRY BREAD 155

CAKES, COOKIES, DESSERTS

CAKES AND ICINGS

APPLE CAKE 165
APPLE CAKE 165
AUTUMN CAKE....................... 166
BUTTER FROSTING.................... 177
COUNTRY UPSIDE DOWN CAKE.......... 171
CRANBERRY-DATE CAKE 170
CRUMB CAKE 170
DATE CHOCOLATE CHIP CAKE.......... 168
DEEP DARK CHOCOLATE CAKE 168
DISAPPEARING DARK CHOCOLATE
    CAKE 168
FRESH APPLE CAKE 165
GRANDMA'S CRAZY CAKE. 170
GRANDMA'S TOPPING 177
HUMMINGBIRD CAKE................. 172
JANE'S CHOCOLATE CAKE. 167
MARBLE CAKE 172
MARY'S RAW APPLE CAKE............. 166
MAYO CAKE. 172
MOLASSES CAKE 173
MOUNTAIN FROSTING 177
NANNY'S HOT MILK CAKE 171
NORTH CREEK WAR-TIME CAKE 173
ROCKY MOUNTAIN CAKE AND
    FROSTING 174
SARATOGA SPRINGS DIRT CAKE 171
SWEET MOUNTAIN CAKE. 174
TOMATO SOUP CAKE 175
TUBE APPLE CAKE 166
UPSTATE CHOCOLATE CAKE........... 167
WHITE CHOCOLATE FUDGE CAKE AND
    FROSTING......................... 169
WILHELMENA CAKE AND MINNEHAHA
    FROSTING 176
YOU NAME IT ICING 176

COOKIES

CAMP MOSS ROCK MOLASSES
   COOKIES 180
EGG YOLK COOKIES 179
GINGER SNAPS 179
MOLASSES COOKIES 180
MOLASSES SUGAR COOKIES 181
OLD FASHIONED FORGOTTEN
   COOKIES 179
PUMPKIN COOKIES 181
SARATOGA SNOWBALLS 181

DESSERTS

APPLE CRISP 183
BLUEBERRIES IN LEMON MOUSSE 184
CHEESECAKE............................. 185
DOUBLE DECADENT BROWNIE TORTE.... 186
GRANDMA'S APPLE DESSERT 183
MOIST AMSTERDAM GINGERBREAD...... 187
PATTIE ANN'S APPLE CRUNCH 184
THANKSGIVING PUMPKIN WALNUT
   TORTE 185
THE ORIGINAL SARATOGA BROWNIES ... 186
WHIPPED CREAM APPLE DESSERT........ 184

PIES AND PUDDINGS

PIES

BLUEBERRY CRUNCH PIE 190
CRANBERRY CRUNCH PIE 190
DEEP DISH APPLE PIE 189
GERMAN CHOCOLATE PIE............... 190
HEAVENLY MOCHA PIE 191
PEANUT BUTTER PIE A LA POTTER....... 192
PEANUT BUTTER PIE 192
PECAN PIE 193
PUMPKIN PIE 193
SARATOGA PEANUT BUTTER PIE......... 192

PUDDINGS

BISCUIT PUDDING 195
DUTCH APPLE PUDDING................ 195
MINNIE'S BREAD PUDDING.............. 195
MINNIE'S RICE PUDDING................ 196
NEE'S SUET PUDDING................... 197
PUMPERNICKEL RAISIN BREAD
   PUDDING 196
SETTLERS RICE PUDDING................ 196

MISCELLANEOUS

ADIRONDACKS BLOSSOMS 202
AWARD-WINNING STEAK MARINADE 200

BAKED APPLE RELISH................... 201
CLIFTON DEVILED EGGS 203
GEISLER PICCALILLI RELISH 201
GRACE SAUCE........................... 199
GREEN MOUNTAIN ONION DRESSING 200
MOUNTAIN RESERVE CATSUP........... 199
NORTHERN SHRIMP DIP................. 202
PIQUANT BARBECUE SAUCE............. 199
SARATOGIAN SALSA.................... 200
3-VEGGIE DILL PICKLES 202

HINTS

A HANDY SPICE AND HERB GUIDE....... 217
APPLE VARIETIES 222
ATTRACTIVE FOOD IS FUN AND EASY.... 230
BASIC GUIDELINES FOR LOSING
   WEIGHT 213
CALCULATING PERCENT FAT............ 207
CHEESE GUIDE 236
ENTERTAINING MADE EASY 226
FAT FACTS 206
FIRST AID IN HOUSEHOLD
   EMERGENCIES........................ 225
FOOD GUIDE PYRAMID.................. 216
FOOD LABELING DEFINITIONS........... 209
FOOD SAFETY GUIDELINES 212
FOOD STORAGE CHART 232
FRUIT CANNING OUTLINE 221
GIFTS FROM THE KITCHEN 228
GRILLING TIPS.......................... 224
"HEART HEALTHY" RECIPE
   SUBSTITUTIONS 208
HOW TO CLEAN A SHRIMP 238
HOW TO CRACK A CRAB 238
HOW TO OPEN A CLAM................. 238
IRON FROM SOME COMMON FOOD
   SOURCES............................. 223
LOW SODIUM SEASONING
   SUGGESTIONS........................ 211
RULES FOR USING HERBS............... 218
SEASONING KNOW-HOW................ 229
SODIUM 210
SUGGESTIONS FOR LOWERING FAT
   CONTENT IN YOUR DIET 205
TERMS USED IN RECIPES 235
THE BEST USE OF YOUR FREEZER MAY MAKE
   MEALTIME EASIER 227
THE NUTRITION FACTS FOOD LABEL..... 215
UNDERSTANDING THE NUTRITION FACTS
   FOOD LABEL 214
UNUSUAL HERBS 219
VEGETABLE CANNING OUTLINE 220

adirondackbb.com

Adirondack B & B Association

50 Charming and Unique
Bed & Breakfast Inns to Choose From

P.O. Box 801, Lake George, NY 12845

NORTH COUNTRY REGION, NY

Jay	Book & Blanket B & B	(518) 946-8323
Keene Valley	Trail's End Inn B & B	(800) 281-9860
Saranac Lake	Branch Farm B & B	(518) 891-0869
Saranac Lake	The Doctor's Inn	(888) 518-3464
Saranac Lake	Porcupine B & B	(518) 891-5160
Saranac Lake	Sunday Pond B & B	(518) 891-1531
Upper Saranac Lake	The Wawbeek Resort	(800) 953-2656
Westport	All Tucked Inn	(888) 255-8825

SARATOGA REGION, NY

Corinth	Agape Farm B & B	(518) 654-7777
Greenwich	Country Life B & B	(888) 692-7203
Hartford	Brown's Tavern B & B	(518) 632-5904
Northville	Inn at the Bridge	(888) 245-8220
Round Lake	Old Stone House Inn	(877) 380-6655
Salem	Bunker Hill Inn	(518) 854-9339
Salem	Salem Scenery B & B	(518) 854-7862
Saratoga Springs	Batcheller Mansion Inn	(800) 616-7012
Saratoga Springs	Brunswick B & B	(800) 585-6751
Saratoga Springs	Geyser Lodge B & B	(518) 584-0389
Saratoga Springs	Saratoga Arms Inn	(518) 584-1775
Saratoga Springs	Saratoga B & B	(800) 584-0920
Saratoga Springs	Saratoga Sleigh B & B	(518) 584-4534
Saratoga Springs	Six Sisters B & B	(518) 583-1173
Saratoga Springs	Union Gables B & B	(800) 398-1558
Saratoga Springs	Westchester House B & B	(800) 581-7613
Schuylerville	Dovegate Inn	(518) 695-3699
Schuylerville	Kings-Ransom Farm B & B	(518) 695-6876

LAKE GEORGE REGION, NY

Adirondack	Adirondack Pines B & B	(518) 494-5249
Bolton Landing	Boathouse B & B	(518) 644-2554
Bolton Landing	Hilltop Cottage B & B	(518) 644-2492
Chestertown	Chester Inn	(877) 558-8001
Chestertown	Friend's Lake Inn	(518) 494-4751
Chestertown	Landon Hill B & B	(888) 244-2599
Diamond Point	Somewhere in Time B & B	(518) 668-9151
Glens Falls	The Glens Falls Inn	(800) 208-9058
Glens Falls	Memory Manor B & B	(518) 793-2699
Hague	Ruah B &B	(800) 254-7549
Hudson Falls	A B & B on the Green	(518) 747-2694
Lake George	Glenmoore B & B	(518) 792-5261
Lake George	Lake George B & B	(800) 348-5113
Lake Luzerne	Lamplight Inn B & B	(800) 262-4668
North Creek	Goose Pond Inn	(800) 802-2601
Putnam Station	Lake Champlain Inn	(518) 547-9942
Queensbury	Crislip's B & B	(518) 793-6869
Schroon Lake	Schroon Lake B & B	(800) 523-6755
Schroon Lake	Silver Spruce Inn	(518) 532-7031
Warrensburg	Alynn's Butterfly Inn	(518) 623-9390
Warrensburg	Cornerstone Victorian B & B	(518) 623-3308
Warrensburg	Country Road Lodge B & B	(518) 623-2207
Warrensburg	Emerson House B & B	(518) 623-2758
Warrensburg	The Glen Lodge B & B	(800) 867-2335

THE MUSEUM

". . . the best of its kind in the world."
THE N.Y. TIMES

A regional museum of history and art, the Adirondack Museum is national acclaimed for its exhibits on life, work, and leisure in the Adirondack region of upstate new York.

Twenty-two exhibit buildings, set amidst green lawns and flowers, look over Blue Mountain Lake 250 feet below. The Museum's Merwin Hill is the setting for native plants and the beginning of a nature trail, and the museum's 7,000 volume library is available for researchers year-round.

The Adirondack Museum opened in 1957, is private, non-profit, and is chartered by the Regents of the State of New York.

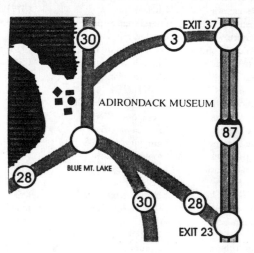

ART & ARTIFACTS

Adirondack Chair

E arly in the nineteenth century, artists discovered the aesthetic possibilities of the Adirondack landscape.

Over 450 paintings by such artists as Thomas Cole, A. R. Tait, and Frederic Remington, and 60,000 historic photographs are part of the museum's collection. Also featured are a fine selection of guideboats, indigenous to the Adirondacks, and one of the largest collections of fresh water craft in the country. Adirondack rustic furniture is housed in an adaptively restored turn-of-the-century cottage. Artifacts represent such traditional occupations as logging and boat building.

Ardis Hughes

Illustrator **Ardis Hughes**
Saratoga Springs, New York

Ardis Hughes was born in Rhinebeck, New York and attended high school in Oneonta, where his father was secretary of the YMCA and his brother later became mayor. During his high school years he took courses in art at Hartwick College. He later went on to Pratt Institute, where he won a scholarship. After his graduation from Pratt, he took a position with Esquire Magazine and then apprenticed with the illustrator, Saul Tepper. During the war years he was assigned to create posters for the Treasury Department, illustrations for Army Talks, murals for Fort Belvoir, and a portrait of General Meade for Fort Meade. Although he was primarily a freelance artist after the war, he was also associated with the Ted Bates and Merrill Anderson advertising agencies.

For the past twenty years he has devoted himself to fine arts, studying at the Art Students League and travelling extensively. His pictures are in public and private collections throughout the world. Since his award of first prize in a national contest at the age of twelve, he has been the recipient of many honours, including the Gold Medal in watercolour at the National Arts Club. Although he is a member of the American Watercolor Society, Mr. Hughes also works in oil and pen and ink, having done portraits for the New York University

Law School, while his drawings have been featured in The American Artist and The Villager. His painting of Carnegie Hall was reproduced for the cover of an entire season's programs, as well as on their 85th Anniversary Album put out by Columbia.

Recently, in order to satisfy his many clients, he has been publishing limited editions of his most popular works as lithographs.

Author Information

❦

Armand C. Vanderstigchel

Trained in the classic school apprenticeship in Europe, Armand has worked various chef positions for conglomerates such as Hilton, Radisson International, Marriott, and Novotel. On a smaller scale he wore the toque in various country clubs and landmark hotels. After being Corporate Chef for the Lessings Corporation on Long Island, Armand rejoined old restaurant friends as Executive Chef of the pretigious Miller Place Inn on Long Island, NY.

Besides being active in the publishing field as author of *Chicken Wings Across America*, *The Adirondack Cuisine Cookbook*, co-author of *The Adirondack Cookbook* and culinary editor of *Dish Du Jour* magazine, Armand teaches various cooking classes in schools on Long Island, New York. As media-host of *The Radio Gourmet* on WGBB 1240am and *Long Island Gourmet TV Show*, emphasis is focused on educating his audience on the importance of utilizing fresh foods in cooking, be it taste or health related. He is a great promoter and fan of regional cuisine here in America, and can be often witnessed at bookstores, festivals, libraries and national TV shows performing live cooking demonstrations with his mobile kitchen.

He is active in the community as a career day chef at schools, fundraiser activist and promoter for organizations such as The American Heart Association, American Kidney Foundation and James Beard House. Using his ethnic European background in the enhancement of New Regional American cuisine, he creates his signature dishes by merging together both cultures.

As a full-time resident of Long Island and part-time of the Adirondacks, he has received recognition on Long Island as "Chef of the Year" by Suffolk Community College's Chef Hall of Fame committee and a returning favorite on various national TV networks such as FOX, NBC, ABC and PBS.

Robert Birkel, Jr.

Robert Birkel, Jr., a former Vietnam Era Naval Aerial Photographer, has been active in the food industry as manager, purchaser, and consultant for Howard Johnson Airport Hotels, Ground Round, Canterbury Ales Restaurants and many other great establishments. He now specializes in food and scenic photography.

His involvement in such organizations such as The American Legion, The Lions Club, Masonic Lodge, and a former member of the Big Brother/ Big Sister Organization known throughout the United States, has brought forth his importance for community involvement.

Today Bob is involved in quite a few projects including co-host of The Radio Gourmet on WGBB Radio 1240am and The Long Island Gourmet TV Show. He is also known as "The Sauerbraten King".

To find out about our other cookbooks:

  ❧ *Chicken Wings Across America*

  ❧ *Adirondack Cuisine*

Log on to: www.Adirondackcookbook.com

A site full of recipes and great links

From late spring to late fall, you will encounter a crowded parking lot at Lakeside Farms Cider Mill. At lunchtime, crowds enjoy the wonderful baked goods, homemade soups and scrumptious signature sandwiches. Almost everybody leaves with a dozen apple cider donuts or fresh baked pie from the bakery. The retail store sells many unique artisan food items, such as local syrup, honey, molasses and cheese. Behind the store, a large cider mill churns out fresh apple cider daily. This is a fun place to visit with the family and a true destination food establishment.

CREAMY BROCCOLI SOUP

3 gal. chicken stock
3 onions, diced
4 to 6 carrots, finely diced
2 red peppers, finely diced
6 to 8 heads broccoli, coarsely
    chopped florettes, (finely dice
    the upper stems)

½ gal. whole milk
1 qt. half & half

    Roux:

½ lb. butter
1¾ c. flour

Seasoning as needed:
Salt, pepper, thyme, garlic, hot
    pepper sauce

Bring stock to a boil. Add onions, wait 5 minutes then add carrots and peppers. When stock returns to the boil, add broccoli. Meanwhile make a roux with the butter and flour. After stock returns to the boil, continue to cook approximately 5 to 10 minutes depending on how tender the broccoli is. Add roux; stir well. Add dairy products. Reduce heat. Season to taste.

Lakeside Farms Cider Mill

Greetings
from the
Adirondack Test Kitchen